Contents

the new
complete manual of
racing &
betting
systems

——— the new ———
complete manual of
racing &
betting
systems

david duncan

foulsham
LONDON • NEW YORK • TORONTO • SYDNEY

foulsham

The Publishing House, Bennetts Close, Cippenham,
Berkshire, SL1 5AP, England

ISBN 0-572-02954-3

Copyright © 2001 and 2004 W. Foulsham & Co. Ltd

Cover photograph © Getty Images

A CIP record for this book is available from the British Library

Neither the editors of W. Foulsham & Co. Ltd
nor the author nor the publisher take
responsibility for any possible consequences
from any action following the information in
this book.

Printed in Great Britain by Creative Print & Design (Wales), Ebbw Vale

Betting and You

Racing is more popular now than ever before. All kinds of people follow the Sport of Kings. Betting shops offer greater comfort and improved facilities and take their place in every high street. Betting is now a respectable pastime and every major meeting receives extensive television coverage. Small wonder that betting turnover has reached record levels, even allowing for inflation. While other spectator sports experience difficulties, racing has consolidated its position and challenges soccer as our national sport.

Also, racing has become international to an extent undreamt of a quarter of a century ago. An English champion racehorse can no longer claim pre-eminence unless it can prove itself in the Breeders' Cup series of races in America in the autumn of each year. British horses now routinely undertake an annual antipodean journey to challenge for Australia's greatest race, the Melbourne Cup, which is a handicap over two miles, while the goings-on in the Dubai desert at Nad Al Sheba in March offer instant world recognition and fabulous sums in prize money and make racing a truly global contest.

The pages that follow are mostly about racing at home, and you have no doubt purchased this book because you like a bet in that arena. If you are honest you will almost certainly admit that you lose in the long run. Most people do and the reason is simple. Unlike the bookmaker who bets along methodical, businesslike lines, the average punter stakes haphazardly according to fancy. This is fatal and plays right into the bookmaker's hands. If, on the other hand, you are prepared to study the form book or follow systems based on established patterns of form and statistics, you give yourself a chance of winning.

No judge of form and no system can pick a winner every time and even the best methods are unlikely to yield more than a marginal gain on outlay but that is still a lot better than losing. Methodical betting along form or systematic lines, although it cannot guarantee success, offers a real prospect of a winning balance.

This book has five parts. Each constitutes a vital element in the armoury of the betting enthusiast who is fully equipped for the battle with the bookmaker.

Part 1 is a complete guide to reading the form book based on the author's own unique method of calculating chances. There is a method of instant handicapping which offers an alternative to conventional techniques of trying to beat the handicapper. In addition, there is a series of shortcuts to winner-finding, arranged according to the type of race to be assessed. Criteria 1 to 24 can, for the most part, be operated by simple reference to a morning newspaper without the necessity of getting involved in a deeper study of form. However, the wise racing fan will probably do best by blending the various guidelines with an analysis of form to arrive at selections with the optimum chance of success.

Whatever strategy or techniques you adopt though, you will be in a position to contemplate a full day's betting at several meetings or the particular card for a meeting you are attending with a confidence about your ability to pick out the best bets that was very likely totally alien to you hitherto.

In Part 2, 12 automatic racing systems are explained. Why 12 when one winning method will do? The answer is that different styles of betting appeal to different people. So you will find in these pages systems for the Flat and systems for the jumps. There are plans for favourites and plans for longer-priced selections. Most focus on win-only betting, but those who feel happier with each-way investments are also accommodated. A few go a stage further and are solely concerned with the staking as opposed to the selection aspect of backing horses. There is an attempt to exploit the excellent racing coverage to be found in the national press. In fact, the 12 systems featured in the following pages cover the whole spectrum of racing. Whatever your betting preferences, you will find something here to interest you.

Each plan has full operating instructions and can be understood by anyone who has only a rudimentary knowledge of racing and betting, so is clear and easy to follow. However, the book is written by an expert, so takes into account that point of view. Some experts scoff at systems. They point out that horses are not machines, that every system can be beaten sooner or later by the long losing run, that the bookmaker always wins in the end, and so on. Now it is certainly true that racing is notoriously unpredictable with the odds stacked against the punter, and for these reasons no one should ever bet more than they can afford to lose on a system, however good it may appear.

Having said that, it is my belief that for the average punter who has no inside knowledge of the operations of a racing stable and no clue about secrets which are always jealously guarded, logical betting, according to some plan based on racing know-how and horse sense, offers the best chance of winning at a pastime which inevitably involves a great deal of risk.

Part 3 contains just such know-how and horse sense in that it explains the professional method of making a 'backer's book', whereby you can back several horses in the same race and still show a good profit – the bookmaker's own system in reverse and the staking system used by most of the great gamblers of yesteryear. Their betting exploits, involving astronomical sums of money, have passed into racing history and become legend.

The old-time professionals often backed two or three, or even more, against the field and today some of their heirs still do, but the professional is willing to bet at odds-on to large sums in a way that the average punter would not contemplate. Yet you can still cash in on the professionals' system in handicaps where the odds take a wide range and good prices are the rule rather than the exception. Betting the day before a big handicap in particular, when running plans are determined and the draw for the race known, may be a profitable strategy. Shrewd punters can get the best of the odds about their fancies and reap a handsome reward if they are successful. Exactly how to achieve this desirable goal, based on the skilful use of betting mathematics derived from percentage probability, is fully outlined in the third part of the book.

In Part 4 there is an analysis of the new betting exchanges. Complete beginners and those who already have some experience of the newest form of gambling on horses will find plenty of advice to guide them through what has been called 'a revolution in betting'. In fact, a betting exchange is a jungle, where the ill-prepared and unwary will struggle to survive. There is no substitute for personal experience, but Part 4 alerts readers to the potential dangers, tells them what not to do, and even makes clear, coherent recommendations for developing a winning strategy in an area where there is as yet no received wisdom about the best ways to proceed.

Our betting manual concludes with a complete guide to the racecourses of Britain, both on the Flat and over jumps. The Racecourse Guide's course descriptions may help you to pick out horses more suited to that particular track or eliminate those which are not likely to run at their best. The effect of the draw is vital in racing. Course modifications, together with new drainage systems have changed much that is familiar in this sphere recently, making some of the old ideas about the draw invalid in many cases. The Racecourse Guide brings you right up to date.

The fate of favourites, trainer tips and a special course classification as a benchmark for conclusions about class, essential to the form reader, are other features which make Part 5 a uniquely helpful guide to betting at a particular course.

Most people follow racing for enjoyment but it is my experience that the pleasure is greatly increased when they manage to make a profit. If you have always lost in the past, then try this book. You will find it interesting to read and you may even be in the happy position of having the bookmaker pay for your pastime.

PART 1

How to Pick Winners

Introduction

The pages that follow contain a detailed form guide to most aspects of modern racing embodying a highly focused philosophy of betting. At the heart of this philosophy is the idea of matching method to a particular type of race.

Anyone who thinks at all deeply about the problems associated with backing horses must surely come to the conclusion that there can never be a single master system or betting technique which will deal successfully with all races in all conditions. There are just too many variables in the sport.

The influence of some factors in racing remains constant. The relative fitness of horses and the state of the going are two obvious ones of major importance which are relevant in every sort of race, but what is vital for successful betting is to have a set of logical and workable approaches which look at individual horses against the background of the different kinds and class of event in which they compete. In terms of selection at least, racing on any one day or at a single meeting should not be viewed as a complete whole therefore, but as a composite of separate and distinct entities, each one requiring particularised analysis according to type.

The opening section of this betting manual is not an automatic racing system, but a comprehensive set of guidelines and criteria designed to help negotiate the perils of betting on all kinds of horses in all kinds of races at all kinds of meetings. Individual experience and preference will determine which of the methods is preferred and used most often.

The form guide that follows is not selective, as the backer must be in order to win. Since it is intended to appeal to as wide a readership as possible, it aims to assist its audience in winner-finding across the whole spectrum of racing. It is, however, only a starting point, a launch pad for a new betting career in which, hopefully, profits will play a prominent part. The specialisation which ought to follow should go far beyond the guidelines, although in some respects the other parts of the book will help to put flesh on the bare bones of the methods of form-assessment explained first. Practice and the flair which may come from experience are needed to complete the process.

Flat (Turf)

The various methodologies featured in this section of Part 1 apply to Flat racing in Britain and are primarily intended for racing on grass. The other code of Flat racing in this country, consisting of all-weather racing at three courses, is so different from the traditional Turf scene that it really calls for a separate treatment in a place other than the present one. For the sake of completeness, however, the Racecourse Guide in Part 5 does contain indicators for the fibresand and polytrack meetings. Also, because the principles of handicapping are always the same, the alternative handicapping method which precedes the criteria for individual types of race can be used for all-weather racing with roughly equal prospects of success.

1
HANDICAPS V. NON-HANDICAPS

The basic distinction for betting purposes, both in regard to selection and arguably staking as well, is between handicaps and those races where differences in weight do not depend on the view of current racing ability taken by the official handicapper. In fact, in only a minority of races in Britain do horses start on absolutely equal terms – even some Classic races, the purest of all tests of the thoroughbred, have an allowance for sex.

There is, however, a world of difference between races where every horse has been given a theoretically identical chance of winning, and conditions races where small penalties for previous successes and allowances for age and sex do not really detract from the goal of establishing the best horse in the race by merit alone. The difference between handicaps and non-handicaps is a very real one and we will begin our analysis by looking at form in the former.

2
PRIVATE HANDICAPS

A handicap race can be a complex problem, and the degree of complexity will depend on the amount of direct and collateral form 'in the book' which is relevant to it. In general, the more form lines that are available, the more complex the problem. Yet the opposite scenario is even worse from the backer's point of view.

A race where the contestants cannot be compared at all by their previous runs against each other, or through the performances of the equine equivalent of third parties, presents an even greater puzzle than one where comparative form is plentiful.

In practice most handicaps fall somewhere between the two extremes. Thus there will be a double difficulty – too much direct and collateral form for some runners and none at all for others. Bridging the gap between the two opposites can sometimes call for skill bordering on psychic intuition that few of us possess.

One way of solving the problem for the average punter is simply to ignore it, or at least to deliberately chose not to become embroiled in the intricacies of weight and distance built up from a multiple of previous races. After all, there are a number of private handicaps available from specialist firms, and most newspapers feature the same thing in the form of race ratings. Experts such as 'Postmark' of the *Racing Post* and 'Formcast' of the *Daily Mail*, do the job of unravelling the form conundrum for us. It is perfectly possible to get by as a racing enthusiast without going further into handicaps than studying a set of published ratings in conjunction with all those other winner-finding aids which are readily available to the betting public nowadays in the racing and national press.

If one feels that it would be impossible to better the efforts of expert journalists, it is still advisable to study closely the principles set out in the ensuing pages, although there is no compulsion to apply them as a matter of course to actual races. Even so, from the knowledge and expertise that will hopefully be acquired, it may be possible from time to time to make vital decisions on which cash depends.

If by contrast, one prefers to make an analysis of handicaps independently, then what follows in the section on 'instant' handicapping, combined with the notes on various aspects of particular types of race, is an excellent solution to the problem.

3
OVERALL V. VERY RECENT FORM

In the main, although consideration is usually given to very recent races depending on the predilections of the individual private handicapper, race ratings arrive at their assessment of each horse's chance by a continuous study of overall ability in relation to other horses running in, approximately, the same class and over a similar distance. The race rating figure which appears by the name of each horse strongly reflects this fact. This can sometimes mean therefore that where a horse is regarded as 'well in' at the weights the conclusion has been drawn from a piece of form which is weeks, perhaps even months old, even though some slight modification has been made for its latest running.

The relevance of old form like this can only be proved in the race but it should not be forgotten that if a horse is shown as 'well in' with a very high figure, this is a comparison based on a difference of opinion with the official handicap ratings which determined the weight that horses have to carry in the first place.

Who gets it right more often: the private handicapper who contrives to have one horse in the ratings a pound or two in hand of the rest of the field, or the official handicapper whose job it is to give a horse in good form just enough weight to allow it to run a series of sound races in its class without actually winning too often?

Private handicaps have their successes but it is the view of this author that backers intending to put down hard cash should always check the last-time-out performance of each runner, whatever significance they attach to newspaper ratings. This is essential, for the fact of the matter is that in a very high percentage of cases a horse's most recent run will give a pretty fair indication of whether or not it is up to winning.

4
WEIGHT AND GRADE

In examining a horse's most recent racecourse run it is not just a matter of assessing performance on that occasion in relation to the weight it carried compared with the weight it is set to carry now. Everything has to be placed in the context of the grade of the races involved in the comparison.

In this respect 7 lb should be seen as a key amount of weight. There are exceptions to just about everything in racing but, as a working rule, it is a fair proposition that the winner of a handicap is unlikely to prove capable of winning again next time out if the weight it is set to carry represents an increase of more than 7 lb in its official rating. There are instances every season of horses raised as much as 10 or 12 lb in the weights repeating a handicap victory. Nevertheless, the case of an animal improving beyond all recognition is just one of those exceptions we must live with. The form reader has no way of anticipating such an improvement.

On the other hand, there are plenty of horses which fail to overcome an increase of only 2–3 lb in their official rating, although in the majority of cases here failure will probably not be solely due to an increase in weight of that order but to any one of several other factors which prevent a horse reproducing its form, i.e. fitness within the form cycle (see Criterion 13), the going (Criterion 14), the draw (Criterion 15), and so on.

In fact we have now arrived at the very essence of the problem with handicaps because, quite apart from such factors, different horses react differently to variations in weight. The cause of different reactions is always a mixture of physical and psychological elements. A big, strong horse with plenty of 'heart' will probably make light of even a hefty increase in its usual weight impost, whereas a pony-sized animal with a weak will to win might well resent even a relatively trivial increase in its burden. Conversely, what will be the reaction to a significant increase in weight of a big, powerful animal which is nonetheless not entirely 'genuine', or of a much smaller horse with a real appetite for racing? Since there are as many different sizes and shapes of horse as there are possible mental attitudes, making an accurate estimate of how a given horse will react to weight variations is a virtual impossibility. It may even be argued that 'weight off' can have a contrary effect on the same horse to 'weight on'. A drop in weight seems to make no difference by way of improvement to the performance of some horses, but an increase of exactly the same amount can often have a definite 'stopping' effect. That is a familiar scenario for any serious form reader. Anyone engaged in handicapping along traditional lines usually assumes that an increase of three pounds in weight will slow a sprinter down by one length but, given the physical and mental differences between horses, that can only be the most general of assumptions. On the other hand, if form in handicaps assessed by weight is to mean anything at all, such assumptions in the guise of rules have to be formulated and applied.

But whatever the effect of weight on horses, and in view of the difficulty in estimating a particular horse's physical and psychological reaction to it, the grade of a contest stands out as the most important factor of all most of the time when trying to assess form from race to race, if only because it is far easier to measure.

Here too seven is the vital number, for in the author's system each grade in the structure of modern racing is equivalent to 7 lb. This can be seen in the following table:

Group One and Two	+21 lb
Group Three	+14 lb
Listed	+7 lb
Grade A Handicap	10–0
Grade B Handicap	9–7
Grade C Handicap	9–0
Grade D Handicap	8–7
Grade E Handicap	8–0
Grade F Handicap	7–7
Grade G Handicap	7–0

This table represents a personal view of the realities of the situation. The official scale for handicaps has considerable variation within it, viz. 60–70 G, 60–70 F, 65–75 E, 80–85 D, 90–100 C, 100–110 B, 110 A. This might be rationalised to 65 G, 70 F, 75 E, 80 D, 90 C, 100 B, 110 A. It is all a matter of opinion of course, but this scale, unlike the one recommended earlier, does not embrace the differences between the various grades above handicaps in the Listed/Group Pattern, and the grades which are available do not divide the classification into equal parts. It makes more sense to use one equal unit of difference throughout, rather than to have overlapping variations of five or 10 units, because the official top rating in an F handicap, for example, can be any of 60, 65 or 70. Also, there is no variation at all between the top of the ratings for some B and all A handicaps, that is 110. It must be remembered, however, that the official classifications are intended to produce competitive races, not to assess them from a private handicapping point of view with the object of trying to pinpoint the likely winner. In this latter connection, consistent use of the key number, seven, is a most useful way of dividing up the range of ability between horses.

In any private handicapper's scale there is always a huge weight difference between a horse of the highest class habitually running in Group 1 and one of the lowest racing ability. The difference on the above scale is 4½ st. Some people may even express surprise that the gulf is so wide. Yet there are authorities in racing who assert that a Derby winner could give a selling handicapper 5 st or more and still beat it. If such a race could be arranged it would be a fascinating one for the form expert and might settle a few arguments!

Be that as it may, what is meant in the table is not that the top weight in, say, a Class D handicap should carry 8–7. The table is for comparative purposes only, and it is the numerical relationship between the grades that is important. For example, a horse carrying top weight in a D handicap will be roughly 21 lb inferior to one similarly burdened in an A handicap. Or put another way, the general class of horses competing in D races will be approximately 21 lb lower than that of the runners in an A handicap.

Therefore, an increase or decrease in a horse's official rating should not be seen in isolation. It has to be related to race grade. A winner last time out carrying up to 7 lb extra on its reappearance has a reasonable chance of success if it is running in the same grade as before. But, if it is down to run in a race of one grade higher, it must find approximately another 7 lb of improvement if it is to succeed. In all it has a 14 lb harder task than it had in its previous race. If it is raised two grades, which is not unusual, it is being asked in real terms to shoulder 21 lb more than last time – 7 lb for the increase in its official handicap rating, and 14 lb (7 lb + 7 lb) for the two rises in class.

No wonder so much money is wasted by unskilled punters who see as the sole justification for a bet just a '1' against a horse's name, indicating a win last time out for an animal now running off an apparently good weight, whose real severity as a burden is not tested by any sound means. The horse might only be carrying '8 st something', but that weight could actually represent a much stiffer task in weight and grade.

Conversely, a winner last time out that is up 7 lb in the official ratings but dropped one grade is in fact racing on the same terms as before. If it reproduces its previous form, it has every chance of winning again.

Sometimes a horse is lowered two grades. Remember, the horse's connections, not the Jockey Club handicapper, determine the class of race they run their horse in. Therefore, from time to time, if winning alone and not prize money is their goal, connections may think they have found a golden opportunity for their horse. If the horse is holding its form and has not deteriorated, it has an excellent chance in the lower grade, provided that it has not been penalised by too great a rise in its official handicap mark.

5
Placed Horses

Obviously, when carrying out a survey of the most recent form in any race that is under review, it is also necessary to consider horses which did not win last time out. Although a horse which ran a very good second will sometimes be raised a pound or two by the handicapper, much to the chagrin of its trainer no doubt, here for the most part we are dealing with horses whose rating remains the same or which is lowered as a result of a poor performance.

In the latter case, however, the reduction is nearly always slight. Whereas a winner of a handicap may be lifted by quite a large amount of weight in a single increase, horses which keep failing to win are moved down the ratings very gradually a pound or two at a time. Therefore a single drop in the weights between races is seldom decisive.

A factor of greater significance which the form reader will frequently have to assess is just how much value should be put on a run where a horse was placed last time out. Again, what significance should be attached to a very poor run when a horse was right down the field?

There have to be extenuating circumstances for a horse which runs pounds below its true form, but it will generally be best to play safe. Taking the view that the horse has quite simply lost its form and the run should be dismissed out of hand will be right more often than it is wrong. The extenuating circumstances need to be pretty compelling to give such a horse a real chance in its next race. Most handicaps are won by horses with sound win-or-place form, or at least which were not beaten far in their previous race. Winners outside this group, with nothing else in their favour, do pop up from time to time, but they fall within the 'impossible' category that the form reader has no alternative but to exclude from his calculations.

For placed horses, however, there is a scale which will measure fairly accurately the distance behind the winner in weight terms. If the weights actually carried by the winner and placed horses are also adjusted by the number of pounds above or below some fixed point, say, 9 st, an exact order of merit revealing by how much weight some horses are superior to others and inferior (or equal) to the rest can easily be constructed.

This is the scale:

Over 5f/6f	1 length = 3 lb
Over 7f	1 length = 2½ lb
From 1m to 1m 3f	1 length = 2 lb
From 1m 4f plus	1 length = 1 lb

Again, the scale is unofficial, but except for one important consideration will be found to be extremely accurate in assessing how placed and close-up horses stand in relation to the winner and each other.

In any finish where there is daylight between the winner and the second, the tendency in many races is for jockeys to ease even horses immediately behind the front two if they have no chance of actually winning. This is, strictly speaking, contrary to the rules of racing, at least if the final placings of animals prominent in the finish of a race are thereby affected. Yet despite the vocal disapproval of each-way backers frequently expressed from the stands, regrettably this is accepted practice on our racecourses and for the most part the stewards turn a blind eye to the breach of the rules.

The problem from the point of view of the form reader is that if full value is given to the distance between second and third, and the distances beyond, the inferiority of beaten horses is often exaggerated. Therefore, give full value only to the finishing distance between winner and second, however great the margin, but halve the distances after that when applying the scale to convert to weight.

Also, although the scale accurately assesses the form difference between winners and runners-up, wide-margin winners last time out do not produce as many winners as those which have won by a narrow margin. Whereas the former have probably had the race run to suit them, the latter have shown battling qualities to get home in front. Tough horses like these with the willingness to fight for the lead are often better betting propositions than facile winners who won unchallenged last time out. This statistical fact is in stark contrast to what many punters believe. The practice, followed by many, of going through the card in search of wide-margin winners is in fact a faulty betting strategy.

CONCLUSION

The first stage in analysing handicaps is now complete. Last-time-out form should always be the best guide. If one is not prepared to look at the most recent form of every horse in the race, one should at least examine with a critical eye the most recent run of any horse which is a probable bet. Or, if the field has been narrowed down to a shortlist of possibles by whatever means, a comparison of the previous outings of each candidate ought to be the final arbiter.

By and large the reader coming to handicapping for the first time will do well to take very recent form at its face value and, even for a sophisticated form enthusiast of long standing, tunnel vision of this kind is no bad thing. Our basic methodology has the advantage of processing vital information reasonably quickly and efficiently; excursions into the forest of races beyond the most recent should be kept to a minimum, however adept readers believe themselves to be at interpreting the vagaries of old or hidden form.

6
INSTANT HANDICAPPING

Last-time-out form in relation to weight and grade should be the main focus of the conventional form reader, possibly combined with an appreciation of the longer view of each horse's chance reflected in race ratings based on a private handicap. Look for very good recent form *and* a high, if not the highest, race rating.

An alternative approach is possible, however. It is based on general, statistical data drawn from the form book and has the advantage of finding favoured horses quickly and automatically, without the backer having to judge the niceties of form. Unique to this book, it has been given the name of 'instant handicapping'.

Instant handicapping is not some miraculous oracle. It will not pick the winner of every handicap. If every single horse indicated by it were backed to win, it would probably not produce a level-stakes profit over an extended period, but what it will do is show readers how to choose a great many winners of handicap races, probably a lot more than they have ever been able to pick before.

The method is based on a basic racing truth: class tells in handicaps as much as in any other horse race. Or, horses near the top of the weights win much more often than those at the bottom. This trend is so pronounced that with the aid of a few simple rules it can be converted into a point at which bookmakers, for all their careful regulation of the odds, may be vulnerable.

Instant handicapping was developed many years ago by the author from a large amount of data which is, inevitably, now dated but which has served him well ever since. For the purposes of this book, however, and as a way of reaffirming the statistical validity of the principles behind the method, another much smaller survey has been undertaken in which the results of 100 Flat handicaps were recorded before being arranged into a meaningful pattern.

May was chosen for the survey. The new Flat season is about five weeks old at the beginning of the month and form has settled down to a great extent. Trainers are still keen to get races into every one of their charges and fields are definitely large compared with later in the year. This is the ideal scenario for demonstrating the ideas which underpin our instant-handicapping methodology.

The point about the sample of handicap winners set out below is that it is purely random. Once the process of recording results on a daily basis was begun, no winner was omitted, whatever its price or position in the handicap, until the 100-race mark was reached.

The largest field in the block of results was one of 29 runners, and the smallest six, but the vast majority of the 100 races had more than 10 runners, often many more. Because in many of the handicaps one or more horses are set to carry an identical weight, it was convenient to assign the positions in the handicap a letter rather than a number – thus avoiding the confusing use of equals signs – where A is always the top weight, B the second horse down in the weights, C the third, and so on. Overweight and the allowance for apprentice jockeys were completely ignored.

SURVEY OF 100 FLAT HANDICAPS

A   4–1 6–1 7–1 8–1 10–1 16–1

B   9–4 4–1 11–2 7–1

C   5–2 5–1 13–2 13–2 7–1 15–2 10–1 12–1 12–1 16–1

D   6–4 100–30 4–1 9–2 9–2 5–1 6–1 6–1 6–1 13–2 13–2 10–1 12–1 12–1 12–1 14–1

E   3–1 9–2 6–1 13–2 7–1 12–1 14–1

F   6–4 9–2 9–2 11–2 9–1 12–1 16–1

G   13–8 7–1 14–1

H   5–2 3–1 4–1 6–1 11–1 16–1

I   5–2 11–4 5–1 9–1 25–1

J   6–1 7–1 14–1

K   4–1 5–1 13–2 10–1 14–1 16–1 25–1

L   11–2 14–1 33–1

M   2–1 7–1 10–1 11–1 16–1 16–1 20–1

N   11–2 15–2

O   6–1 13–2 12–1 20–1 20–1 20–1 33–1

P   8–1

Q   15–8 3–1 7–1

R   11–2

S   —

T   —

U   16–1

V   —

W   12–1

The preceding table reveals some highly significant points which ought to be the subject of further analysis. The quite high number of wins recorded by K, M and in particular by O, where some big prices would have yielded a good level-stakes profit, are almost certainly something of an aberration, and would probably not be repeated in another survey. More likely some other letter or letters would have an exceptional run of good fortune but, although the sample of 100 races is small enough to allow for this kind of luck to play a part, nevertheless there is a clear, and to some extent predictable, pattern in the figure as a whole.

If the general proposition that high weights in handicaps do best and bottom weights do worse is correct and that the weights in between win in approximate proportion to that model, then what you would expect to see is a triangle. With the exception of the two top weights, that is what you have. Looking at the figure from the bottom up and from left to right, the hypotenuse of the triangle can be drawn in from the 12–1 of W to the 14–1 of D.

There is a very good reason to explain why the top two positions have done relatively badly. The handicapper who, according to the most uncharitable view, never forgets, tends to be hard on horses which show an exceptional run of form or even run just one exceptional race. Such horses rise rapidly to the head of the weights within their class. Their measure is taken and they are no longer capable of winning off their high rating. Once this has happened, a horse might remain too high in the weights for the rest of its racing career.

This is not an exceptional scenario. It is a situation which, to a greater or lesser degree, occurs all the time and certainly to the extent that any method of betting in handicaps needs to have built into it some device by which animals so afflicted are identified and excluded for betting purposes.

Leaving refinements apart for the moment, it is clear from the figure that the four positions C to F are the best consecutive positions and it is around this area that the vulnerable point for the bookmaker occurs. If there had been an equal distribution of recorded victories, the strike rate for weights would have been $100 \times 4/23 = 17.39$ per cent. The actual strike rate for the positions C to F is in fact much higher, at 40 per cent of the sample.

The author knows from other data, however, that there may be some element of lucky aberration in the F position. Since our final methodology will not abandon the highest weights entirely, it is also worth noting that the five weights A to E produced a total of 43 per cent of the wins. Put another way, over two-fifths of all the handicaps in the survey were won by one of the top five in the weights.

It is also possible to draw some pretty definite, general conclusions about the starting prices of winners. Below are the 100 results arranged according to this factor, where the data has been put into bands of starting prices reflecting various levels of confidence within the racecourse betting market. Once again there appears to be an area where the bookmaker looks vulnerable to the backer who works from statistical record.

Up to 2–1	5 winners
9–4 to 4–1	14 winners
9–2 to 15–2	39 winners
8–1 to 10–1	9 winners
11–1 to 14–1	17 winners
16–1 to 20–1	12 winners
22–1 or over	4 winners

The price range of 9–2 to 15–2 is outstanding with 39 per cent of all winners contained within it. The ranges 9–4 to 4–1 and 11–1 to 14–1 are roughly equal and both produce slightly more winners than 8–1 to 10–1. But, when it comes to choosing a favoured group of prices on which to concentrate, the very narrow 8–1 to 10–1 band added to 9–2 to 15–2 is surely best for the punter.

Horses quoted 9–4 to 4–1 do not offer value in terms of likely profitability from a by-no-means-exceptional strike rate of winners; and 11–1 to 14–1 chances, though clearly more remunerative individually, are in fact very plentiful in any typical handicap with a fair number of runners. This would reduce the overall profitability from successes, and indeed, would probably result in an actual loss overall. Also, they are impossible to identify from newspaper forecasts, as they are usually included among the unspecified 'others'.

On the other hand, an unbroken price band from 9–2 right up to 10–1 inclusive offers the punter a readily identifiable, consecutive group of horses from within the normal betting-forecast range. Even if on occasion some of them start and win at longer odds than 10–1 they would still fall into our net. The survey, derived solely from starting prices, showed a strike rate of 48 per cent from the 9–2 to 10–1 band, or nearly half the races. This is definitely the odds range which should be the focus of the punter's attack on the bookmaker.

RULES

We are now in a position to lay down the rules of the instant handicapping method, which are as follows:

1 Concentrate on the top five horses in the handicap, including all horses set to carry equal fifth weight. Ignore apprentice allowances.
2 Strike out, however, any horse due to be ridden by a jockey claiming either seven or five pounds.
3 Rate the form figures of the two top weights in the race by these scales:

   Six-figure form
   – winner in last three races: 2 pts per win
   – winner in previous three: 1 pt per win
   – placed (2, 3, 4) in any race: 1 pt each place.

   Five-figure form or less
   – winner last time out: 3 pts
   – winner in previous races: 2 pts per win
   – placed (2, 3, 4) in any race: 1 pt each place.

   Strike out any horse with a total of less than 4 points from six-figure form, less than 3 points if it has only run five times in all, or less than 2 points if it has run four times or less.
4 Consider only horses quoted between 9–2 and 10–1 inclusive in the betting forecast of the newspaper you use for betting purposes.

Rule 3 imposes a minimum form qualification in order to eliminate those top-weighted no-hopers of which the handicapper has probably taken full measure, as well as those which find themselves at the top end of the handicap for technical reasons which have nothing to do with racing ability, such as failure to meet qualifying standards for a realistic weight.

Rule 2 eliminates horses ridden by very inexperienced apprentices. They are seldom value for the weight concession. Horses so ridden rarely win, for the presence of a 'chalk' jockey in the plate of a highly weighted runner is in fact a sure sign that a horse is 'not off' today.

It was gratifying to find that although there had been a considerable gap in time since the rules of instant handicapping were originally formulated, the survey of a block of recent results did not call for any modification in the rules. The instant handicapping method appears as good now as when it was created.

How often can you expect to win with it? We have already admitted that it is not a magic oracle, but the punter who turns to it as a selection method still has every right to expect some very good days.

Take, for example, the following day's Flat racing. There were two meetings and three handicaps at each meeting. The complete 'instant' record was as follows:

GOODWOOD

3.10   7f   Class C

09100–0	CHAMPAGNE RIDER	Form count: 1.	Eliminated
0–01852	MISTER RAMBO	Form count: 2.	Eliminated
6/7035–6	CHEWIT	L. Newman (5).	Eliminated
090–244	PRINCE BABAR	7–1.	Selected
200–066	BOOMERANG BLADE	Not 9–2 to 10–1.	Eliminated

Probable SP: 6 Peartree House, 7 Hyperactive, Prince Babar, 8 Bintang Timor, Karameg, Mister Rambo, 10 Second Wind, 11 Elmhurst Boy, 12 Amber Fort, Chewit, Welcome Gift.

Selection: Prince Babar

Result: Gift of Gold (9th in the weights) Won 25–1
Prince Babar 5th 7–1

3.40   1m 6f   Class B

00133–4	SALMON LADDER	Form count: 4, but not 9–2 to 10–1.	Eliminated
320–224	MURGHEM	Form count: 5, but not 9–2 to 10–1.	Eliminated
11200–9	PAIRUMANI STAR	10–1.	Selected
145320–	MONTALCINO	Not 9–2 to 10–1.	Eliminated
7000–07	TURTLE VALLEY	Not 9–2 to 10–1.	Eliminated

Probable SP: 9–2 Afterjacko, 5 Little Pippin, 6 Zilarator, 7 Livius, Montechristo, 8 Tensile, 10 Pairumani Star, 12 Murghem, Salmon Ladder, Turtle Valley, 14 Quedex.

Selection: Pairumani Star

Result: Pairumani Star Won 12–1

5.20   5f   Class E   Apprentice race

760–206	FORGOTTEN TIMES	Form count: 1.	Eliminated
366154	BEWARE	Form count: 4. 7–1.	Selected
1246–00	ECUDAMAH	8–1.	Selected
00000–0	SIHAFI	7–1.	Selected
000–000	POLAR MIST	10–1.	Selected

Probable SP: 4 Beyond The Clouds, 5 Forgotten Times, 7 Beware, Sihafi, Nightingale Song, 8 Ecudamah, 10 Polar Mist, Dancing Lily, Half Tone.

Selections: Beware, Ecudamah, Sihafi, Polar Mist

Result: Polar Mist Won 12–1
Sihafi 4th 9–1
Beware 5th 11–2
Ecudamah 9th 15–2

NEWCASTLE

3.20   1m   Class E

114423	SIGN OF THE TIGER	Form count: 6. F. Goode (3) 5–1.	Selected
43167–0	TOP OF THE CLASS	Form count: 3.	Eliminated
7–88	HAIKAL	Not 9–2 to 10–1.	Eliminated
662440	DONTBESOBOLD	Not 9–2 to 10–1.	Eliminated
619–00	MARVEL	Not 9–2 to 10–1.	Eliminated

Probable SP: 9–4 Mister Clinton, 5 Sign Of The Tiger, 7 Alpathar, 8 One Domino, Nowt Flash, 10 Top Of The Class, Flying Carpet, 12 Watergold.

Selection: Sign Of The Tiger

Result: Sign Of The Tiger Won 6–1

3.50   2m   Class D

111112–	VIRGIN SOLDIER	Form count: 8. 6–1.	Selected
41–6	FREETOWN	Form count: 3. 11–2.	Selected
790708–	PASS THE REST	Not 9–2 to 10–1.	Eliminated
17–6000	YES KEEMO SABEE	Not 9–2 to 10–1.	Eliminated
418–890	GIVE AN INCH	Not 9–2 to 10–1.	Eliminated

Probable SP: 7–2 Generous Ways, 5 Kagoshima, 11–2 Freetown, 6 Virgin Soldier, 7 Legendary Line, Old Hush Wing, 10 Sposa, Northern Motto.

Selections: Virgin Soldier, Freetown

Result: Virgin Soldier Won 10–1
Freetown 2nd 3–1

4.20   5f   Class E

187–0	CAUTIOUS JOE	Form count: 2. B. McHugh (7).	Eliminated
885787	AVONDALE GIRL	Form count: 0.	Eliminated
634–36	DAWN	R. Cody-Boutcher (7).	Eliminated
250–960	TWICKERS	8–1.	Selected
101600	FRILLY FRONT	7–1.	Selected

Probable SP: 6 Naissant, 7 Frilly Front, Bollin Ann, 8 Twickers, Record Time, 10 Dawn, Angel Hill, 12 High Carry, Tancred Times.

Selections: Twickers, Frilly Front

Result: Bollin Ann (6th in the weights) Won 6–1
Twickers Unplaced 12–1
Frilly Front Unplaced 10–1

Thus the following successes and failures emerged for the day:

> Loser in one pick
> 12–1 winner in one pick
> 12–1 winner in four picks
> 6–1 winner in one pick
> 10–1 winner in two picks
> Two losers in two picks.

It would be wrong to expect such a spectacular return too often. The examples do demonstrate, however, the very real potential of the method in a difficult area of racing speculation.

Several horses are often indicated in the same race. This is unavoidable and it is left to the reader to decide exactly how to use the instant handicapping method. You might make a choice based on your reading of form or you may prefer simply not to bet when the method indicates more than one horse. Or again, you might decide to back all the possibles in a race, dividing the stakes equally or regulating stakes more systematically as explained in Part 3.

At all events, instant handicapping is a viable alternative to conventional ways of assessing form in handicaps. Selections are fully automatic, no judgement is required on the part of the punter, and it is the work of a few minutes to check out the daily indications. If attracted to the method, one has every chance of finding many winners in the future.

There is no need to take my word for it. Some time after the first edition of this manual was published, I received from a Mr Doug Miller a Christmas card which was annotated, 'Dear David

Duncan, your "instant handicapping" system has changed my betting balance from the colour red to the colour black! Many thanks. Here's to a prosperous New Year.' It was gratifying to hear from a reader in this way that the manual had been so successful in creating a winning punter who had previously struggled to show a profit from his racing.

On the other hand, we have said that specialisation pays the biggest dividends, and there now follows a series of criteria in which very specific guidelines are given for various types of race.

7
CRITERION 1 – FIVE-FURLONG SPRINT HANDICAPS

Even more than with handicaps in general, sprint handicaps over the minimum trip are usually won by horses near the top of the weights which are also well to the fore in the betting.

1   Concentrate on the top half-dozen in the weights (slightly more in very big fields).

2   Concentrate on a similar number of horses at the head of the betting.

3   Winners last time out frequently win again. But even over this minimum trip where weight might be thought to have less effect, an increase of more than seven pounds in the ratings may well be enough to prevent a repeat victory.

4   Horses which have been running well without winning or even being placed can and do win sprints. Here form from some time ago can suddenly become indicative of a probable win, although the horse has been just short of concert pitch in very recent outings. The market on the race compared with the betting forecast often provides the clue that a sprinter is 'off' today.

5   Five furlongs is a specialist distance both for horses and trainers. Never ignore lightly the chance of a runner trained by one of the small number of handlers who specialise in winning sprint handicaps. They have purple patches from time to time in these races when every runner from the stable suddenly improves by leaps and bounds. They even win with 'cast-offs' from other stables.

    D. Nicholls and J.M. Bradley are the current 'sprint kings'. One of the 'secrets' of the success of trainers who target sprints is that they focus on making a horse quick from the stalls. Speed at the gate is usually the difference between winning and losing in these races.

8
CRITERION 2 – SIX-FURLONG HANDICAPS

These events are not the object of specialisation to the same extent as races over the minimum distance. However, more than in the latter, the key here is winning form over the trip, although not necessarily last time out.

Therefore:

1 Consider only horses which won last time out or which have won at least one of their last three runs or which have won at least two of their last six runs.

   This rule will have a severe 'pruning' effect in many races, but strict adherence to it will pay off over time.

2 Ignore horses in the bottom third of the weights.

3 Provided a horse is not hopelessly overburdened by being put up a huge amount in the weights as a penalty for a facile win, ignore the study of weight. It may not help much in six-furlong handicaps.

4 Even races of this type with enormous fields are seldom won by a horse priced over 16–1. The betting market on the course is far and away the best indicator for the shrewd punter who can spot when money is 'talking'.

9
CRITERION 3 – TWO-MILE PLUS HANDICAPS

There are not a lot of these races but horses at or near the top of the handicap are much the best. Class tells over a distance of ground.
Therefore:

1   Concentrate on the top third of the handicap.

2   Consider, say, only the first five in the betting in races of 16 or more runners, and roughly *pro rata* for races with fewer contestants.

3   Look for horses which are ultra consistent as revealed in the six-figure form summary. It is not necessary to insist on a preponderance of winning over placed form, but too many '0's in the form line make a staying handicapper a suspect betting proposition.

10
CRITERION 4 – FORM FIGURES IN ALL HANDICAPS

It is possible for a backer to find winners of handicaps consistently by simply studying the three-figure form lines of the runners, either in conjunction with other factors or even in isolation. The merit of this approach is that not many handicappers actually record the most favoured figures.

The sequences established as those producing most winners in handicaps, after a large amount of research are, in approximate order of merit:

Top Rank	101 131 011 112
Second Rank	321 311 121 122
Third Rank	111 211 114
Handicaps for 3-y-os only and nurseries	11 21

11
CRITERION 5 – MAIDEN WINNERS FIRST TIME IN A HANDICAP

Horses, three-year-olds for the most part, which have won a maiden race and which are now running in a handicap race for the first time, have a poor record. They hardly ever go on to win a good class handicap (A to C) immediately and are suspect propositions in races of lesser class.

Maiden-race winners made favourite to win their first run in a handicap are especially poor value as a betting medium. Some of them, running in big handicaps and trained by a fashionable trainer, are sometimes at very short odds. They hardly ever win but punters are 'taken in' in droves time after time. The Newmarket trainer L. Cumani, however, is one leading handler who is something of the exception who proves the rule.

12
CRITERION 6 – NURSERIES

The days when nurseries, that is handicaps for two-year-olds, were the medium of betting coups by clever stables have long gone. Nevertheless, the market related to very simple form study is a fair guide and these events are by no means as formidable as races for older horses.

1   The first four in the betting are heavily favoured (first five in fields of 16 or more runners).

2   As a general form prescription, winners last time out are to be preferred to seconds in their previous race which in turn are better than thirds and fourths.

3   Unlike three-year-olds, many two-year-old maiden winners go on to score in a nursery handicap at the first time of asking, but be wary of the winners of sellers. However low their weight, the rise in class will nearly always put paid to their chance.

13
NON-HANDICAPS – BACKING AND OPPOSING FAVOURITES

Although it is a view that has been challenged in some quarters in recent years, traditional racing wisdom holds that the backer's best chance lies in trying to find the winners of non-handicaps and that those races in which the handicapper has an influence should be avoided by the serious punter. It is a fact in support of this view for instance that both on the Flat (turf) and over jumps (hurdles and chases) approaching 80 per cent of all winners in stakes races emanate from the first three in the betting forecast. On the other hand, handicaps, judged either from the point of view of betting forecasts or the actual market on races, are nothing like as consistent. No category of handicap under any code of racing can boast the same kind of statistic.

However, even if a non-handicap race can be narrowed down to just three possibles much of the time, which one of three will actually win remains a major conundrum. Also, the odds available for 'live' candidates in non-handicaps are on the whole some way below the rate of return for fancied runners in handicaps.

In all except the most competitive conditions races, given the expertise of both bookmakers and backers in reading form, *the favourite should win,* but will rarely be at a generous price. If the backer opts for a horse which is not favourite, even though it is second or third favourite, this generally means that the indications of form are being ignored.

The secret of winning in this area of betting, as in all others, is to find enough winners at prices good enough to ensure an overall profit. In practice, finding the right blend of first, second and third favourites is a feat beyond most punters.

As a starting point to solving this perennial problem, the following question should be to the fore of the reader's mind every time a non-handicap race is considered as a potential betting proposition:

> **If the favourite is, theoretically, the best horse in the race at the weights, but only 35 per cent or so**

of all favourites actually win nowadays, is the
favourite in the race under review one that is
likely to succeed or fail?

It is a simple-enough question but one with enormous significance
in determining how the backer should proceed. In this respect
statistics can be a great help, at least if one is comfortable with
statistics in racing to the point where they may sometimes
contradict a personal opinion.

For the purposes of this book, a survey of 500 conditions races
on the Flat was undertaken. Betting-forecast favourites were
arranged by their odds, and the number of winners and losers in
each of four price ranges carefully recorded.

The outcome was as follows:

Horses quoted at odds-on in the betting forecast   54.8% won
Horses quoted from evens to 6–4 inclusive   55.6% won
Horses quoted from 13–8 to 11–4 inclusive   26.1% won
Horses quoted at 3–1 or over   9.1% won

There are small but variable profits to be had from random betting
on favourites in the first two categories, although too small
probably to satisfy the ordinary punter wagering in moderate
stakes. Forget about profit and loss for the moment, however, and
consider only the winning percentages. Surely, for anyone who
backs a lot of horses regularly, the following prescriptions, derived
from the above survey, must make sense.

1 Back all odds-on chances in the betting forecast to win.

2 Back all horses quoted between evens and 6–4 to win.

3 Back some horses quoted at between 13–8 and 11–4 to win, but
   in some races with a betting-forecast favourite in this price
   range, find an alternative selection.

4 Automatically oppose any horse quoted as favourite at 3–1 or
   longer in the betting forecast with some other selection.

I personally see nothing wrong in principle with betting at odds-on but, for the many who do not like laying the odds, the first rule could be amended to read:

> **When the favourite is odds-on in the betting forecast, do not oppose it with a bet on some other selection.**

Eyebrows will no doubt be raised in some quarters at such a set of sweeping generalisations which restrict the backer's freedom of action across the board in a number of vital respects when it comes to backing favourites. But, hopefully, readers will grasp the point that is being made, even if they ultimately reject some or all of the prescriptions as automatic betting tactics.

When attending a race meeting with the intention of having a bet on every race, or when going down the day's cards in the morning newspaper with a view to having a bet, it is usual to pick out some favourites and avoid others. Hitherto this process will have been entirely subjective, governed by one's own knowledge, prejudices and preferences.

But, how often is this right? How often does one pick out one 6–4 chance that gets beaten and disregard another horse at the same price which wins? More often than one cares to admit is almost certainly the answer.

Instead of relying on personal judgement of form, suppose we make the above conclusions a set of absolute, inviolable precepts based on statistics, not fallible human judgement. This will then be right more often than not. Perhaps one should not bet on every race at a meeting (although bookmakers do) and be more selective in betting from home, but the general point remains valid.

As a first step in assessing any race, the favourite's chance should be examined and action taken accordingly. If punters are prepared to put their faith in statistics, the aforementioned quartet of rules provide an automatic *modus operandi* to guide their betting actions.

Needless to say, many will reject such a mechanistic approach. But even the most confident and talented reader of form will find food for thought here, and although not wishing to adopt every one of the four rules as a matter of course, some readers may be prepared to let non-handicap betting be influenced to a greater or lesser extent by them.

Within the main survey of 500 races a number of other possibilities concerning the favourite were considered. The results of this secondary investigation are set out below. Remember that only non-handicap races are within its scope.

Where the betting-forecast favourite was at odds against, but was replaced as favourite in the actual racecourse market, 22.7 per cent of the original favourites won.

Since there was a 6.8 per cent level-stakes profit on outlay from backing all horses which met this qualification, the view often touted among some media pundits and others that a favourite which drifts in the market 'cannot win' is simply not true. On balance it is better to back the drifter than to oppose it, certainly unless there is a good and sufficient reason to account for the lack of confidence reflected in the betting market.

On the other hand, the one time when a big drift in the market can be viewed as a potentially accurate indicator of an imminent poor performance is at Group level, especially in Group One and Group Two. These are big races, and every move of the candidates at home and on the racecourse is, as far as possible, scrutinised for fitness and well-being. If information that a horse is not 100 per cent for some reason reaches the racecourse betting ring, and this information results in a drift in price, then in the main such information proves accurate, not always but usually. At all other times it is no bad thing that a horse drifts in the betting, and the statistics bear this out.

Another frequent circumstance surrounding favourites was investigated and the outcome was as follows:

Where the favourite was at odds against in the betting forecast, but was backed down to start at odds-on in the racecourse betting, 55.6 per cent of such favourites actually won.

Unfortunately here things are not quite so clear-cut, for backing all non-handicap favourites which behaved in this manner produced a level-stakes loss of 24.3 per cent overall, despite the high percentage of winners. Clearly there is nothing in this circumstance to help the backer in a positive sense, although an important negative conclusion can be drawn, namely that in statistical terms at least there needs to be a very good reason to bet against the trend and oppose a favourite which shortens up to odds-on in the pre-race betting exchanges.

One other question was asked in assessing the results of the survey. This concerned the fate of betting-forecast favourites quoted at odds-on in the morning newspaper, but which drifted out to odds against on the course, although still remaining clear favourites. The finding in this respect was that there are very few such horses. No clear trend emerged, with about half winning and half losing, but it would be pointless to cite exact figures because the sample was too small for any serious statistical conclusion to be drawn.

It is hoped that this survey is of value. Even if readers are unwilling to act to the letter upon the conclusions which emerged, thereby making them an automatic part of non-handicap betting strategy, at least the realities of the situation are now known in the case of the various betting scenarios discussed. And, in the uncertain world of backing horses, certain knowledge is a precious commodity.

The survey focused on non-handicaps in general, but non-handicaps can be broken down further into a number of different types, far more in fact than is the case with handicaps. This opens up an obvious avenue for specialisation, and specialisation is the backer's best chance of winning in the long run. Good recent form, especially last time out, is as always the racing enthusiast's greatest ally and most effective weapon in the struggle with the layers. However, it may pay to apply this guiding principle to one or perhaps just a few of the various kinds of stakes race – hence the analysis of main categories which follows, although space prevents a full and separate examination of some of the sub-categories, especially those which are grouped together under the heading of 'conditions races' in the guidelines to be found in the next few pages.

14
Criterion 7 – Group One/Two Races for Three-Year-Olds and Over

For betting purposes one of three possible form profiles is generally found in the races which make up the top flight of British racing. There is the very competitive event with plenty of runners. Many have high-class form and there are quite a number of horses which hold a reasonable chance of winning. The Classic races, with the usual exception of the much less competitive St Leger, are invariably of this type. At the other extreme we find races with relatively small fields that have 'cut up' to such an extent that an odds-on favourite, which on all known form should win, apparently dominates proceedings. In races of the third sort, where just two or three horses seem to have a real chance, the punter has a straightforward choice, but knows only too well that it is easy to be on the 'wrong one'.

In the case of the presence of a 'hotpot' or 'good thing' in the field, on balance it is best not to attempt to 'buy money' at very short odds. Odds-on favourites in Group One or Group Two are more reliable than their counterparts further down the racing scale, but they are not infallible, and from time to time they flop – to the astonishment of the racing *cognoscenti*. Horses, even horses of the highest class, are not machines.

The better bet is to ignore the presumed 'certainty' and to go for an 'each-way steal' as it is sometimes called. This is a horse with sound form that might just upset the favourite. If such a horse has an outstanding chance of finishing in a place, it will be good business to back it each-way, even though the punter is prepared to accept the loss of the win part of the wager. Once in a while there is a shock result and the backer on the only realistic alternative to the favourite will reap a handsome reward. Even if the favourite wins, its very short price inflates the odds for the rest of the field to an unrealistic level. The each-way better is therefore almost certain to break even, even though the bookmaker will pay only one-fifth the odds for a place, or in the case of some firms, only one-sixth when the favourite in a non-handicap starts at odds-on.

It does not do, however, to oppose every odds-on chance in a big stakes race with each-way bets. The horse chosen for a win-

and-place bet should be as outstanding for a place as the favourite apparently is for a win. If the backer can additionally find even a slight chink in the favourite's armour such as doubtful stamina or a tendency to prefer different going, then the each-way steal is truly a 'bet-to-nothing'. For example, the race for the 1999 St Leger threw up precisely such a bet. The odds-on favourite Ramruma had won the Oaks on soft ground but, on both form and breeding, there was a substantial doubt as to whether she would stay the extra distance of the Doncaster race on the very firm ground that prevailed at Town Moor. By contrast Mutafaweq, a Royal Ascot winner on lightning-fast ground, seemed certain to stay every yard of the St Leger trip. The outcome is history. Mutafaweq ran out the winner of a hard-fought contest and rewarded the 'each-way thieves' at a handsome 11–2, while those who had 'laid the odds' on Ramruma lost their cash on a gallant filly that could only finish an honourable second.

Where one of these races looks very open, it should be remembered that this is the top level of racing and that form still works out well. The favoured form figures cited in Criterion 4 are especially effective as a winner-finding aid in this class of competition, although here 111 stands out and the remainder are fairly equal in rank. Conversely, inconsistent animals with poor form figures should be left severely alone. Statistics tell us that it is highly unusual for the winner of such events to be outside the first five in the betting.

Most Group One and Group Two winners are horses with established form at the highest level that have been specifically prepared for their races as part of a career strategy. Therefore the backer should be wary of the type of animal which, on the strength of a single brilliant run, is suddenly asked to break into the highest echelons of competition. This certainly applies in Classic trials in the spring of each year, when fitness gives an advantage to precocious types that cannot be sustained in the big race itself.

Even when connections are prepared to go to the considerable expense of supplementing a horse for a big race, it is generally one of the established stars which succeeds, and the newcomer is found to just lack the class necessary to repeat its impressive performance at the lower level. Recently, there have been a few exceptions to this trend but, generally speaking, even the top yards often get it wrong in these cases, at least in so far as prize money for a win, though not necessarily a place, is concerned.

Since Classic and other Group One and Two contenders are now trained with the utmost tenderness to ensure that they hold their form, a long absence is no barrier to success in an important stakes race. These days, far more than in the past, the best horses are prepared at home for their long-term objectives, in contrast to lesser animals which are expected to earn their keep on the racecourse by the alternative route of winning a few races from a lot of runs. Participation in actual races at Group level is kept to the minimum compatible with establishing a reputation for stud purposes as much as for gathering prize money. Fitness can therefore be taken on trust in racing's showpiece events.

15
CRITERION 8 – GROUP THREE/LISTED RACES

GROUP THREE RACES

For different reasons a great many Group Three races are just as competitive as the most open Group One event, but form is far more suspect here when it comes to trying to spot winners.

A typical Group Three race might be made up of one or two horses dropped from Group Two (though rarely Group One), horses which habitually compete at this Group Three level and several hopefuls graduating as winners from Listed races or even jumping directly from winning a big handicap to this much tougher grade. Fields are on the medium to small side, but recent form, even last-time-out form, can be extremely difficult to assess in this mixed company. However, the shrewd backer who bears in mind the following points can keep ahead of the game:

1 Horses that have had a number of outings in Group Two but which have never quite succeeded at that level are not likely to fare much better in Group Three. The drop in grade is nearly always more of a warning sign than a recommendation.

2 Listed race winners can and do graduate without too much difficulty to the higher grade. A good win last time out in a Listed event is one of the more reliable indicators of a potential Group Three winner.

3 Very few good handicappers make the grade in Group class, for to do so means they have been seriously underestimated in the early part of their careers. The exception is a lightly raced three-year-old which, by its racecourse performances, has demonstrated that it is improving so quickly that it ought to experience little difficulty in competing against established Group Three performers. Consecutive wins in handicaps is almost invariably the first signpost to success in Group Three for this type of improving three-year-old but, unlike most good winners of Listed races, they are not inevitable winners in Group company. Some make the grade and some do not.

4 The leading stables dominate Group One and Group Two. Group Three is a far more democratic affair. Do not be put off a horse with apparently winning credentials in Group Three just because it is trained at one of the less-fashionable yards.

5 In so far as race distance is concerned, Group Three sprints are far and away the most reliable from a form point of view.

6 Over other distances the betting forecast is frequently a poor guide. Winners start at all kinds of prices. However, paradoxically, actual racecourse favourites are reasonably sound bets. They only win according to the statistical average for all non-handicaps, but starting prices are on the whole well above average. In a race where the form indicators are confused, the market leader is often the best bet. Stakes on these and, indeed, on all horses in Group Three, should be kept on the low side.

LISTED RACES

Listed race winners are a mixture of improving horses and older animals that have been established for some time at this level. Failed Group Three horses are best avoided.

The improvers are three-year-olds for the most part. They may have arrived by the handicap route or could have done well in conditions races of the better sort, but they are nearly always readily identifiable by their racecourse performances.

Older horses are much more 'in and out'. They tend to win occasionally from a mixture of races in Listed company itself, a few tilts at Group Three and not infrequent pot hunting in Class B or C conditions events. It may well be extremely difficult to tell from the form book when their time to win is due.

However, in medium-sized fields particularly, the betting forecast is a fair guide. More than in Group Three races, the first three in the betting forecast account for the majority of winners but favourites have only an average record, judged by the criterion of profit and loss at level stakes. To bet confidently in Listed races calls for a specialist in this area of competition.

Horses from Listed company dropping into handicaps are not automatic winners. They will receive no concession in the weights from the handicapper and need everything in their favour to succeed.

16
CRITERION 9 – CONDITIONS RACES

This group of races makes up the entire non-handicap racing programme below Listed class. It consists of events actually called 'conditions' races, classified stakes in which only horses whose official rating does not exceed a specified figure may compete, auction races, selling races and those events restricted to apprentice or amateur riders. Maiden races are another large group of non-handicaps and these will be dealt with separately. It is also possible to combine some of two types of race in one, a device which is sometimes employed by racecourse executives to add variety to their cards. For the purposes of betting, the student of form should draw a clear distinction between the relatively small number of races labelled 'conditions' events and the rest.

'Conditions' races are 'open' races, entry for which is not restricted in any of the ways that define the composition of other kinds of non-handicap. They are the best class of non-handicap below Listed events and are graded B to D. Featuring only animals of some ability in the main, form works out extremely well in them. Favourites have an above-average record – in the region of 50 per cent win. Consequently, since they were introduced in 1993, a number of systems exploiting this high percentage of winners with various staking plans have appeared.

The other types of non-handicap are a mixture of events competed for by inferior animals. On the whole, form is unreliable and the backer should proceed carefully. From time to time circumstances throw up a runner with an apparently excellent chance on form that has the appearance of a banker. But starting prices are unlikely to be generous and as with all horses of inferior class, however outstanding in relation to the opposition, reproduction of known form cannot be taken on trust. The added complication of an indifferent ride from an apprentice or amateur jockey adds to the need for caution in those races restricted to this kind of assistance from the saddle.

On the whole, whereas conditions races, especially of classes B and C, are a sound medium for form readers in which to bet, the backer should not habitually bet in non-handicaps below that standard. The risks are too great relative to the possible rewards.

17
CRITERION 10 – MAIDEN RACES

Usually restricted to three-year-olds but occasionally open to older horses as well, almost by definition these races feature animals with unexposed form. Horses that have never run but which may be capable of winning are an additional complicating factor. A measure of caution is therefore needed in maiden races, both in regard to betting in a race itself and to drawing form conclusions for the future from it.

Since a few top yards tend to 'farm' all classes of maiden race by dint of the superior ability of the animals generally at their disposal, the name of the trainer of a runner is usually more important than anything it has accomplished so far on the racecourse. This is particularly true of southern and Newmarket-based raiders operating on northern tracks. Where a horse trained by a top handler has put up at least one promising racecourse performance, there may be a sound case for a good bet. Even on some of the smaller tracks in the north, opinions can take a wide range in maiden events, and starting prices for raiders from the most fashionable stables, many of which do not bet, can be worthwhile.

Note also maidens from the big Newmarket stables that are described as 'backward' or 'bit backward' on their initial racecourse run. The chances are that the horse will be a very different proposition next time out and may be something to bet on. Other significant comments in the official form book on the running of maidens are 'scope' or 'good sort'. Again, a horse so labelled from a big yard is almost certainly bound to improve rapidly and put its initial, warm-up run well behind it next time out.

Backers should also be aware of another factor that applies particularly in maiden races, namely that it is very bad policy to back a maiden filly to beat maiden colts. No filly's form should be taken at face value at least until she has got her head in front at the business end of a race. Even in races confined to fillies, maidens are not generally trustworthy racing machines. Paradoxically, fillies of the very top class are arguably the most reliable of all thoroughbreds on the racecourse, but in maiden races if you never back a filly you will probably be the richer for it in the long run.

18
CRITERION 11 – TWO-YEAR-OLDS

Methods in training juveniles have changed radically in the last 20 years or so. Only genuinely precocious, speedy types which may not have much of a future in their second season are exploited to the full as juveniles. With the remainder the aim is as far as possible to educate them for a three-year-old campaign, with winning at two only a secondary consideration.

This is very bad news for the modern punter, and is reflected in the steep decline in the percentages of winning two-year-old favourites at many courses. Nevertheless a two-year-old with good form, and winning form in particular, is still a sound betting medium if demonstrably superior to its rivals by a comparison of racing records.

A sound system for all two-year-old races is to confine bets to the first three in the betting forecast and to keep to those horses which won or were at least placed last time out. A successful, particular application of this strategy is explained in detail later in this book in the section on systems.

The study of comparative times, based on the principle of comparing the time of a juvenile winner against the standard for the distance with the times recorded by older horses over sprint trips at the same meeting, can also be a fruitful source of future winners.

Two-year-old form nowadays is at its most reliable in August, September and a dry October because all juvenile form is by then largely exposed. Additionally, the better class two-year-olds which have been given plenty of time to come to hand are now on show.

19
CRITERION 12 – CLAIMING RACES

Claiming races, or 'claimers', are near the bottom of the scale in terms of the overall racing programme, being ranked only marginally superior to sellers and races for apprentice and amateur riders. Officially non-handicaps, in reality they are a sort of half-way house between handicaps and non-handicaps. Their non-handicap status is confirmed if, as sometimes happens, one or just a small number of horses stand out when the weights are compared with the official ratings for themselves and their rivals. The difference is that in a claimer, trainers nominate the sum of money for which horses can be 'claimed' by someone else, though this right is seldom exercised. This gives the horse a handicap mark and determines the weight to be carried – hence the divergence with the Jockey Club handicapper's official assessments.

In the US such races and variants of them are much more plentiful, presumably because Americans dislike the power of the official handicapper to influence results, connections preferring to rely on their own estimates of their charges' ability to determine how they are placed in races. Claiming races are contested by horses of most classes, with very good horses sometimes competing for rich purses. The racing culture of the US is very different to that of the UK, however.

In this country, claimers were introduced to add interest to the racing scene but, in fact, they are not popular with punters and most trainers. They are invariably contested by poorer quality animals which connections are prepared to risk losing. Quite often there has been some physical or other training difficulty. Most fields for claiming events include a few downright bad horses of selling-plate class. For these reasons it usually pays to follow a simple rule which more often than not will separate out the 'quick' from the 'dead':

Ignore the bottom third of the field in the weights completely and examine most closely the top third.

Horses in the middle of the weights can go either way in terms of the overall class of the race. A study of the official ratings, which are published in the racing press (but not in daily newspapers), may reveal the tendency of the middle zone.

Where a horse that is the 'spot horse' of a published private handicap or of newspaper race ratings also emerges as 'best in' when the weights are compared with the official ratings, it is a runner which, on form, should win. Claimers are usually won by one of the first three in the betting forecast.

20
CRITERION 13 – FITNESS

A vital factor in determining whether a horse can win is its current state of fitness. In a non-handicap a horse's fitness can be more-or-less taken on trust once the season has passed its initial, opening phase. Unraced two-year-olds and three-year-olds which may be given an educational run are the obvious exceptions. In handicaps, on the other hand, probably no other single factor influences results so much.

The reason is that many horses are raced in handicaps when not at their absolute peak in order to secure a favourable handicap mark that will enable them to succeed when they are finally trained 'to the minute'. Whether a handicapper is 'off' or 'not off' in today's race can sometimes, but by no means always, be inferred from a study of the dates of its races in relation to how they ran in them. Look out for the horse that begins to improve early in the season after a poor run or two.

Similarly once a horse's season is reasonably advanced it may be given a rest at some point to recuperate. Again, look for much improved form following a mid-season lay-off of about a month or slightly more. The horse will have been 'let down' and then gradually brought back to its peak. It could soon be in the winner's enclosure.

A further clue to a horse's readiness to win a handicap can be gained by examining the distances over which it has been running. Every horse has an optimum trip and in the case of all but unexposed three-year-olds the form book usually provides the necessary information. The official handicapper is probably aware that a horse is not doing itself justice because it is running over a distance either too long or too short for it but the unwritten rules of the game say that the horse should be dropped in the weights after several poor runs. When an animal has had two or three races at the 'wrong' distance and is suddenly put back to its best distance, this can be taken as a strong clue that its trainer is finally satisfied with its handicap rating. Then it becomes a trier with a real chance of winning.

There are other important points about fitness which must be noted by the form reader:

1   Generally speaking, any Flat horse which has not run for about 28 days or more has a slight question mark about its fitness in a handicap.

2   The time lapse that will return a horse fit and well to the racecourse after a rest is related to the distance of the races in which it competes. Sprinters can reappear within a few days with no loss of form. Stayers need much longer to recuperate. Two-year-olds should have a lay-off of at least 10 days if they are not to be damaged.

3   There are exceptions, but horses in general hold their form for no longer than a month. After that some deterioration from the peak of well-being is to be expected. The start of a fresh 'form wave' can sometimes be detected from a close study of the form book, as explained above.

4   A gradual rise in the level of a horse's form is usually more reliable than sudden and spectacular improvement from one race to another.

Be wary of a horse that runs really well after a long absence. It quite often fails to reproduce the form next time out.

In this respect the top trainers make fewer mistakes than their less fashionable counterparts. They have the luxury of time on their side, whereas the average handler is subject to pressures which may prevent him or her from preparing the horse in the best possible way. Connections want to see their horse run and trainers need cash flow, even if it only comes from place money in small races. The result is that horses may be rushed in a way that top yards, with wealthy owners having lots of horses, can avoid.

Even so, any horse coming back with a big run after a long rest is not certain to go on, whoever trains it.

21
CRITERION 14 – THE GOING

Next to fitness, the going preference of individual horses is the single most important factor in determining whether they will show their best form on the racecourse.

A liking for a particular type of going can improve a horse by many pounds. Conversely, dislike of the prevailing ground conditions, if pronounced enough, can ruin a horse's chance of winning a race completely.

Most horses like one type of ground – somewhere between firm and heavy – and dislike the opposite. There are, however, a minority of horses that are equally effective on any going. Good going is neutral in the sense that, whatever their preferences, all horses will run reasonably well on it.

In terms of the conformation of the thoroughbred a few observations here may help the racing enthusiast who combines form with paddock study and race-reading.

A horse with a rounded action, particularly at the forelegs, will most likely have a preference for some give in the ground. Sharp-actioned horses tend to need fast ground. Big, heavy-topped animals will be happiest on softish going because its reduces the pressure on their forelegs. Horses that dislike firm ground tend to dislike running downhill.

The conformation of a racehorse is the study of a lifetime, and compressing observations about ground preferences and physical build of a horse into one small paragraph will perhaps have done readers of this book no real favours. Fortunately, however, once a horse has raced a few times, its going predilections can usually be divined from the form book. In the absence of clues from the form record, a horse's breeding is frequently indicative of its preferences, and here it is the sire and not the dam which, nearly always, is the determining influence. In cases of doubt the tables set out in Criterion 16 will provide a fairly accurate indicator of how the state of the ground is likely to affect the offspring of leading sires.

There are three other major points which the backer should keep in mind about the going:

1 Heavy ground generally favours front-running horses.

2 When the ground is fast, favourites and form horses tend to win. When it is soft, form is suspect and heavy conditions usually see more outsiders winning than usual. Therefore wise backers adjust their stakes when extremes of going prevail.

3 Do not put much faith for the future in form achieved on heavy ground, unless there is a long spell of wet weather, as there sometimes is in the autumn.

22
CRITERION 15 – THE EFFECT OF THE DRAW

In all kinds of race up to a distance of a mile, and occasionally even further, the draw has an influence on the outcome of races at some courses, although the degree of influence can vary even on the same course due to the position of the starting stalls, going conditions, jockeys' tactics, and so on. On a small number of courses the draw has the same effect whatever conditions prevail on the day. In big fields especially, the draw can make an immense difference to results, even to the point where some horses badly drawn 'may just as well have stayed at home', as the saying goes in racing circles.

Despite all the evidence there are some punters who do not trouble themselves with this vital factor. This is folly. The result of the Temple Stakes run over five furlongs at Sandown in May 2000 provides a good example. The going was heavy and it was known in advance that high numbers were likely to be favoured. However, in a field of only 10 runners, backers ignored the known effect of the draw and made Sampower Star, drawn on the outside at 3, favourite for the race.

The result was as follows:

		Drawn
Winner	PERRYSTON VIEW	10
2nd	PROUD NATIVE	8
3rd	RAMBLING BEAR	9
5th	SAMPOWER STAR 11–8 fav	3

beaten 5l, ¾l, 5l, 3l, a total of 13¾ lengths.

Another example of just how potent an influence the draw can be is taken from the Beverley meeting of Saturday, 24 August 2002. High numbers on the straight course at the Yorkshire track are known to be heavily favoured, and the following race is just one of the many that could have been chosen from any Flat season to illustrate the point.

SPORTING OPTIONS BETTING EXCHANGE H'CAP
5f. Going: Good to Firm (Good in places). 19 ran.
No 1 stall vacant – non-runner.

		Drawn
Winner	BEYOND THE CLOUDS	13
2nd	CASH	15
3rd	MUNGO PARK	16
4th	BELLS BEACH	17
5th	TIME N TIME AGAIN	20
6th	SIR SANDROVITCH	19
7th	KISSING TIME	18
8th	SPEED ON	14

Thus the eight highest drawn horses in the field of 19 occupied the
first eight places home.

Enough said?

23
CRITERION 16 – BREEDING

Genetic influences in thoroughbred racehorses are very strong. One influence is that a stallion transmits its going preference to its progeny. The tables below show this preference for the leading sires in so far as deviations from good ground are concerned, although there are many sires who have no really pronounced preference and

FIRM	
AFFIRMED	KINGMAMBO
ALHAARTH	LION CAVERN
ANABAA	MACHIAVELLIAN
CAERLEON	MTOTO
CASTEDDU	MUHTARRAM
CLANTIME	PIVOTAL
COZZENE	POLISH PRECEDENT
DILUM	PUISSANCE
DISTANT RELATIVE	SHARROOD
DISTINCTLY NORTH	SHIRLEY HEIGHTS
GONE WEST	SINGSPIEL
GREEN DANCER	SIZZLING MELODY
GREEN DESERT	WOODMAN
KAHYASI	ZILZAL

SOFT	
ACCORDION	LINAMIX
BAHRI	LODE
BERING	RAINBOWS FOR LIFE
BRIEF TRUCE	SABREHILL
CHARNWOOD FOREST	SADLER'S WELLS
DOYOUN	SCENIC
FIRST TRUMP	SELKIRK
GRAND LODGE	SHEIKH ALBADOU
HENNESSY	ST JOVITE
HERO'S HONOR	THEATRICAL CHARMER
JAVA GOLD	TURTLE ISLAND
KING'S THEATRE	UNFUWAIN

transmit none to their progeny. The progeny of the sires that are listed have shown a marked preference for one extreme of going or the other.

The preferences shown on page 59 are only tendencies. The progeny of a sire with a distinct preference for soft going are certainly capable of winning on firm, although this is the less likely of the two scenarios. Similarly, it is not impossible for an animal by a sire who is known to prefer firm to win on soft ground. For the strength and class of the opposition are obviously important factors, at least as far as an individual race is concerned, and these tables do not take this into account.

On the other hand, it is fair to say that horses by the sires in the 'firm' table will, in all probability, prefer firm and will usually, but not necessarily, dislike its opposite of soft. Progeny from the 'soft' table may well dislike firm, but positively love soft, though here again the positive emphasised in the table does not imply a corresponding negative as an infallible rule. The fact remains that most horses prefer one or other of the types of ground, but it is also true that horses with a marked preference will, like any other, act perfectly well on good going.

It may be that some newcomers to racing will not treat these stallion tables with the respect they undoubtedly deserve. 'Surely,' the tyro might argue, 'something as particular as a liking for one kind of going or a dislike for another is so individual to each horse that its parentage has little to do with it?' In fact, though nothing of this sort is ever absolutely true in racing, a stallion's influence in that respect is one of the most solid rules in the entire sport for, by and large, a thoroughbred tends to take its physical characteristics from its sire. The form book is the best guide to a distinct preference for the prevailing ground, or a dislike of it but, faced with a horse unexposed on an extreme of going, one can be remarkably 'clued up' as to whether it will be able to produce its best form on it, while other punters are merely stumbling about in the dark.

Two-year-olds only have a limited amount of racing and in their case stallion influence can be a very useful factor in forming judgements, in default of definite evidence from the form book. Opposite are the 25 most successful sires of two-year-olds of the last few years, measured by the percentage of wins to runs. An indication of the going preference that each sire transmits to its offspring is also included.

LEADING SIRES OF TWO-YEAR-OLDS	
BARATHEA (soft)	LINAMIX (soft)
BERING (soft)	MACHIAVELLIAN (firm)
DANZIG (good)	RED RANSOM (good)
DAYJUR (good)	SADLER'S WELLS (soft)
DIESIS (firm)	SEEKING THE GOLD (good)
DIXIELAND BAND (firm)	SELKIRK (soft)
EL GRAN SENOR (good)	SHEIKH ALBADOU (soft)
FAIRY KING (soft)	SILVER HAWK (——)
GONE WEST (firm)	STORM BIRD (good)
GREAT COMMOTION (good)	STORM CAT (——)
GROOM DANCER (firm)	WARNING (firm)
IRISH RIVER (soft)	ZAFONIC (firm)
LEAR FAN (good)	

National Hunt

There are those who assert that weight does not matter very much in National Hunt racing and that, by contrast, jumping is the paramount factor in determining results, at least in steeplechases.

In my opinion such people are wrong about weight, and only partly correct about jumping. Two or three pounds might not make the difference they often do on the Flat, but 'over the sticks' it is still weight that is used to bring horses together in handicaps, and it is weight that separates them at the finish of a race.

That jumping is crucial in this branch of equine sport is surely self-evident. On the other hand, it should be realised that speed and stamina are two other essential ingredients in the make-up of a successful National Hunt horse. An animal may be a very safe jumper, but it will not win races unless it is capable of laying up with and passing rivals at key moments while possessing the capacity to see out its races full of running at the business end of a contest.

What many people fail to understand is that jumping is just as important in hurdling as in chasing. Only a very superior hurdler jumps cleanly every time without touching the obstacles or losing momentum. Over a distance of two miles or more, how a horse performs at the hurdles can make a difference of many lengths in determining where it finishes in a race.

Since form is a compound of weight, jumping ability, stamina, speed through a race and acceleration at the end of it, the problems presented by National Hunt racing are every bit as complex as those peculiar to the Flat. Few people really know how to go about solving this complexity from a betting point of view, and this section of the book, like the previous one for the Flat, takes one through every stage of analysing a lot of information that is relevant to the inherent problems. The object is to locate sound selections which can be backed with a reasonable expectation of overall success.

24
HANDICAPS

Form in handicaps can still be defined as recent past performance against the background of weight ratings and race grade but its assessment needs to be informed by a consideration of the special characteristics of jump racing. This will be dealt with in relation to race type from Criterion 17 onwards. As an introduction to these specific guidelines, however, we will once again examine the concept of 'instant handicapping' as applied to races over obstacles. Firstly something needs to be said about jumping form in general.

Races over jumps are now officially graded, as are Flat races, but there are some points of variation which reflect differences between the two branches of the sport.

This is the National Hunt scale:

Class A Grade 1
Class A Grade 2
Class A Grade 3
Class B
Class C
Class D
Class E
Class F
Class G
Class H

Thus there are 10 ranks. The difference between the top of the very top rank and the top of the bottom tier is, as on the flat, 4½ st, if seven pounds is unofficially allotted to each rank.

Over jumps, however, horses of the very highest class sometimes compete in handicaps, particularly in chases, whereas on the Flat such animals are expressly disqualified from doing so. On the Flat, therefore, all Group One, Group Two and Group Three events, and practically all Listed races, are non-handicaps. Under National Hunt rules, on the other hand, handicaps may extend as far up the scale as Grade 2 of Class A. Only Class A Grade 1 is an exclusively non-handicap grade in the manner of a Flat Group race. Also, at the other end of the scale, Class H is used to accommodate two special categories of National Hunt horse, namely hunter chasers and National Hunt Flat horses.

These few distinctions apart, the two scales are in essence much the same, and our basic form-reading methodology for the Flat can be applied equally well to National Hunt. A comparison of official weight rating related to grade of race for each horse, with the same data from every runner's most recent public run, is similarly valid as a measure of the most relevant form available and of the prospects that can be inferred from it.

25
INSTANT HANDICAPPING

Once again 100 races in a single, uninterrupted block, one for handicap chases and one for handicap hurdles, were used to provide some basic data from which to draw conclusions. Just as before, the sample is a fairly small one in relation to, say, the total number of races in a season, but it will be adequate to confirm the author's experience of jump racing over many years in so far as handicap races over jumps are concerned.

The outcome of the survey of 100 steeplechases, arranged into a single 'handicap of results' was as follows:

SURVEY OF 100 HANDICAP CHASES

A 2-5 4-6 4-5 6-5 11-8 13-8 15-8 2-1 2-1 9-4 9-4 100-30 7-2 4-1 4-1 9-2 5-1 5-1 5-1 11-2 11-2 6-1 7-1 9-1

B 11-10 11-8 11-8 9-4 5-2 7-2 6-1 6-1 6-1 8-1

C 4-5 6-4 7-4 7-4 2-1 9-4 5-2 7-2 9-2 9-2 5-1 7-1 7-1

D 13-8 3-1 3-1 7-2 4-1 4-1 5-1 5-1 11-2 6-1 8-1 10-1 16-1

E 4-7 3-1 3-1 3-1 7-2 7-2 4-1 9-2 5-1 5-1 11-2 13-2 7-1 12-1 12-1

F 7-2 4-1 6-1 7-1 16-1 40-1

G 11-2 6-1 6-1 7-1 8-1

H 4-1 6-1 7-1

I 7-4

J 9-2 12-1

K 10-1 25-1

L 9-4 16-1 16-1 40-1

M

N 9-4

O

P

Q 12-1

The picture here is remarkably similar to the one derived from the survey of Flat handicaps. The same triangular pattern occurs to confirm that in handicap chases, too, horses near the top of the weights predominate among winners. As the handicap descends, winners get fewer and fewer to the point where they tail off to none at all (the biggest field in the survey was one of 18 runners).

Just as on the Flat, handicap chases were dominated by the five handicap positions A to E with 75 per cent of the total races in the survey won by them. There was some immediate falling off of the incidence of winners at F, then the strike rate fell dramatically.

Therefore in the instant handicapping method, the top five weights, including any horses set to carry equal fifth weight, should form the core of selections in handicap chases. Given the very impressive array of winners from the highest weighted horse of all, there is no need here for a special rule to deal with the most heavily burdened horses which was considered necessary for the Flat. Indeed, in this particular sample of handicap chases at least, a simple level-stakes bet on the top weight alone would have produced an outcome close to the break-even point. It might be possible with just a little refinement to devise a system around top weights in handicap chases as a trouble-free automatic bet. One could certainly do a lot worse. If, however, the idea is to find the largest possible number of winners in these races, then it is necessary to go further down the handicap. Once the fifth position in the weights has been decided upon as the cut-off point, there has to be some way of singling out the best bet or bets from the group of runners indicated thereby.

As with the Flat, once again the obvious way to narrow down the five favoured weights in a handicap chase is to consider probable starting prices. The price bands used for the Flat would not be helpful here, however, for the merest glance tells us that the odds about winners are on the whole much shorter. Therefore, a different set of odds groupings was adopted to reflect this change in the overall starting price picture.

The new price bands, together with the number of winners accruing in each, were as follows:

Up to 2–1	20 winners
9–4 to 4–1	28 winners
9–2 to 13–2	28 winners
7–1 to 10–1	13 winners
(including 7 winners at 7–1)	
11–1 or over	11 winners

Thus 56 per cent of all the winners started at from 9–4 to 13–2 inclusive. If this price range is extended to include the single price of 7–1 which alone accounted for seven winners in the survey, the percentage rises to a very impressive 63. Horses at 2–1 or less should be excluded because they do not represent value, given the comparatively low number of winners produced.

We now have a second simple rule with which to reinforce the basic strategy of considering only the top five weights in handicap chases: back only horses quoted at between 9–4 and 7–1 in the betting forecast of the newspaper consulted.

Once again the problem of the difference between actual starting prices and betting forecast estimates arises. Yet this is not really a significant drawback. The forecasts produced by representatives of the Press Association are in fact just as accurate in their own way at assessing the chance of runners based on form and expressed in prices, as is the racecourse market in producing odds which similarly reflect chances based on form *and* the opinion of backers expressed through the amount of money staked. The betting forecast can only be a substitute for the actual market in the Ring but it is still a very good substitute.

A more fundamental objection to our two-rule system for handicap chases is that fields in the sample were generally much smaller than those used for the Flat survey. It could be argued therefore that there is a statistical skew in the survey that tends to invalidate its conclusions. When a lot of races have fields of less than double figures, as is the case for handicap chases, the smaller number of runners outside the top five are bound to do much less well in percentage terms than when many races with much larger fields are considered. This is true, but there is still no getting away from the fact that 75 per cent of winners came from just five favoured weights. What was wanted was a straightforward and generally applicable overview which did not cloud the issue by placing artificial upper or lower limits on the size of fields.

So, a survey derived from taking the results of handicap chases just as they come is surely perfectly valid. The truth of the matter is that though many handicap chase fields are on the small side, the higher-weighted horses still visit the winner's enclosure more frequently than lighter-weighted rivals. Our system is doing no more than reflect the realities of the situation, imperfect as the survey in support of it may be in terms of strict statistical method.

Instant handicapping in steeplechases may indicate one, but very often more than one, runner in a race. In the latter case, as on the Flat, the final decision is left to the reader who may prefer to wait for single-selection races or make an informed choice from two or more qualifiers using other form precepts, or even back more than one horse in a race if the odds make this economic.

Thus no extra system rules are necessary. The Flat race rule of excluding apprentice jockeys is not suitable for jump racing – in National Hunt sport there are many competent riders who are not fully fledged professional jockeys but who, by and large, do an excellent job on their mounts. Two rules alone, operated in handicap chases, where small fields are the norm, may produce many winners at sound though not spectacular starting prices.

When we turn to consider handicap hurdles, the situation is different and far less encouraging for the backer. The results of the survey of 100 races of this type revealed that the reputation of handicap hurdles for being especially difficult is perfectly justified.

SURVEY OF 100 HANDICAP HURDLES

A   1-3 7-4 2-1 5-2 100-30 4-1 6-1 11-1

B   4-6 5-4 15-8 2-1 2-1 2-1 4-1 9-2 6-1 6-1 9-1 12-1 12-1 14-1 25-1

C   8-11 11-8 13-8 7-4 2-1 5-2 3-1 4-1 5-1 6-1 13-2 13-2

D   5-4 5-2 3-1 7-2 9-2 5-1 8-1 10-1 20-1

E   2-1 4-1 6-1 13-2 13-2 8-1 8-1 8-1 10-1 12-1 18-1

F   10-11 evens 9-4 11-4 100-30 9-2 6-1 6-1 10-1 10-1 10-1

G   7-4 7-2 7-2 11-2 11-2 6-1 6-1 7-1 8-1 66-1

H   4-1 11-2 7-1 7-1 12-1 12-1 20-1

I   5-4 4-1 11-2 8-1 9-1 14-1

J   6-1 14-1 25-1

K   9-4 7-1

L   4-6 12-1

M   7-2 12-1

N   6-1 20-1

The largest field in the survey had 22 runners. With no winners below 14th position, clearly low weights in these races must be avoided even more scrupulously than in other handicaps.

The overall picture is again triangular, but this time the shape is neither so clear nor so defined as in earlier surveys, with the triangle itself dominated by a rectangle within it emanating from B to F. The consequence of this blurring is that the handicap snapshot here is of less value when trying to discover an 'edge' that can be exploited against the bookmaker.

Winners in depth are found in consecutive positions as far down the weights as the eighth or even ninth position, while the highest weights of all cannot be said to be decisively favoured over those slightly further down. In fact the optimum range for winners is B to G, that is, the six positions immediately below the top weight. Positions B to G accounted for no less than 68 per cent of winners.

Keeping to just five positions as a possible system focus in the style of previous versions of instant handicapping would yield 58 per cent winners, when the best five consecutive positions, B to F, are taken. But would one be justified in singling out this group as the sole material for betting when A and G, and even H and I, are so close to its component positions in terms of winners? Betting on B–F alone would exclude A, G, H and I, all good sources of winners. The alternative of a group including these positions would be so large that perhaps four, five or more qualifiers might be left after other, not too stringent, criteria have been applied to weed out the weakest runners.

Lacking an outstanding, small grouping therefore, probably the wisest thing to do is to abandon the basic instant handicapping concept as a hard-and-fast system rule. All that can really be inferred of value from the survey is the fact that when for some other sound reason a horse is backed in the B to G section of the handicap, it is well over 2–1 on (32–68) that it will be in the winning area of the handicap. Some readers might find this reassuring.

An analysis of the starting prices of winners in the races surveyed is similarly unhelpful. The findings are summarised in tabular form – with each X signifying a win – in order to make the point as graphically as possible, although the same price bands as for handicap chases have been used.

Up to 2–1	XXXXXXXXXXXXXXXXXXXXX
9–4 to 4–1	XXXXXXXXXXXXXXXXXXXX
9–2 to 13–2	XXXXXXXXXXXXXXXXXXXXXXXXX
7–1 to 10–1	XXXXXXXXXXXXXXXX
11–1 or over	XXXXXXXXXXXXXXXXX

The even distribution of winners across the full range of prices means that here too no statistical bias exists for the punter to exploit. Also the 21 horses which won at 2–1 or less suggests that when form horses do win one of these races, the odds available for them are likely to represent very poor value.

In handicap hurdles, therefore, the instant handicapping concept is not really a viable one. Neither weight nor price can be used to pinpoint winners and to the best of my knowledge nor can any other statistical criterion.

The reason for this is not hard to fathom. There are a great many moderate horses that can be trained with some prospect of winning a handicap hurdle of some kind. Provided it has just enough speed and stamina to keep in touch in lowly company and has been properly schooled with the necessary racecourse experience, a very indifferent performer may be able to take advantage of a handicapping system that gives every runner the chance of its moment of glory. Even so, some horses are beyond redemption but, with the exception of novice hurdles, in no other sort of race do so many poor horses regularly compete to the extent that they do in handicap hurdles.

The conclusion is inescapable. Strictly speaking one should refrain from betting in handicap hurdles for the simple reason that there are, as a general rule, no more difficult races for the backer in the whole of racing. However, the punter attending a race meeting might want an interest in every race, or one could see handicap hurdles as a source of the occasional winning outsider needed for betting plans. To cover this situation, Criterion 18 is included, which offers a theory for finding winners for these races. First, however, we will set out some specific guidelines for handicap chases.

26
CRITERION 17 – HANDICAP CHASES

Instant handicapping showed how the vital factors of weight and price can be converted into a simple formula for races of this kind. Even if you do not use the weights and betting forecast in the way suggested, they must still be weighed carefully in the balance of form for the conventional analysis of handicap chases. Jumping is the other factor that needs to be assessed in such an analysis.

This is really a job for the expert race reader and one, moreover, who is able to see a great deal of the racing over fences which takes place during the season. This in effect means someone professionally engaged in racing, although not even a professional can view every race on every course. However, there are several ways in which jumping can be assessed from the armchair, perhaps not as effectively as the ideal, but for all that, reasonably accurately.

1 Post-race comments in the official form book can be most instructive. Every runner's performance is covered by such comments, and a horse which jumped cleanly throughout a race will have no tell-tale comments about blundering at its fences.

2 The form book sometimes gives very specific clues. For instance 'j.w.' is a comment that is used occasionally. It means in fact that a horse which 'jumped well' put in an outstanding round. The sparing use of this deliberate understatement makes it a comment that should be especially noted when assessing a chaser's prospects in near-at-hand engagements.

3 Another way of assessing the jumping talents of any horse is to look at its performances and, where applicable, its last-time-out performance in particular, judged against the background of the courses recognised as being difficult in a jumping sense.

A horse which ran well to win or finish close up at a meeting where the fences are noted as 'testing', 'stiff' or 'severe' in our Racecourse Guide has undoubtedly put up a good performance. Even if a horse got tired and struggled at one or more of the closing fences as the pace of its race gradually built up towards the finish, a good run on a severe track is worth far more in form terms than a similar run on an easy course.

4 A final indicator of jumping ability depends on a straight-forward interpretation of the six-figure form lines which appear on racecards. A chaser which has fallen, unseated rider, refused or pulled up in several of its most recent races is obviously a suspect jumper, or at least one running out of its class. Such a horse is likely to sacrifice its chance at the fences, and there must be a serious doubt as to whether it will complete the course in a current engagement. Only a significant drop in grade might enable it to compete on equal jumping terms with lesser rivals than it has been meeting.

Picking the winners of handicap chases need not be too daunting a task therefore. One's choice should be based on the following criteria:

a) weight indicates that it is one of the better-class horses in the race;
b) recent runs, and preferably the most recent of all, have indicated a sound level of current form and jumping ability;
c) a quote among the first three or four in the betting.

A horse that meets these requirements could provide a ready-made winner, or at least one that, on form, certainly ought to be.

27
CRITERION 18 – HANDICAP HURDLES

Here are a few hints to help those who insist on betting in these races:

1 If a horse is to win a hurdle race against seasoned animals of roughly equal ability, it will need experience and plenty of it. Very few hurdlers, whatever their natural talent, realise their potential without this prerequisite. The surest way to establish whether a horse has such experience is to check whether it has already won a handicap hurdle race. Regardless of the grade of the race and irrespective of how it performed last time out, no bet should be laid on a handicap hurdler which has only won, so far, in novice company.

2 We have seen that there is a definite statistically favoured weight range in handicap hurdles beginning somewhere just below top weight. This means that horses near the bottom of the weights in these races are not likely to win because they are usually outclassed by better hurdlers.

3 Some horses are able to run up a sequence of wins in handicap hurdles. The reason is that extra weight does not easily stop a horse with a measure of hurdling talent at the top of its form. Any winner of a handicap hurdle may survive a quite steep rise in its official rating and still win again, if not immediately, then at least in the not-too-distant future.

4 By contrast, weight tells in hurdle races over the longer distances, particularly when the ground is soft or heavy. Therefore, one's betting response to weight and weight rises should be modified in races of 2m 6f or more.

5 In races over shorter distances up to 2m 2f (2½ miles is the 'in-between' distance) the ability to quicken at the end of a hurdle race is important, far more important than in chasing. Any evidence of such speed in a horse's racing record is a big plus

which, when combined with good or improving form last time out, suggests a horse which has what it takes to win.

6 Keep stakes to a minimum if betting in handicap hurdles however good a horse's chance seems to be. Appearances can be deceptive in races of this kind.

28
NON-HANDICAPS

As we have seen, there are a number of important differences between National Hunt and Flat racing, but there is also much that is common to both sports. In the general matter of reading form and the betting-forecast odds derived from it, we are justified in repeating the statistically based prescriptions for staking on non-handicaps according to price which could be applied on the Flat. National Hunt favourites on the whole have a slightly better record, but the difference is not all that great. The prices of favourites laid down to determine specific courses of betting action on the Flat are identical over jumps:

1 If a horse is quoted at odds-on, there is a greater chance of it winning than losing. You should not oppose it.

2 Favourites quoted at between evens and 6–4 are more likely to win than lose.

3 Those put in as favourite at from 13–8 to 11–4 inclusive will win and lose in the approximate proportions of one winner to every three losers. There may be occasions when such favourites are worth backing.

4 There is only about a 10 per cent chance that a favourite quoted at 3–1 or more in the betting forecast will win.

For the person who is comfortable with the principle of automatic rules in betting, the four precepts set out above may prove invaluable. Even those who are not prepared to be quite so restricted in how they bet would almost certainly benefit from keeping them in mind as general standards in non-handicap betting. It is possible to be more open-minded, however, depending especially on the category of race in which you are considering having a bet.

29
CRITERION 19 – NOVICE HURDLES

Novice hurdle races are open to horses which, before the beginning of the season, have not won a hurdle race of any kind. Here are some tips for dealing with them.

1 The technique for jumping hurdles is different from that for steeplechasing. It is flatter and faster, and some horses have it naturally. Others must learn it.

Either way, as we have noted already in the case of handicap hurdlers, all horses need experience over hurdles before they can shine, even in lowly company. Schooling at home is no substitute for the racecourse. Some horses need a whole season in novice company before they master the technique tolerably well; they will almost certainly never aspire to be more than average in the hurdling sphere.

2 For the same reasons one should generally avoid Flat horses having their first run over hurdles. Similarly, horses coming on from National Hunt Flat races, even if they have won a 'bumper', should be given time to prove themselves in the new arena. The relatively few horses from these two categories which win first time up are more than made up for by the army of horses that do not.

3 Also, again because of the demands imposed by the obstacles, hurdlers seldom win if backward. A racecourse run to bring a hurdler to its peak is far more necessary than for a Flat racer or a chaser.

A good ploy is to regularly check the form book for those novice hurdlers noted as 'backward' or a 'bit backward' on their initial outing. They will definitely improve next time out.

4 The introduction of penalties for winners in novice races has reduced quite noticeably the number of hurdlers which run up a sequence of victories, contrary to what happens in handicap hurdles where experienced horses seem to be able to defy weight increases. Certainly there has been a decline in the strike rate of

first and second favourites in novice hurdles which is difficult to account for otherwise.

5   A win last time out, therefore, is not always the recommendation it ought to be. With prices on the cramped side, it may be better to look instead for improving sorts which ran a good second or third last time.

30
CRITERION 20 – NOVICE CHASES

Novice chases are mostly about jumping, not speed. They have the reputation of being one of racing's biggest lotteries because it is believed that 'dodgy' jumpers abound in them. As a consequence betting in novice chases, even on favourites, is almost universally considered a high-risk business.

Yet again, this category of race need not be excluded from the betting repertoire, provided one learns to recognise the types of horse involved. Timing is also very important.

There are three main sorts of novice chaser:

1   One significant category, though a minority, consists of the type of animal which has always been seen by connections as a good chasing prospect. Such expectations will have been based on breeding, physical conformation and the general demeanour of the horse. Any runs over hurdles, which will almost certainly have been limited in number, have been primarily for experience as part of a horse's education. Some top-class chasing sorts bypass hurdles altogether.

Such horses can be difficult to identify for those not intimately connected with the sport. The stay-at-home enthusiast must rely on racing annuals and the daily racing press to gain information about the most prominent among them. But those that do not attract publicity can be extremely difficult to spot.

They will generally be racing over fences for the first time as five-, six- or even seven-year-olds. Their hurdling career, if they had one at all, will have been short and unambitious. They will not be rushed, however, and will probably have one or two runs in lowly novice chase company before suddenly being catapulted into a much higher grade. This is a decisive point in their career, the stage at which to step in and bet, provided that a genuine, top-class chasing prospect has been correctly identified. A win in top novice company may be the prelude to a sequence of victories, but prices thereafter will be on the short side.

2 A second category of novice chaser is the good hurdler which is sent chasing as it grows older and at the point in time where it has begun to lose its speed in races over the smaller obstacles. Many horses of this type make the grade over fences and some of them go on to take their place in the very top rank of chasers. Complete failures over fences are comparatively few.

Though courage is needed on the part of the backer, the time to bet on animals like these is on their steeplechase debuts. If they are successful, prices are bound to be short in subsequent runs and a victory is much less assured when they take on the better class of chaser at the next stage in their career.

3 Finally there are horses which failed in the main as hurdlers and are sent chasing if not exactly as a last resort, then at least because it has become obvious that they lack the ability to compete with speedier animals in the hurdling arena.

Very few of these horses do well over fences and should be studiously avoided by the shrewd student of form. There will be exceptions, but their success is unpredictable. It is much safer to disregard such types altogether, at least until they have proved themselves by a win in fair company.

In the lower grades, novice chasers in general, once they have had a bit of racing, are sometimes a sound bet in handicaps against more experienced chasers. They get into handicap chases with a low weight and can jump round well clear of jaded horses with a lot of races under the saddle.

This does not apply to the better class of handicap steeplechaser, however, where jumping ability, in most cases born of experience, is paramount. There has always been a tendency, among some trainers at least, to run an exceptional novice against good, seasoned chasers too soon. The wisdom of trying to strike while the iron is hot may be justified from the connections' point of view but, as far as betting is concerned, it is a sound dictum never to back a novice in top chasing company. The stiffer the task for the novice, the more this applies. The history book is full of inglorious failures, and the few exceptions are there to prove the rule.

31
CRITERION 21 – CONDITIONS RACES

Never bet in National Hunt Flat races because form is so unexposed. However, non-handicaps for experienced hurdlers and chasers meeting on more-or-less equal terms tend to be won by form horses at any grade. The form figures cited in Criterion 4, as well as the general prescriptions based on betting forecast prices set out in the opening part of this section on jump non-handicaps, may assist readers to find plenty of winners.

32
CRITERION 22 – HUNTER CHASES

Fewer favourites win now than ever before, and in very recent times there seems to have been a general decline in the reliability of form in these events. Why this should be is difficult to say. Perhaps increased competition, combined with better training facilities at home for every permit holder, has produced a situation where not even an apparent 'good thing' can be counted upon to win, as was once the case. Also, it is possible that a better class of horse is to be found in the point-to-point field these days as a result of greater economic prosperity all round. This means that fewer animals stand out on form once they arrive in the racecourse arena to compete under rules.

In these circumstances backers need to modify their view of the typical hunter chase. It no longer offers the regular prospect of a good bet at reasonable odds. Shock results are now much more frequent, and much greater care needs to be taken in making selections.

One factor, however, remains unchanged. By and large a young hunter with good point-to-point form is a better proposition than the National Hunt 'has-beens' which sometimes end their careers in this sphere of competition. Part of the problem is that knowledge of form from point-to-points is outside the competence of most ordinary punters. Even among professional racing journalists, not many can claim to be experts in a branch of the sport which only becomes relevant to racing under rules for just a few months each year.

33
CRITERION 23 – DISTANCE, GOING AND FITNESS

As a general rule and excluding the top yards, the legion of jump trainers and permit holders up and down the country are far less focused than the Flat training fraternity when it comes to placing their horses. Over jumps, horses are often run at the wrong distance or on the wrong type of course or on the wrong going. The really gifted student of form can sometimes cash in.

Over fences, two and a half miles is a specialist distance. Especially on good going on an easy to only moderately testing track, the distance specialist will beat genuine two- or three-milers nearly every time when it has its trip.

Over hurdles the difference between two miles and two and a half miles, or between two and a half miles and three miles, is not nearly so important.

Apart from the summer and autumn months when only horses needing a fast surface race under National Hunt rules, most jumpers are at their best on good ground, although they can handle soft. However, very heavy ground will obviously inconvenience some winter jumpers, though others have a particular liking for 'bottomless' going. In this respect it should be remembered that official going of 'heavy' over jumps is very different to the much less severe 'heavy' of the Flat.

It might be thought that because they compete over longer distances and often in tougher conditions than Flat animals, National Hunt horses would need a longer period of recuperation between races. However, the statistics quoted in this connection on pages 145–46 of this book suggest, paradoxically perhaps, that the most successful jumpers are those running within a relatively short time of their last outing. The figures here are very similar under both codes of racing, and jumpers, like the Flat horses, do best in statistical terms when reappearing within a fortnight.

34
CRITERION 24 – BREEDING

Over the jumps, breeding as it affects performance, though evidently significant in imparting class and ability, is much less useful for the student of form than on the Flat.

In fact, in the main, breeding can be ignored by those whose focus is on finding winners. Once a horse's career is some way advanced, stamina and going preferences can be inferred from the form book far more accurately.

However, for those who might like to develop an interest in this aspect of National Hunt sport, here is a list of stallions who have been the major influences of the last decade. If all other things are equal, a horse by one of these top-class jumping sires may be preferred over one who is less well-bred, and this might just enable the backer to make the right decision when trying to decide which competitor is most likely to come out on top.

LEADING NATIONAL HUNT STALLIONS	
ACCORDION	LE BAVARD
ARDROSS	LE MOSS
BE MY NATIVE	MANDALUS
BUCKSKIN	MONTELIMAR
CALLERNISH	OATS
CARLINGFORD CASTLE	ORCHESTRA
CELTIC CONE	OVER THE RIVER
CRASH COURSE	PHARDANTE
DEEP RUN	ROSELIER
FURRY GLEN	SADLER'S WELLS
IDIOT'S DELIGHT	STRONG GALE
ITALIC	SUPREME LEADER
KAMBALDA	THE PARSON
KEMAL	TORUS
KING'S RIDE	ZAFFARAN
LAFONTAINE	

35
Five Golden Rules of Handicap Betting (Flat or Jumps)

1 With the exception of instant handicapping based on a statistical approach, all the form-related methods of picking winners in the preceding sections are, in the main, more effective in higher, rather than the lower, grades of handicap.

2 Keep the bulk of handicap betting to fields with a maximum of about 10 runners, and never bet in a field of more than about 16 runners if trying to find the winner in a single pick.

   Simple mathematics dictate that the fewer runners opposing the selection, the greater the chance of being on the winner in those races where every horse has a theoretically equal chance on an official estimate of form.

3 As a general strategy, back more than one horse in the race when betting in handicaps. Two single points on two horses is better value than one point each-way on a single selection, unless there is a very good reason to know that the latter has a quite exceptional chance of reaching a place at remunerative odds.

4 When a horse is priced at 10–1 or over in the actual betting market on a handicap race, bet at Tote odds if available.

5 Do not bet more than you can comfortably afford to lose and never chase your losses.

FIVE GOLDEN RULES OF BETTING IN NON-HANDICAPS (FLAT OR JUMPS)

1 In a non-handicap race the favourite almost always has the best theoretical chance of winning. There needs to be a good reason for opposing it with a bet on another runner.

2 Do not bet beyond the first three in the betting except when there is statistical evidence to suggest that a broader approach may be successful.

3 Good form last time out is the primary qualification for a potential winner. This is even more important in a non-handicap than a handicap.

4 Non-handicaps for older horses are dominated by a small group of elite trainers. The overall and current form of a top stable is usually as significant as the actual form of individual horses. This applies particularly to maiden races.

   Two-year-old stakes races, however, are much more competitive and are won by trainers at all levels in the training hierarchy.

5 Do not bet more than you can comfortably afford to lose and never chase losses.

37
THE RULES OF STAKING

There is absolutely nothing wrong with level stakes as a staking system, though in practice it requires a lot of discipline always to have the same amount on every single selection. Most backers vary their stakes according to fancy and a personal estimate of the strength of a selection. This is the opposite principle to level stakes. For most people, not blessed with unerring judgement, it is one of the worst ways to stake, despite its popularity. Big stakes tend to go on losers, small stakes on to winners – not always but often enough to make this a losing game in which the backer does not exploit successes to the full financially.

The problem with level stakes as a method, strictly applied, is that the accumulation of a worthwhile profit is inevitably slow, so that the patience of Job is required on the backer's part. One way out of this bind is, very gradually, to increase or decrease the general level of staking as profits build up or losses mount. A lot of money-management skill is needed for this strategy, but the effort is well worth making.

VALUE

Where bets are not placed at starting price, the backer should seek 'value' in the odds taken about horses backed. However, if anyone could devise a method of accurately assessing value in the odds in relation to a horse's precise mathematical and form chance, this would in effect be the infallible racing system. All the backer would have to do would be to bet only when the odds on offer were above the selection's true chance of winning, which could similarly be expressed in odds. In the end a credit balance would be bound to accrue.

In terms of reality, however, one way in which the punter can improve his/her position against the bookmakers' trading edge is to keep to small fields. Fewer runners against a selection improves its chance of winning in mathematical terms. Also, the bookmakers' over-round, which is explained in Chapter 52, is less in small fields.

VARIATION IN THE ODDS

The use of a staking plan, even when the backer is in the unlikely position of always being able to take an exact price, can never be a perfect solution to betting. This is because it is impossible to predict in advance the pattern of winners and losers which, if known, would enable punters to maximise profits. They would simply back the winners and disregard the losers!

For most backers who must bet some of the time away from the course or the betting shop where definite odds are obtainable, the lesser difficulty of variation between betting forecast quotations and the eventual starting price can be enough to reduce the efficiency of automatically regulated staking. However ingeniously devised a plan is in relation to the type of selection, the probable percentage of winners and the expected level of odds, frequent deviations from the expected starting price norm will upset the long-term financial balance of a great many staking methods. This will reduce the chances of obtaining maximum gain or minimum loss from any series of wagers.

INCREASING STAKES AFTER LOSERS

Staking plans of this type should be treated with extreme caution. By definition they involve chasing losses and, in the real world of a limited betting bank, winners may not pay for losers as they are expected to do. Too often increasing stakes on a losing run gets backers into deep trouble quickly and, whatever the theory, in practice they find themselves forced to give up with only a hefty loss to show for their endeavours.

One the other hand, where the expected percentage of winners is reckoned to be high, and by this something in the order of 70 is meant, mild increases in stakes will often marginally enhance the profit that would have accrued with level stakes. In this respect percentage is at least as important as starting price, for if a percentage of 70 plus is more or less guaranteed, the all-important maximum losing run that can devastate plans of this type will be on the short side.

INCREASING STAKES AFTER WINNERS

Such systems can do little harm and may do some good if used sensibly. By increasing stakes gradually, using cash from the bookmaker, it may be possible to enhance profits significantly. However, the strategy is as much dependent on the pattern of winners and losers as any other form of staking plan. An adverse pattern can occur for any staking plan, even one calling for increasing stakes after winners. One objection to all plans of this type is that it is virtually impossible to avoid having the largest stake of all on the loser which terminates a run of winners.

Increasing stakes after winners works best with selections that give a high percentage of winners, and that means favourites or near-favourites for the most part.

Staking 1/10, 1/12 or 1/15 of the betting bank and then increasing or decreasing the stake by the same fraction throughout according to the ebb and flow of winners and losers is a fundamentally sound method of betting although, without an exceptionally high percentage of winners, the conversion of wins into a worthwhile, overall profit can be a lengthy process.

MULTIPLE BETS

Bets of the Yankee, Heinz, Lucky Fifteen or Round-the-Clock variety should be avoided by the serious backer. Unless nearly all selections are correct, the high wastage in stakes from losers can eat into profits in a devastating way in bets involving full cover on doubles, trebles and accumulators on a larger number of selections. These bets are promoted by bookmaking firms in their advertising and with good reason from their point of view. Singles and, as we shall suggest later, doubles (but not trebles and accumulators) are the surest key to the layers' safe.

The 'WEEKENDER' bet, however, which is the final system in Part 2 of this book, is a sound example of a multiple bet. This is because it works on the principle of permutation and not of full cover. Full cover immediately writes off a disproportionately high number of individual bets within the whole, every time a loser is backed. Limited permutation, on the other hand, budgets for losers and can enhance profits by exploiting winners to the full at reduced stakes in the form of fewer bets when compared with the unrealistic blanket coverage of a Yankee or Heinz.

GROUP BETTING

A generation ago one national newspaper's leading tipsters always gave three selections for every handicap in their panel of tips for a meeting. In a more demanding age this concept of finding 'the winner in three' has been quietly consigned to history, but from a staking point of view in handicaps it remains a very sound approach.

As already stated in one of our 'Golden Rules', several selections to win a handicap outright is superior mathematically to the drastically reduced odds for a place that are part of each-way bets.

Backing a small group to win against the field – two, three or even more if prices allow it – is the recommended basic procedure for all handicaps. Even the biggest handicaps, such as the Royal Hunt Cup, the Stewards' Cup and the Cambridgeshire, can be tackled in this way with real prospects of success. The full methodology for this form of group betting is described in Part 3.

If one embraces the concept of several against the field, individual wins may be smaller but much more frequent. In the long run one should gain financially by adopting this more cautious approach.

RACECOURSE BETTING

Many people who go racing for an afternoon's sport are often in the position of backing a couple of winners, but somehow contrive to emerge with a loss on the day. They may even have an exceptional day and back more winners than that but still have very little to show financially for their efforts. Faulty staking is nearly always the cause. Add to this all the days when the typical racegoer does not find a winner at all and the result is that, combined with the high entrance money and other expenses, visits to the racecourse can be a very expensive business indeed.

Following the rules set out on page 89, however, will give one a sporting chance of getting it right on the racecourse, unlike the experience of so many fellow racing enthusiasts.

RACECOURSE STAKING PLAN

1 Stake 1 point on a single selection in non-handicaps (including any claiming race not labelled a 'handicap'), until a change of stake is called for by these rules.

2 In handicaps stake ½ point and ½ point on two horses, or ⅓ point on each of three horses, until a change of stake is called for.

3 If a winner is backed at evens or odds against (or money is at least doubled on total outlay in a handicap), stakes should be increased by 1 point in subsequent races (plus ½ point twice or plus ⅓ point three times in handicaps).

4 If an odds-on winner is backed (or winnings do not double the total outlay in a handicap), stakes should not be changed as a result of that winner, except when Rule 7 applies.

5 A single-selection winner at odds-on (or a winner which does not at least double the total money staked in a handicap) does not count as a 'winning race' for system purposes, except in Rule 7.

6 If a second winner is backed at evens or odds against (or the total money staked is at least doubled in a handicap, making a second winning race), stakes should be increased by 1 point (plus ½ point twice or plus ⅓ point three times in a handicap) on the NEXT RACE ONLY. If a loser, the stake reverts to 2 points or the handicap equivalent on several horses.

7 After three winners at the meeting, whether at odds-on or odds against (including any handicap winners where the stake was not at least doubled), stakes must be IMMEDIATELY reduced on all remaining races to ½ point and must not be increased again under any circumstances.

   Stakes on handicaps are thereby reduced to ¼ point for each of two horses, or ⅙ point for each of three horses.

All this looks horribly complicated at first sight, but it is really quite simple. After one winning race at evens or better the stakes are increased to 2 points, and after two winning races the stakes rises to the maximum of 3 points before reverting to 2 points or even only ½ point if three winners at any price have been found.

One variation of this racecourse staking system is allowed, although some readers may look askance, having been lectured in the section on level stakes about the inadvisability of varying staking according to personal whim. This second version permits the backer to choose between the next race only *or* the next-but-one race only, when increasing to 3 points after a second 100 per cent-plus winning race. It may or may not have anything to do with the non-mathematical 'law of averages', but winner-loser-winner, which Americans call the 'skip-hit' technique in betting, is often a more achievable sequence than two consecutive winners. Be that as it may, provided there are at least two races left on the card in which to bet, the exceptionally skilled punter could well benefit from the element of selectivity implied in taking such an approach. With or without the corollary, however, this racecourse staking plan is founded on a betting strategy that is eminently sensible.

One view put forward by gamblers of the less cautious kind is that one should always play up winnings when ahead, thus going for a really big profit. This is fair enough up to a point, but not to the extent that all the gains so far accrued are put at serious risk.

The rules of the recommended system are common sense and represent a compromise between trying to maximise profits in a sensible way and 'going for broke'. The plan is based on what might be called the principle of 'reasonable maximum expectation'. Winnings are played up from early successes in the hope of making a worthwhile profit on the day, but not at the risk of handing all gains made back to the bookmakers. If three winners have been found on a visit to the racecourse, one has become a hostage to fortune. Therefore stakes near the end of the card are reduced, not continually increased, the opposite of the approach that would be adopted by the out-and-out gambler.

This plan is worth a try when next visiting the racecourse. It may be better, however, to test it out on some cards from a newspaper before actually visiting the course in order to find out if it is suitable. One should soon see the point of a plan which aims to strike a balance between the actual, the probable and the only remotely possible.

Here is an example of the plan in action:

		Basic stake	Adjusted stake (if any)	Result	Profit/ loss
1st race	Non-handicap	1 pt	—	Lost	−1
2nd race	Handicap	½ pt ½ pt	—	Won 4–1	+1½
3rd race	Handicap	½ pt ½ pt	½ pt ½ pt	Lost	−2
4th race	Non-handicap	1 pt	1 pt	Won 7–1	+14
5th race	Handicap	½ pt ½ pt	1 pt 1 pt	Lost	−3
6th race	Non-handicap	1 pt	1 pt	Won 4–6	+1⅓
7th race	Handicap	—	¼ pt ¼ pt	Lost	−½
					Total: +10⅓

Level stakes: −1, +1½, −1, +7, −1, +⅔, −1. Total: +5⅙

This plan will usually improve the level-stakes position, given some winners, but it is only fair to show also how things can go wrong if there is an unfavourable pattern of results.

Below can be seen what happens if the three winners at 4–6, 4–1 and 7–1 are rearranged in the very worst possible order:

		Basic stake	Adjusted stake (if any)	Result	Profit/ loss
1st race	Non-handicap	1 pt	—	Won 7–1	+7
2nd race	Handicap	½ pt ½ pt	½ pt ½ pt	Won 4–1	+3
3rd race	Handicap	½ pt ½ pt	1 pt 1 pt	Lost	−3
4th race	Non-handicap	1 pt	1 pt	Lost	−2
5th race	Handicap	½ pt ½ pt	½ pt ½ pt	Lost	−2
6th race	Non-handicap	1 pt	1 pt	Won 4–6	+1⅓
7th race	Handicap	—	¼ pt ¼ pt	Lost	−½
					Total: +3⅚

Thus even when the winners are put in the worst possible order, the level-stakes situation is only 1⅓ points better, which is a very creditable performance for the staking plan.

It seems only fair to change things round one final time with a view to putting the plan in the best possible light:

		Basic stake	Adjusted stake (if any)	Result	Profit/ loss
1st race	Non-handicap	1 pt	—	Won 4–6	+⅔
2nd race	Handicap	½ pt ½ pt	—	Lost	−1
3rd race	Handicap	½ pt ½ pt	—	Won 4–1	+1½
4th race	Non-handicap	1 pt	1 pt	Won 7–1	+14
5th race	Handicap	—	¼ pt ¼ pt	Lost	−½
6th race	Non-handicap	—	¼ pt ¼ pt	Lost	−½
7th race	Handicap	—	¼ pt ¼ pt	Lost	−½

Total: +13⅔

This is quite significantly superior to level stakes – hence the recommendation for the plan. Without being overly ambitious, thereby risking a serious dissipation of any gain, there is a real prospect of boosting profits and making a day at the races worthwhile in financial terms.

It always pays, however, when contemplating the use of any staking plan to work out the worst-case scenario and what that will mean in terms of total financial liability. In this case that liability is not 7 points at level stakes. It is worse than that and comes about only if one winner is backed and this winner occurs in the worst possible position in the progression. On any seven-race card this is what could happen:

1st race	Won evens	+1
2nd race	Lost	−2
3rd race	Lost	−2
4th race	Lost	−2
5th race	Lost	−2
6th race	Lost	−2
7th race	Lost	−2

Total: −11

A single winner at odds-on would not be a problem because the expensive stake increase is only triggered by a winner at odds against, or as in this case, by one at evens. The above sequence may seem unlikely, but it is by no means a freak result. It is shown here in fairness to the reader who has the right to be fully informed about any bet which these pages might inspire. That said, I believe the racecourse plan is still a good one and well worth a trial for anyone who is prepared to accept a little extra risk for the possibility, and in my view the probability, of quite a bit more gain.

STAKING LEVELS

The Golden Rule of all betting will stand repeating yet again – never bet more than you can afford to lose, and never chase your losses.

38
BETTING ON HORSES – FORM, THE VITAL KEY

From time to time the Government of the day appoints a Royal Commission charged with looking into various aspects of the gambling industry. In 1978 one such Commission did something none of its predecessors had done before and which its successors have not attempted since. It enquired into the relationship between punters and bookmakers, specifically with a view to establishing whether the former has any realistic chance of winning at the expense of the latter.

The studies the Commission had carried out went into considerable detail and were quite complicated from a statistical point of view but, broadly speaking, it came to the conclusion that horses at short prices were much better material for the punter than outsiders.

Over the quarter of a century before the 1978 Commission this situation had remained remarkably constant, even if things varied somewhat from year to year. It was found that if all horses which started at 6–4 on, or shorter, could somehow have been backed by one punter, that punter would actually have shown a small amount of profit on the total outlay. The fact that every horse in this odds range was considered means that the random principle alone was tested. No attempt was made to pick and choose by the application of form criteria of any kind. What would have been the result, therefore, had the imaginary punter been able to bring to the problem the kind of winner-finding aids discussed in the present book cannot be known, but if form has any value at all in racing, then the outcome must surely have been even more advantageous.

The Royal Commission also found that, in the long period covered by its survey, backing every horse priced at over 9–1 and less than 20–1 would have resulted in losses amounting to something in the region of 35 per cent of turnover. With horses at 20–1 or more the picture was even bleaker for the punter – a loss of about 70 per cent of total stakes would have accumulated over the years.

The 1978 Commission's findings were not new, however, and nor was the type of investigation it had conducted original. Its work had been largely anticipated by E. Lenox Figgis who in the world of gambling was better known by his pseudonym of 'Midas'.

Figgis, a chartered accountant and actuary by profession, pursued his interest in probability and gambling to the point where he published under his own name *Focus on Gambling* in 1951. This book was issued by the firm of Arthur Barker Ltd and in it Figgis considered all the most popular gambles of the day. Football pools, greyhounds, cards and horse racing were among them, with much of his most interesting material being presented in a brilliant series of appendices.

In Appendix XVII, Figgis surveyed the complete starting price returns for the 1951 Flat racing season. He found that backing all horses which started at 4–1 on or shorter showed a profit on outlay of almost 10 per cent. Horses with a probability of winning of between approximately 30 per cent and 20 per cent according to the starting price (odds of 5–2 to 4–1) accumulated an overall loss of around 4 per cent on turnover. Longshots priced at 20–1 or more produced a loss of 77 per cent. Throughout his survey Figgis adhered to the random principle of betting by which every horse at a given price or in a given price range was included in the reckoning.

The analysis of E. Lenox Figgis, confirmed by the Royal Commission nearly 30 years later, was replicated in one way or another in the years that followed by a series of studies, mostly American, undertaken by professional economists, academic statisticians and games theorists, as well as by several authorities on gambling. The exact rates of loss for various odds and price ranges differ at various times and in various circumstances, but the broad conclusion has always been the same. Short-priced horses in the odds-on category, which can sometimes be extended to include those at a shade of odds against, will often randomly produce a profit. As the odds lengthen, the more the backer can expect to lose in percentage terms, with rank outsiders a complete disaster from a random point of view, a clear warning to those punters habituated to backing them.

Anyone who came to this manual therefore with the preconceived opinion that betting is a 'mug's game', that 'there is only one winner – the bookmaker', and so on, must surely revise their views to some extent. Betting on horses, even random betting, can sometimes pay.

However, the imprimatur bestowed by the Royal Commission obviously requires modification from the point of view of the practical needs and desires of the ordinary backer. The gains accruing from very short-priced horses were tiny in comparison with the outlay that would have been involved in achieving them. It is very difficult to convert a very small gain into a profit the punter will consider worthwhile. That is where the preceding pages, and indeed this book as a whole, come in, with methods of selecting short-priced horses for maximum profitability discussed at several places in the text.

Also, the unfavourable position for the punter when it comes to outsiders, noted by Figgis, the Royal Commission and the rest, is not the whole story. True, the punter who shuns short-priced selections in favour of longshots is flying in the face of statistical reality. Judged from a random point of view at least, they are making things difficult for themselves.

Yet, because they are looking for a lot for a little, many punters stick to outsiders as the best hope of achieving this aim. And it is my considered opinion that they are not entirely wrong to do so.

For example, it has been shown earlier that 'instant handicapping', particularly in Flat races, will pinpoint many long-priced winners, though it is admitted that profits overall are by no means automatic and that skill and flair on the part of the punter are also needed to overcome the many losing races that go with the winners at big prices. Nevertheless, it can be done, as letters I have received from readers confirm.

> *'Since buying David Duncan's book I have won £500*
> *net using his handicap system on page 24 with only*
> *20p stakes in a 'Yankee' bet which costs £2.20,*
> *picking the top 3 horses by weight and the first 3 in*
> *the betting forecast. Thank you, sir!'*

Thus we have two pieces of evidence from very different sources – one from a Royal Commission, one from a typical racing enthusiast, that backing horses is not a completely lost cause. Far from it. Contrary to the belief of many, it need not always be the bookmaker who wins.

An individual punter with the 'Midas touch' can win and win consistently. For the 'Midas touch', read the study of form and racing statistics. Harnessed to sound judgement and sensible staking, form is the key to the bookmaker's safe. It may not be easy, there may be many a slip along a hard road, but readers *can* acquire the 'Midas touch' from this betting manual. Part 1 has explained in great depth a logical method of studying form in general and of applying it to particular kinds of race. Part 2 will deal with racing systems which, for some, may be a similar route to at least a little of the bookmaker's cash.

PART 2

Racing Systems
to Help You Win

39
THE BEST OF THE PRESS FORM PLAN

Facts and figures are important to any serious follower of racing. For the system operator they are absolutely essential. Fortunately we have never had it so good in terms of the racing coverage offered regularly by the national press. Detailed race cards with extensive form analysis and skilfully compiled betting forecasts, course statistics plus selections by acknowledged experts are a feature of the sporting pages of every popular newspaper. Nowadays the racing fan is given so much help that winning might seem a relatively simple task.

However, it is not simple, far from it. Even with the embarrassment of riches to be found in the racing pages, the wheat still has to be sorted from the chaff. The problem of finding enough winners to yield a profit over a reasonable period of time defeats most of us.

One possible answer is to look very closely at the tips given by the racing correspondents retained by the various newspapers. They are professionals; they travel regularly to race meetings and they are paid to make a thorough study of every aspect of form. A method of betting based on their selections ought to offer a reasonably trouble-free road to success.

In fact, the typical newspaper correspondent who makes a selection in every race manages an overall ratio of approximately one winner to three losers. At first sight this may not seem too satisfactory. It is a worse average, for instance, than the general percentage of winning favourites. It must be remembered, however, that the newspaper tipster's successes include a spread of winners at all prices up to the occasional 20–1 outsider. The fact that the strike rate of winning press selections does not depend on strings of horses at short prices prompts me to suggest that in terms of potential profit they are probably the best of all readily available betting propositions.

Some backers have a favourite tipster whose selections they follow regularly. Almost everyone has a clear preference for one correspondent above all others, even if they don't always blindly follow the advice given. The BEST OF THE PRESS system recommends concentrating on the tips of one's preferred newspaper pundit. The idea, however, is not to back a selection in every race but to single out only those runners which have the highest statistical chance of winning.

One way of doing this is to examine closely the performance figures of each horse your tipster chooses. Performance figures are the record of a horse's placings on its last three outings which precedes the name of each runner on the standard race card. It is a well-known fact that some three-figure combinations produce a far greater overall percentage of winners than others. Moreover, the best of them show a remarkably high level of consistent success. My figures, based on many years of research for both Flat and jumps, and equally valid in handicaps and non-handicaps, are set out below. Note that there are also form figures for two-year-olds and other lightly rated animals.

Last Three Outings

011	121	321	421
101	112	122	221
311	211	114	131
111	411		

Two Career Outings Only

11	31
21	41

One Career Outing Only

1

The operating instructions for the BEST OF THE PRESS plan are very simple and require only a few minutes' work each day. Examine every selection of your chosen tipster and pick out only those which have recorded one of the above performance combinations in their most recent outings. In this way you locate up to two or three horses per day that have a double plus factor in their favour. They must be regarded as bets of the highest quality.

Nothing guarantees a profit in racing but this system has real potential for consistent success. In summer or winter you are automatically on some of the best bets your newspaper has to offer. Moreover, the selective process need not end there. The discerning backers who use their own judgement to pick and choose may be able to pinpoint one horse a day which comes close to being the perfect wager.

40
THE SPECIALITY SYSTEM

Specialisation pays or so they say. Given the right temperament, this probably applies as much to betting matters as to any other sphere of activity and this plan is to help you win bets on two-year-olds. Certainly one could do a lot worse than to concentrate on this particular aspect of the racing scene for the majority of bets. This is a great deal more sensible than jumping around from one expedient to another, clutching at every straw in the wind, always in search of the elusive big win that so seldom materialises.

To my mind two-year-olds are an excellent medium for such an approach. Competing regularly over uniform sprint distances, juveniles run to form to a remarkable degree. They are fresh and bring to their racing a zest that is all too often lacking in older horses, many of which are definitely soured by over-exposure. By contrast, consistency is the hallmark of two-year-old racing.

If you can be content with small but regular profits from fancied runners at the less spectacular end of the odds range, then it might well suit you to study the youngsters very closely. By going about it in the right way there is every chance that you could enjoy a successful season's betting with a sound capital gain at the end of the campaign to reward you for your efforts.

Two-year-olds perform within predictable limits to such an extent that a few simple tests can be used to pinpoint the best potential bets in a most effective way.

First, it is desirable that any two-year-old which carries a backer's money should have won or been placed second on its previous run. Obviously in the course of a season's racing there are plenty of examples of youngsters that were third, fourth or unplaced last time out that go on to win their next race. On the other hand, statistics show quite clearly that winners and seconds are quite outstanding. Here are the results of a survey for three full seasons:

Last Time Out	Percentage of Wins Next Outing
first/second	41 per cent
third/fourth	25 per cent
unplaced	34 per cent

When it is considered that first and seconds in the nature of things are vastly outnumbered by the others, then it is apparent that 41 is a very good percentage indeed. Clearly they offer a very high statistical chance of success.

Needless to say, there are sound reasons for this excellent strike rate. Two-year-olds do reproduce their form more consistently than any other type of horse. If a youngster wins or finishes close up in a race, then unless it is asked to rise sharply in class there is every chance that it will be there or thereabouts in its next.

Over the same three-year period it was found that the win frequency for favourites in two-year-old non-handicaps (nursery handicaps were excluded because of their highly competitive nature) was 38.2 per cent and for second favourites 21.3 per cent. Note that both figures are adjusted to correct the discrepancy arising from the duplication which occurs when there are joint favourites or joint second favourites.

A combined percentage for winning first and second favourites of nearly 60 is so impressive that it seems pointless to look beyond it for the second rule of two-year-old betting. You are strongly advised to focus your attention only on the likely favourites; that is, the first two in the betting forecast of a reliable sporting or daily paper.

A two-year-old, like any other thoroughbred, needs to be fully fit to do itself justice on the racecourse, However, it is standard practice among all good trainers to give their charges a periodic rest. Horses are not machines; they cannot be kept at their racing best indefinitely without a break. In this respect they are no different to human beings who go to work regularly and need a holiday from time to time in order to recharge their batteries. The surest sign that a horse has been 'let down' is a prolonged period of absence from actual competition. When it does eventually return to racing after a lay-off, it may have done a good deal of work at home but there is no substitute for a gallop under racing conditions to bring a horse right up to its absolute peak.

Therefore the punter is advised to back only two-year-olds which are running within one month of their previous public outing. This is a guarantee of a horse's racing fitness and enables one to be fairly certain that no complications have developed regarding general physical well-being which might detract from its ability to reproduce its form. The third rule goes a long way to giving grounds for confidence that a horse is being backed which is fully fit and well.

The three conditions for betting in two-year-old non-handicaps may be summarised as follows:

1 Only back horses which finished first or second last time out (just second in races for maidens at starting).

2 Concentrate on the first two in the betting forecast of the newspaper used for racing purposes.

3 In no circumstances back any two-year-old which has not run in public for over a month (say, 30 days).

These are rules from which no one should deviate. They will produce a short list of possibles from which to make one or more selections each racing day. The final stage in the process is left to the backer. One may feel confident enough to rely on personal reading of form or class. One may prefer to make use of the undoubted expertise of newspaper correspondents to arrive at a final choice. However, there is one guide which requires special attention. I refer to the comparative time test.

Two-year-old racing is peculiarly well suited to a close study of comparative times. Except for a minority of mile events, all juvenile races are decided over sprint distances, and it is in sprints that time is of most value as an aid to finding winners. Riding tactics have little impact on calculations in races that are usually run flat out from start to finish. A two-year-old capable of recording a fast time should always be watched very closely.

Most readers will be familiar with the concept of comparative times by which each recorded race time can be classed as faster or slower than the standard for course and distance. The specialist racing press show this comparison in the following way:

Ayr	5f	58.40s (+1.60)
Goodwood	5f	56.50s (−0.20)

Goodwood   6f   1/12.10s (+2.30)
Newmarket   7f   1/26.44s (+1.94)

The vital information is contained in the brackets. Here is shown the number of seconds and tenths of a second the winner was faster (–) or slower (+) than the standard. In this way the comparative value of performances on the clock can be readily assessed even though races were run over different courses and over different distances.

Clearly from this set of figures, the horse which won or finished close up second in the Goodwood race over five furlongs where the standard was bettered by 0.20 seconds would be an obvious first choice.

There is one problem with comparative times. Races are run on different going. Obviously it is much easier to run a fast time on firm or good ground than on soft or heavy. In assessing times, therefore, some experience is needed in making an appropriate allowance for ground conditions but the time test is so valuable in evaluating two-year-old form that the effort to acquire expertise in this area is well worth making.

Looking closely at the winning times recorded by older horses on the same card is one of the best ways to evaluate the merit of a two-year-old's performance against the background of the prevailing ground conditions. If a juvenile winner or a good second did a comparative time which is close to, or even better than, the best time of the day set by an older horse, this is clearly a very sound performance. Or is the two-year-old race faster or slower against the standard than most other times recorded that afternoon? How does the two-year-old compare with a good handicapper or a selling plater, or even with a Group race winner running on the same card?

When all the racing appears very ordinary, time may be the only satisfactory key to making an accurate assessment of a piece of juvenile form. And here do not forget the draw. Were the two-year-old winner and the runner-up well drawn or badly drawn in a big field? Performances need to be upgraded or downgraded in the light of this factor. The effect of the draw should also bear on the analysis of a race currently under review. Is the fast two-year-old well or badly drawn? Check these influences out in the Racecourse Guide in Part 5. You will get a lot closer to a true estimate of the chance of a two-year-old in which you are interested.

One other factor should be considered when betting on two-year-olds. This is the time of year. The situation alters from month to month, so that a betting strategy needs to be tailored to changing circumstances very precisely. The following points should be borne in mind:

APRIL

The new season has hardly begun and most juveniles are unknown quantities. Try to find one good two-year-old bet each day and keep stakes to an absolute minimum.

MAY

Form has started to settle down but there are still plenty of youngsters who have yet to show their true potential, and the going can be changeable. Stick to one bet a day with a slightly increased stake.

JUNE

By now a fairly clear picture of the new crop of two-year-olds has emerged and summer is officially here, so there should not be too many variations in going or form. Keep to a single selection but bet with confidence.

JULY AND AUGUST

Traditionally the best months of the year for the backer, July and August should bring really fast ground when short-priced horses monopolise the winner's enclosure. Now is the time to cash in with two or even three selections a day, backed in singles and doubles with one's maximum stake.

SEPTEMBER

Suddenly a lot of form becomes suspect. Classy types given plenty of time as a prelude to a three-year-old campaign at a high level appear for the first time or improve by leaps and bounds. Very likely they will upset juveniles which looked good earlier in the year. Many of the latter begin to show the effects of a long campaign, fields get more competitive and the going can change very quickly with variable weather conditions. Stakes should be dropped sharply and care must be taken not to dissipate gains from a successful spring and summer.

OCTOBER

Every horse is competing for its winter training bill, fields are huge and heavy ground plays havoc with form. Long before November comes, the betting book should be closed for the year.

So a fully planned programme of two-year-old betting has been mapped out. The three basic rules should provide a small number of potential bets each day. The final process of selection gives one plenty of scope to exercise personal skill. The SPECIALITY system is thus interesting to work. In the hands of a careful operator, the system has all the prerequisites of a successful method of backing horses.

41
THE MIDSUMMER METHOD

This is a system for summer bets in selected non-handicaps.

July and August are the backer's months. Form on the Flat has had plenty of time to settle down, and firm ground sees small fields and more predictable results than at any other time of the year. Favourites and near-favourites go in with monotonous regularity. The MIDSUMMER method offers a sporting chance of cashing in when circumstances are most favourable to the punter.

The general percentage of winning favourites rises sharply in every kind of race during the summer months but there are a number of categories which, according to the records, are particularly good for backers. These include maiden races for two-year-olds and non-handicaps confined to three-year-olds, of which stakes races and maidens are the two main types.

As far as two-year-old maiden races are concerned, the fact that they are restricted to non-winners means that competition is not strong. One or two horses usually stand out on what they have achieved so far and for the most part they are able to confirm their form advantage in the actual race. In this they are helped by midsummer conditions for, with the exception of mudlarks, the average thoroughbred is more reliable on fast ground than any other type of going.

Much the same reasons account for the high success rate of winning favourites in three-year-old non-handicaps. Halfway through the season on firm surfaces, the form of three-year-olds works out exceptionally well. In maiden races opposition is not strong, and the fancied horses have it to themselves. Clever trainers can exploit a good three-year-old. At the smaller meetings, particularly in the north, leading yards with a monopoly of the better-bred horses have a huge advantage which results in a very high percentage of winners. As for stakes races, many of these feature class horses which, almost by definition, can be expected to run to form. So three-year-olds competing on equal terms, without the intervention of the handicapper, offer relatively easy pickings for the discerning backer of favourites.

The system bet is a daily double on market leaders in these types of race. There is plenty of racing at this time of year, usually at least three meetings a day, and probably more with evening racing, even in the middle of the week, so there will be quite a number of possible bets from which to choose. Do not be too ambitious. On most days one or two of the supposed 'certs' will go down. Keeping to just two horses a day cuts down the risk of the unexpected, but nearly inevitable, actually happening to you. If one does make a habit of backing everything that seems to have an above-average chance on paper, one is bound to suffer from a percentage failure rate that statistics say must be within the region of 30–35 per cent at least. There is no profit in that, even if the occasional multiple bet comes up. Rather than indulging in trebles and accumulators, it is far better to put the daily stake on just the two best bets of the day in two 2-point singles and a 1-point double. Five points a day spread in this way maximise the opportunities that midsummer offers. Avoid horses likely to start at prohibitive odds and just one winner will return your daily stake a lot of the time, and there will be plenty of days when both selections win. Most weeks you should be in profit after five or six days of systematic betting.

A punter taking advantage of favourable conditions in favoured races will not be the bookmaker's ideal customer. However, any pangs of conscience should soon disappear when the end of August comes with a handsome credit balance to testify to the wisdom of betting steadily and sensibly on the best available bets at the best time of year for backers.

42
THE STAR CHOICE METHOD

Many readers will be familiar with the Jockey Club's 'Pattern Race' classification by which the top non-handicaps for the various age groups are divided into Group One, Group Two, Group Three races according to their status and value. The STAR CHOICE method concentrates only on the very highest echelon of Flat racing, that is, the Group One weight-for-age races run over middle distances.

Chief among these are the five Classic races – Newmarket's 2000 and 1000 Guineas, the Derby and Oaks at Epsom and finally the St Leger run at Doncaster in the autumn. Other races which fall into the elite category are four big events in July and August. They are the Eclipse Stakes (Sandown), the King George VI and Queen Elizabeth Stakes (Ascot), the Sussex Stakes (Goodwood) and the International Stakes (York). The Prince of Wales's Stakes at Royal Ascot over 10 furlongs in June and the one-mile Queen Elizabeth II Stakes on the same course in late September are two other well-established races which have now acquired the very highest status. The Champion Stakes, decided at Newmarket near the end of the season, completes the cycle of the greatest races in the British calendar.

The STAR CHOICE approach is ultra-selective and seeks to pinpoint only the best for the best. To win any one of this sequence of top races takes a horse of the highest class. Hence the basic premise of the system:

In such races any horse which has failed to win its last two races in similar or lesser company cannot be said to have a good chance.

Think about this carefully. Spelled out like this, the idea seems self-evident but an examination of any of the top weight-for-age races shows how many runners can be eliminated. In the majority of cases most of the candidates fail to measure up to this standard. Yet if a horse has failed recently in inferior or even similar company, where is the confidence about it winning one of the great races which bring together the best horses from the leading stables in England, Ireland and sometimes France? If, on the other hand, we confine ourselves only to those animals which have achieved the comparatively rare feat of two recent victories in roughly the same standard of racing, then surely we have something to be on.

The STAR CHOICE method has, therefore, only one simple rule:

> **In the top weight-for-age races on the Flat, back any horse which has won both its two most recent outings, provided at least one of them was a Group One, Group Two or Group Three event.**

Group categories for big races are shown clearly in form books and in the form summaries that appear in the racing papers on the day of the race, so there should be no difficulty about determining qualifiers.

The formula will often single out only one horse for a big race. Sometimes two or three will qualify. The best advice is to back them all. Unlike most of the runners, these horses boast unbeaten form in approximately similar company. Given the prestige at stake, they are sure to be trying for their lives. They are bound to go close to winning. Backing more than one in the same race is justified to make certain of being on the right horse. Part 3 explains how to back several horses in the same race at various odds for an identical profit, whichever wins.

What about starting prices? 'All odds-on', I can hear the cynics saying. Not true, for opinions always take a wide range in the great races and the prices for qualifiers can extend to 10–1 and occasionally even more. Yes, there will be short-priced favourites too but, while there is no such thing as a racing certainty, records show that they are in the banker class.

The STAR CHOICE system isolates only the cream of the bets in the top sphere of British racing. Look in racing annuals for past years and check the idea out. One will be agreeably surprised, not only by the number of winners from this system, but also by the odds sometimes freely available about them. It must be remembered that the performance of any racehorse, even one of the very highest class, is to some extent governed by the laws of chance but these animals definitely have unrivalled potential as betting propositions.

43
THE BARRAGE PLAN

The BARRAGE Plan is an old formula for backing two-year-olds which down the years has made steady, if unspectacular, profits by cautious betting on form horses. Here the system is brought right up-to-date to take into account all the latest trends in juvenile racing in Britain.

The rules are as follows:

1 Only those horses which are first, second or third in the betting immediately before the 'off' in two-year-old non-handicaps may qualify for a bet. Where there are two or more horses quoted in equal third place in the betting, these are all considered for possible selection.

2 From the first three horses quoted in the betting in a race, there will be two horses to back, a principal selection with a large stake, and a danger selection with a smaller stake.

3 The horse with the best placing last time out of the three becomes the principal selection. Horses which did not finish first, second, third or fourth, or which have never run, are all counted as 'unplaced' and rank equally. Where a horse was disqualified last time out, its original finishing position before disqualification is counted as its placing.

4 The horse with the second-best placing becomes the danger selection.

5 If two or more horses were identically placed last time out, the one which is shorter or shortest in the betting takes precedence.

6 Where two or more horses were identically placed last time out and are at the same price in the betting just before the 'off', the one quoted at the shorter or shortest price in the betting forecast of the newspaper being used for systems purposes is taken.

7 There is a two-point stake to win on the principal selection and a one-point stake to win on the danger.

The examples below should clarify any doubts about the exact application of these rules.

Position in betting	Place last time out	Betting decision
1	2	Principal selection
2	0	
3	3	Danger
1	3	Danger
2	unraced	
3	2	Principal selection
1	1	Principal selection
2	1	Danger
3	1	
1	0	Principal selection
2	0	Danger
3	0	
1	4	
2	3	Principal selection
3	3	Danger
1	3	
2	4	
3=	2	Danger
3=	1	Principal selection
1	4	
2=	1 ⎫	Rule 6 applies for principal
2=	1 ⎭	selection and danger
1	1	Principal selection
2	0	
3=	2 ⎫	Rule 6 applies
3=	2 ⎭	for danger

1=	unraced ⎫	Rule 6 applies for principal
1=	0 ⎬	selection and danger
3	unraced ⎭	

The main change in the rules has been the elimination of the betting forecast as the chief factor for choosing between the market leaders, although in situations where everything else is equal in the actual betting, recourse to a newspaper must still determine the final order in the way illustrated above where Rule 6 is quoted.

Where a clear choice through the actual betting market alone is possible, however, that is now a much better option, given the fact that two-year-old racing is more competitive than ever before and also because juveniles do less racing than they used to, leaving their ability more unexposed than once was the case. The betting forecast is no longer any sort of guide to merit at big meetings, unlike the racecourse market. Although this calls for the system operator to monitor very closely betting movements from the course before making a bet, which is much less convenient than bets made from the betting forecast of a morning newspaper, the actual market has always been the best option in reality.

As long ago as August 1990, a piece in *The Times* newspaper gave an account of a 'risk research' unit based at Southampton University with financial support from Ladbrokes and others. The unit looked into betting on horses and found that backers who watched market movements right up to the time the horses came under starter's orders were the most successful. Incidentally, the unit also found that for those betting on the racecourse, the punters who watched the horses' behaviour from the time of their arrival in the paddock up to going into the starting stalls also put themselves at an advantage over those who ignored this factor and made their bets much earlier.

The upshot of all this is that the betting forecast is eliminated from the BARRAGE Plan as far as possible, and the actual betting market is now made the chief arbiter of what to back.

Here are the results of the BARRAGE formula at the most important festival meetings of the 2003 Flat season:

ROYAL ASCOT

Tuesday
2.30 race

Principal selection	SABEEH	£20	Lost	−£20.00
Danger	BOTANICAL	£10	Lost	−£10.00
				−£30.00

Wednesday
3.05 race

Principal selection	ATTRACTION	£20	Won 13–8	+£32.50
Danger	CATSTAR	£10	Lost	−£10.00
				+£22.50

5.30 race

Principal selection	PEARL OF LOVE	£20	Won 11–10	+£22.00
Danger	MILK IT MICK	£10	Lost	−£10.00
				+£12.00

Thursday
2.30 race

Principal selection	KHELEYF	£20	Lost	−£20.00
Danger	RUSSIAN VALOUR	£10	Won 4–1	+£40.00
				+£20.00

Friday
2.30 race

Principal selection	SILCA'S GIFT	£20	Won 5–1	+£100.00
Danger	TOLZEY	£10	Lost	−£10.00
				+£90.00

Saturday
4.55 race

Principal selection	WATERSTONE	£20	Lost	−£20.00
Danger	HOWICK FALLS	£10	Lost	−£10.00
				−£30.00

Total profit from meeting: £84.50

NEWMARKET JULY MEETING

Tuesday
2.50 race

Principal selection	ATTRACTION	£20	Won 4–7	+£11.43
Danger	PEARL GREY	£10	Lost	−£10.00
				+ £1.43

4.00 race

Principal selection	JOSEPHUS	£20	Won 7–2	+£70.00
Danger	ANDEAN	£10	Lost	−£10.00
				+£60.00

Wednesday
2.15 race

Principal selection	HOLBORN	£20	Lost	−£20.00
Danger	BYRON	£10	Lost	−£10.00
				−£30.00

4.00 race

Principal selection	PSYCHIATRIST	£20	Lost	−£20.00
Danger	REIDIES CHOICE	£10	Lost	−£10.00
				−£30.00

Thursday
2.15 race

Principal selection	CHESTER LE STREET	£20	Lost	−£20.00
Danger	BAYEUX	£10	Lost	−£10.00
				−£30.00

4.00 race

Principal selection	NOYAC	£20	Won 3–1	+£60.00
Danger	DU PRE	£10	Lost	−£10.00
				+£50.00

Total profit from meeting: £21.43

GLORIOUS GOODWOOD

Tuesday
4.25 race

Principal selection	FOKINE	£20	Lost	−£20.00
Danger	CARRIZO CREEK	£10	Won 5–1	+£50.00
				+£30.00

5.35 race

Principal selection	TAHREEB	£20	Won 6–4	+£30.00
Danger	FINDERS KEEPERS	£10	Lost	−£10.00
				+£20.00

Wednesday
2.40 race

Principal selection	LUCKY STORY	£20	Won 6–5	+£24.00
Danger	THE MIGHTY TIGER	£10	Lost	−£10.00
				+£14.00

5.00 race

Principal selection	KUNDA	£20	Lost	−£20.00
Danger	TAROT CARD	£10	Won 2–1	+£20.00
				£00.00

Thursday
2.40 race

Principal selection	MAJESTIC MISSILE	£20	Won 9–4	+£45.00
Danger	DALLAAH	£10	Lost	−£10.00
				+£35.00

4.25 race

Principal selection	ITHACA	£20	Won 2–1	+£40.00
Danger	SAHOOL	£10	Lost	−£10.00
				+£30.00

Friday
5.00 race

Principal selection	SECRETARY GENERAL	£20	Lost	−£20.00
Danger	PSYCHIATRIST	£10	Won 7–2	+£35.00
				+£15.00

Total profit from meeting: £144.00

YORK AUGUST MEETING

Tuesday
4.05 race

Principal selection	RULE OF LAW	£20	Won 15–8	+£37.50
Danger	CELTIC CAT	£10	Lost	−£10.00
				+£27.50

Wednesday
3.30 race

Principal selection	GRAND REWARD	£20	Lost	−£20.00
Danger	BALMONT	£10	Won 7–2	+£35.00
				+£15.00

4.05 race

Principal selection	CONVINCE	£20	Lost	−£20.00
Danger	HARRY UP	£10	Lost	−£10.00
				−£30.00

4.35 race

Principal selection	FINDERS KEEPERS	£20	Lost	−£20.00
Danger	GREAT EXHIBITION	£10	Lost	−£10.00
				−£30.00

Thursday
2.25 race

Principal selection	SILCA'S GIFT	£20	Lost	−£20.00
Danger	CARRY ON KATIE	£10	Won 3–1	+£30.00
				+£10.00

Total loss at meeting: £7.50

To summarise, therefore, here is the consolidated account for the 2003 Flat season:

Royal Ascot	+£ 84.50
Newmarket (July)	+£ 21.43
Glorious Goodwood	+£144.00
York (August)	–£ 7.50
Total profit	+£242.43
Total outlay:	+£720.00
Percentage profit on outlay	33.7%

Given the fact that these examples of the BARRAGE Plan in action are all worked on a short sequence of races, this is quite a creditable performance. Note that all the meetings are in the summer months of June, July and August when systems based on form horses at the short end of the market do best. As soon as the rains come in early autumn and fields begin to swell in size, as happens every backend, results can be expected to be much less consistent.

However, the four festival meetings above are obviously only the top of the tree. Equally sound results in high summer may be anticipated further down the class scale at less important venues. Here the key is to choose the right kind of two-year-old non-handicap in which to operate, for much weaker betting markets produce some very short-priced favourites that would upset the mathematical balance of the staking on two selections per race. But if races are carefully analysed with a view to avoiding those with a likely odds-on favourite, the BARRAGE can still be a profitable bet for a shrewd operator.

It is rare in racing to come across such a neat little system like the BARRAGE which consistently delivers the goods, even though some readers may not be comfortable with backing two horses per race at short odds. Nevertheless, in the right hands this plan has the potential to be a steady winner. The abolition of betting tax and a strict adherence to market movements, rather than relying on the much less reliable betting forecasts of newspapers, combine to make the BARRAGE more potent than ever as a profit-maker. It must be accepted that there is still a fine balance between success and failure, at least in the short term, and there is no possibility of spectacular gains, just a marginal profit from fancied horses in non-handicap races.

If it is felt that margins are too small to make the use of the plan truly worthwhile, profits may be enhanced by the use of doubles without too much extra risk in the following way:

TWO SELECTIONS IN EACH OF TWO RACES

Two principal selections	2-point double (one bet)
Principal selection with	
danger in other race	1-point doubles (two bets)
Both dangers	1-point double (one bet)
Total outlay:	5 points on four doubles

Here again, any race with a possible odds-on favourite should be omitted in favour of a more open contest. Also, when two races chosen for a doubles bet are widely separated in time, it will be necessary to use a betting forecast as an indicator of the final selections, at least in the later event.

As we saw in an earlier chapter, specialising in two-year-olds can be an interesting and rewarding way of backing horses, for with specialisation comes knowledge and, hopefully, more accuracy in choosing winning selections. The BARRAGE is an excellent way of capitalising on the knowledge and expertise thus acquired.

44
THE KEY RACES METHOD

Most of the big races in the British racing calendar have been established for well over a century and a half. Moreover, the actual fixture list has changed little in terms of the time of year at which most important events are run. In these circumstances it is not surprising that definite patterns should have evolved which determine how horses are prepared for big races and that is the focus of this system.

Individual trainers may have their own methods of preparing horses on the gallops but season after season the big winners follow similar paths to success. These are governed by the far-from-limitless opportunities offered by a largely unchanging programme of meetings and races. This is the justification for the 'key race' theory of betting. In many cases the key to the results of top races is to be found in earlier races which traditionally provide important clues. It is simply a question of discovering the seasonal pattern and applying it to the current year.

Below is an analysis of the top races according to the key race idea. Allied to the study of form, it should enable you to back a lot of big winners.

THE CLASSICS

Readers are referred to the STAR CHOICE method earlier in the book, but the following is a more specific guide that may help you to choose between several possible candidates.

2000 Guineas (1m, Newmarket, early May)
Two-year-old form is frequently as important as the spring trials, but with so many top three-year-olds nowadays given a very easy time as juveniles, it is not necessarily those at the top of the two-year-old ratings which come out and run prominently in the first Classic for colts. However, the Dewhurst Stakes, over the last seven furlongs of the Rowley Mile, remains a highly significant indicator from the previous autumn. The Craven Stakes is the best three-year-old trial.

Despite all the confusion in the form which seems to attend

most modern renewals of the 2000, nearly all winners win their previous race, and the Classic itself seldom goes to a horse outside the first five or six in the betting. If a horse that was beaten last time out is to win, most likely it ran in the Craven Stakes.

1000 Guineas (1m, Newmarket, early May)

The first Classic for three-year-old fillies comes barely a month after the start of the new Flat season which is very early in the form cycle of a typical member of the equine fair sex. There are a number of trials in April which can consequently confuse the picture. The Nell Gwyn Stakes, run at Newmarket a fortnight before the Classic, has proved highly misleading in recent times, and the Fred Darling Stakes at Newbury may be a better guide. On the other hand, there are plenty of examples in the record book of a filly succeeding first time out in the big race.

Two-year-old form, therefore, is very much the key. One of the leading half-dozen fillies in the 'International Classification of Two-Year-Olds' form a group which often includes the winner. Most French-trained winners of the race have also won the Prix Imprudence at Longchamp in April. Top fillies occasionally cross the Irish Sea for the race; their chance should never be lightly dismissed.

Oaks Stakes (1½m, Epsom, early June)

Winners of the 1000 Guineas used to have a good record, and placed horses from the Newmarket Classic also do well, although in an age of specialisation fewer fillies challenge for both races than used to be the case. Look for a contender placed in a Group One race over a mile at two or three, or the winner of a Listed or Group race at 10f or more. If a filly has won at 10f plus at three, in either a Pattern or non-Pattern race, she should not have been subsequently beaten. These rules account for every Oaks winner of the last decade.

Though not a race for big outsiders, the Oaks cannot be said to be a favourite's race either. Market leaders only win in their turn.

Derby Stakes (1½m, Epsom, early June)
The Derby is an international event featuring challengers from England, Ireland and France. There are many trials but no one race consistently provides the best clue. The race is seldom won by anything but a genuine stayer – hence the failure in the race of so many 2000 Guineas winners, whose speed is often blunted by the extra four furlongs.

Favourites or near-favourites dominate the race, so look for a well-backed candidate which has won at or close to a mile and a half in top company. This usually cuts the field down to a few live contenders from which the winner may come. An interesting feature in recent times has been the number of winners which were given an easy time at two. Top class two-year-old form is, therefore, no longer a necessary credential, as was once the case.

On the other hand, 35 out of the last 40 Derby winners won over 7f or more as juveniles, and some of the others were unraced at two. This is a most interesting statistic and might lead to the elimination of a fancied candidate or two with a fair degree of confidence.

St Leger (1¾m, Doncaster, early September)
Nowadays winners of the race take many routes to Classic glory, and races such as the Derby, Irish Derby and Great Voltigeur Stakes at York have seen their influence diminish over the years, with many St Leger winners emerging late in their second season from outside the ranks of the established stars. However, at least a place, if not a win, in a Group One or Two race, is a qualification most of them have.

The race has become very much one for favourites. If opposing the favourite, bet each-way, for fields seldom get much above double figures and one could 'steal' a win as well as the inflated place money if the market leader goes down at a short price.

WEIGHT-FOR-AGE AND CONDITION RACES

Ormonde Stakes (1m 5f, Chester, early May)
This important early season test for senior horses seldom falls to anything but a form horse. The best trial by far is the John Porter Stakes in mid-April. The Group Three Newbury race over 1m 4f 5yd was renamed, probably only temporarily, the Dubai Irish Village Stakes in 2003. Winners of it, or those who finished close up behind the winner, dominate the results of Chester's middle-distance test a month later.

Coronation Cup (1½m, Epsom, early June)
Epsom's big middle-distance event used to be dominated by Classic winners of the previous year but nowadays, with so many good horses retiring to stud at the end of their three-year-old season, the race usually goes to one of the second eleven. The Jockey Club Stakes at the Newmarket Guineas meeting is probably the best single 'key' race. French raiders should be noted, especially if the home side appears to lack quality. The Prix Ganay over 1m 2½f at Longchamp in late April is the most informative French trial.

Queen Anne Stakes (1m, Ascot, mid-June)
The Lockinge Stakes at Newbury is an important 'key race' for this tough contest which produces winners at all kinds of prices. Examine the chances of the placed horses in the Lockinge, as their record in the last decade is superior to the actual winner.

St James's Palace Stakes (1m, Ascot, mid-June)
One of Royal Ascot's showpieces, the race often goes to one of the first four in the 2000 Guineas, though many are beaten between their good run on the Rowley Mile and their victory in this event. The winner of the Irish 2000 Guineas must also be considered if contesting the race. Runners from France are not all that frequent but they have an above-average record if already established as one of the top French milers. This is definitely not a favourite's race; most winners come from the middle order of the betting.

Prince of Wales's Stakes (1¼m, Ascot, mid-June)
Now a Group One championship race, it seldom falls to a horse
outside the first two in the market.

Hardwicke Stakes (1½m, Ascot, mid-June)
There are two clues to Ascot's big middle-distance test for senior
horses – the Jockey Club Stakes at Newmarket and the Coronation
Cup at Epsom. Most years the winner of the Hardwicke contests
one or both of these races, without necessarily winning. The race is
a Group Two affair, and the difficulty with the good, older horses
that compete at this level is that their form tends to be very in and
out. Look for one which has shown a spark of brilliance in the past,
even if recent runs have not produced a win. Alternatively, the race
often goes to a late-developing, lightly raced animal which has
recently improved to the extent that it looks capable of making the
grade in this company. Most winners come from the middle rank
in the betting.

Coronation Stakes (1m, Ascot, mid-June)
The race often crowns the achievements of a winner of the Irish
1000 Guineas, or is a consolation prize for a filly which ran well in
the English 1000. The race has Group One status, however, and a
late-developing filly can sometimes shock established stars. Given
the right material, the big guns among the Newmarket training
elite make a speciality of this.

Lancashire Oaks (1½m, Haydock, early July)
Now open to four-year-olds, the race is still on the agenda of the
Epsom Oaks failures. Any filly which finished in the first half-
dozen at Epsom should go close.

Eclipse Stakes (1¼m, Sandown, early July)
This is a race of the very highest class open to three-year-olds and
upwards over 10 furlongs. Milers as well as 12-furlong horses can
win if they have the class. It takes a real top-notcher to succeed in
the race, and nearly all winners have at least one Group race victory
to their credit during the current season, with many having been
also, at least, placed in a Classic either this year or last. The record
of favourites, however, is only average. The Prince of Wales's Stakes
at Ascot has been the best single guide.

King George VI and Queen Elizabeth Stakes (1½m, Ascot, late July)
Above-average winners of the Epsom and Irish Derbys often win but only if they have the overall form to suggest that their Derby win was not a one-off. But winners of the Eclipse Stakes, though stepping up in distance, often have a vital edge in speed on going that is usually fast. Three-year-olds have by far the best record, for it appears that the scale of weight-for-age favours them at this time of year.

Sussex Stakes (1m, Goodwood, late July or early August)
Three-year-olds dominate this showdown between the best milers at Glorious Goodwood. The St James's Palace Stakes may have a bearing, and Royal Ascot form generally comes out on top. The first three in the betting have a virtual monopoly of results, though it may not be easy to pick the right one.

International Stakes (1¼m, York, mid-August)
Now established in the very top echelon of racing, York's big test used to provide consolation for horses that ran well in the Epsom Derby. But in recent times all three-year-olds seem to struggle against the best older horses. Favourites do badly and outsiders win far more often than is usual in a Group One contest. Not a race in which to 'go for broke'.

Yorkshire Oaks (1½m, York, mid-August)
The form of the top staying fillies has moved on a bit since the beginning of June, but those who made the frame in the Epsom Oaks are still most likely to succeed. The Oaks at Epsom is after all the premier Classic for fillies over the distance. Races like the Ribblesdale Stakes at Royal Ascot, the Nassau Stakes at Goodwood and the Irish Oaks at the Curragh, though sometimes having a bearing, can also be something of a blind alley in the York race.

The race is now open to four-year-olds and over, and a really top-class member of this age group will often see off the Classic generation, especially if no outstanding stayer has emerged from among the younger animals.

Park Hill Stakes (1¾m, Doncaster, early September)
Known as the 'fillies' St Leger' and run over the full Classic distance, the race has become much less important in recent years. Classic fillies seldom appear nowadays, and the race usually goes to an improving sort from a top English yard. The ability to stay, as established by the racecourse test, or, failing that, a staying pedigree, is the vital form factor to look for in a probable winner.

Queen Elizabeth II Stakes (1m, Ascot, late September)
This is now a world-class race and the winner will usually take the title of 'champion miler'. Anything less than top-class form should be disregarded. However, the presumed 'good thing' frequently gets turned over. Three-year-olds seem to have the edge over older horses.

Champion Stakes (1¼m, Newmarket, mid-October)
Run over the straight 10 furlongs at Newmarket in the autumn when even some of the best horses have had enough for the season, this prestigious weight-for-age race is one of the trickiest in the calendar. An English Classic winner, either a three- or four-year-old, and not necessarily the one at the shortest price, is often the best solution. Fillies are at their peak at this time of year and they have an outstanding record. French raiders sometimes win at a very good price.

THE CUP RACES

Gold Cup (2½m, Ascot, mid-June)
In an age of speed, very few horses are able to produce top-class acceleration at the end of a marathon distance. Those that possess this rare quality will nearly always have established their reputation and will start as a hot favourite. They usually win. In an average year, however, with no outstanding horse in the field, the way is open for unfancied horses to overturn a weak favourite.

Form is hard to assess because of the extreme distance. Breeding is often a better guide. Look for a tough, staying sire, with plenty of stamina close up on the dam's side. The Henry II Stakes at Sandown in May is the best single trial. The Yorkshire Cup has also been a sound guide in recent years. In both of these trials pay attention to beaten horses as well as the winners.

The French sometimes send over a challenger, but French predominance in stayers' races is very old history indeed, and their runners usually struggle against the home side.

Goodwood Cup (2m, Goodwood, late July or early August)
An obvious choice is the Gold Cup winner if that horse contests the race but the price is bound to be short. The race used to be run over five furlongs further. The reduction in distance has produced more competitive fields, but form is that much more reliable. Do not look beyond the first three in the betting but remember that Goodwood is a course for specialists. Tough, older stayers often beat off the challenge of young pretenders.

Doncaster Cup (2¼m, Doncaster, early September)
This is very definitely a favourites' race. Winners of the Yorkshire Cup, Ascot's Sagaro Stakes, the Henry II Stakes or the Goodwood Cup which occupy the leading position in the market ought to be something of a banker bet. The Gold Cup form, by contrast, is not always upheld on Town Moor.

Jockey Club Cup (2m, Newmarket, mid-October)
Fields are small. Yet prices are, relatively speaking, often generous. If form indicates a reasonably certain winner, the result is likely to confirm the analysis and pay a handsome dividend. The horse with the best credentials usually wins at more than fair odds. The Doncaster Cup winner or one of the first three home in the Goodwood Cup is a small group that often contains the winner.

TOP SPRINTS

King's Stand Stakes (5f, Ascot, mid-June)
Horses from three-years-old to six are on the recent score sheet for what is invariably a very difficult race to call. More important than age, a victory in at least one Group race in recent runs is a useful qualification. The Temple Stakes at Sandown remains the best single trial, as it has been for many years.

Golden Jubilee Stakes (6f, Ascot, mid-June)
Formerly known as the Cork and Orrery Stakes, this hot sprint is now the centrepiece of the final day of the Royal meeting. The Duke of York Stakes over the same distance at York's May meeting has been the biggest source of winners in recent times. Not a race for real outsiders, statistically it is 6–4 on that the winner will come from one of the first three in the betting, a better average than one would expect in such a competitive race.

July Cup (6f, Newmarket, early July)
This is a very hot race these days and it often pays to stick with the two traditional guides, the Golden Jubilee Stakes and the King's Stand Stakes, both run at Royal Ascot. The French challenge only occasionally but, if a runner from across the Channel is in the field, the hint should be taken. Horses of all ages win.

King George Stakes (5f, Goodwood, late July or early August)
Placed horses from the King's Stand Stakes at Royal Ascot often land a good consolation prize in this Group Three sprint, one of the feature races at Glorious Goodwood.

Nunthorpe Stakes (5f, York, mid-August)
The market is not always a good guide and the 'key race' picture is confused. The state of the ground is often the deciding factor. A horse needs the going to be exactly to its liking if it is to have that split-second edge over other flying machines. Check out the form book and the stallion guide on page 59.

Haydock Sprint Cup (6f, Haydock, mid-September)
Here too the ground is often decisive among sprinters that are very close on form. Outsiders seldom win but actual favourites do not have a particularly good record either.

Diadem Stakes (6f, Ascot, late September)
The race is often run on heavy ground, and the going is frequently the deciding factor. Most winners have won at least one race in Group Three or better.

BIG HANDICAPS

Lincoln Handicap (1m, Doncaster, late March)
Much depends on the draw in the season's first big handicap, so small stakes are advised. Fitness is the key with most runners making their seasonal debut. Look for those horses which have shown that they come to hand early by winning in the first month of the previous season. Live candidates should also have good win-and-place form in fair handicap company at the back-end to have a real chance of success in this highly competitive race. Recent form on the all-weather can also confer a decisive advantage.

Chester Cup (2¼m, Chester, early May)
Run round Chester's tight turns, the race is not so much a test of bottomless stamina as it might first appear. Just as important is a top-class jockey who can judge the pace on the tricky track. Horses that have already recorded a win in the first weeks of the season should be noted. Key races both from last and the current season are the Cesarewitch, the Queen's Prize at Kempton in April, and the Chester Cup itself. A prominent run (1st to 5th) in one of these races for out-and-out stayers is a vital clue for those prepared to dig really deep into the form book. For a big handicap, most winners are surprisingly well fancied.

Royal Hunt Cup (1m, Ascot, mid-June)
There are numerous good mile handicaps in the weeks leading up to Ascot's annual cavalry charge, but the Victoria Cup over 7f of the course at the previous meeting on the Heath has developed into an excellent trial. There is always a huge field for the Hunt Cup and favourites have a very poor record. Very highly weighted horses struggle too. Big stables tend to monopolise the race, and the small trainer is seldom able to make an impact.

Wokingham Handicap (6f, Ascot, mid-June)
One of the most open handicaps of the year, this big sprint is another race where heavy betting is asking for trouble. However, somewhat surprisingly, practically all winners in the last decade have corresponded to a distinct form profile. Find a horse which finished in the first three in a Grade B or Grade C handicap on a

Class A course (see the RACECOURSE GUIDE at the back of this book), and you have a live prospect to bet on.

Northumberland Plate (2m, Newcastle, late June)
The 'Pitman's Derby', as the race is known, usually falls to a well-backed candidate. The Queen's Prize at Kempton in mid-April, the Chester Cup and the Ascot Handicap at the Royal meeting are three races for stayers that can give useful hints.

John Smith's Cup (1¼m, York, mid-July)
The North's top midsummer handicap attracts the biggest Flat racing crowd of the year after Derby Day and Royal Ascot. The draw is the most significant factor in finding the winner. No horse drawn in double figures has won for well over a decade. Horses of all ages succeed, but three-year-olds have the best record, scoring about 50 per cent of the time. An improving candidate of this age with plenty of good, recent form is an obvious choice most years, but there will be four-year-olds and five-year-olds which have been running well in big handicaps that also need to be considered.

Outsiders can, and do, win from time to time, but it is best to stick with the market leaders, though the outright favourite is seldom good value in terms of price and does not win very often.

Stewards' Cup (6f, Goodwood, late July or early August)
There is no key formula to the race, with winners coming from many directions. However, two factors are most important. Three-year-olds are just coming into their own against older horses at this time of year, and this age group should be examined as closely as any other. Also, a good draw is a virtual necessity for success. Check the earlier results on the straight course in big fields at the meeting to establish this year's bias, but if you can pick out a horse with the speed to lie up with the pace and which has a draw in the high 20s, you will have recent history on your side and a chance of finding the winner.

Ebor Handicap (1¾m, York, mid-August)
There are no easy solutions to this most open of staying handicaps.
The class of the race is always very high, so lightweights are up
against it, save for the unexposed three-year-old which might just
fool the handicapper. Valuable staying handicaps at Newmarket,
Ascot and Goodwood are the best guides.

Ayr Gold Cup (6f, Ayr, late September)
An each-way bet on a horse which got into the frame in one of the
several sprints at Doncaster's big September meeting often pays a
dividend. Outsiders rarely win; well-backed horses (up to 14–1)
usually do.

Cambridgeshire (1m 1f, Newmarket, early October)
This is usually the most difficult handicap of the year. Horses
which finished in the first four in the Royal Hunt Cup represent
good value and can win at a big price. Beauchamp Pilot, the 2002
winner, though starting at the relatively modest price of 9–1, was
one such horse, having finished third in the big Ascot handicap.
Among the market leaders, look out for a horse which has suddenly
begun to improve dramatically in the last month or so.

Cesarewitch (2¼m, Newmarket, mid-October)
Great reserves of stamina are needed for this end-of-season
marathon. Many winners are either established stayers with a
biggish weight to match their form or improving three-year-olds
down at the bottom of the handicap. Form is hard to assess for a
race over such a long distance but note very carefully the entries of
'clever' trainers who like to bet. Well-backed horses generally do
well.

BIG RACES OVER JUMPS

Gold Cup Handicap Chase (2m 4½f, Cheltenham, mid-November)
The first big race of the jumping year is over an extended two and a half miles, and many of the best handicappers at this 'in-between' distance contest the prize. Though there are exceptions, genuine two- or three-milers are probably running in the wrong race. Most winners have had a preparatory race in the current season but this is not essential. A win, or at least a good place last time out, is desirable as evidence that a horse is capable of going on to win such a competitive event. Look for a 'class' horse carrying 11 st or more, or a lightweight with excellent form figures. Ten-year-olds or over are best forgotten in a race for up-and-coming young chasers. Favourites do well, and the first four or five in the betting are statistically favoured. Rank outsiders are highly suspect.

Hennessy Cognac Gold Cup Handicap Chase (3m 2½f, Newbury, late November)
Most winners have at least one warm-up race, and quite a few have two or more. Top trainers 'farm' the race, and the smaller handler is bound to struggle in the face of competition from the big yards. Despite the wide difference in race distance, Cheltenham's Gold Cup Handicap in November is sometimes a reliable guide. Favourites do far better than might be expected in such a keenly contested handicap, and the middle rank in the betting dominates when the actual market leader fails to pull it off.

King George VI Chase (3m, Kempton, late December)
The cream of the chasing ranks is on show in the premier mid-season jumping prize but the race does seem to require special talents, perhaps because speed is at a premium over Kempton's easy three miles. At one time, horses often won in consecutive years but, with competition ever more intense, the race is now a much more open affair. Hence challengers from overseas must be considered alongside the best Britain has to offer, for the invaders often come out on top. Favourites do reasonably well, sometimes at a generous price. Rank outsiders should be forgotten.

Tote Gold Trophy (2m ½f, Newbury, early April)
Although a five-year-old winner pops up from time to time in this big handicap hurdle, horses aged six or seven do best in fairly equal measure. High-weighted horses struggle in such a competitive race. Realistically, 11 st 7 lb is the upper limit for success, but horses right down at the bottom of the handicap are not particularly favoured either. Before Spirit Leader won at 14–1 in 2003, every winner in the previous 10 years had started at between 9–4 and 10–1 inclusive. In that time, all winners, like Spirit Leader, too, had without exception been placed in the first four on their last run.

Racing Post Handicap Chase (3m, Kempton, late February)
Though a handicap, a horse with a touch of class is needed for this hotly contested race. Therefore, ignore lightweights and outsiders. By applying a basic form qualification, it is possible to cut out a lot of losing bets in all but an atypical year: most winners were at least placed last time out and also won a minimum of one of their last four races.

Champion Hurdle (2m, Cheltenham, mid-March)
Two or more victories by the same horse has always been a feature of the history of hurdling's crown. Also, most horses beaten one year are not very likely to win the next. Concentrate on young horses if you think there will be a new champion. The prices of winning favourites tend to be poor in a race where heavy gamblers tend to 'get stuck in' on a presumed 'certainty'. However, there is plenty of each-way value, and this is often the best bet in the race for the average punter.

Queen Mother Champion Chase (2m, Cheltenham, mid-March)
In what is very much a race for specialists over the minimum trip, previous winners must be considered again. Failing that, last year's second or third may win or go close. Avoid very young and old horses; nine- and ten-year-olds have the best record. Keep to the first three in the betting.

Cheltenham Gold Cup Chase (3m 2½f, Cheltenham, mid-March)
Top-class conditions races are the best guide. Handicap form, however impressive on the surface, is best left alone. An animal needs to be at its absolute peak to win, so veterans of over 10 years old have little chance. By contrast, novices in their first season over fences are rarely good enough. Most years it pays to concentrate on the first four or five in the betting.

The King George VI Chase at Kempton on Boxing Day is historically by far and away the best trial, though it is the beaten horses, not the winner, that the statistically minded punter should concentrate on if any chink in the Kempton victor's armour is visible. However, the Cheltenham showdown itself has been a poor guide to the King George VI Chase the following season, for nine months is a long time in National Hunt racing.

Grand National Handicap Chase (4½m, Aintree, early April)
Stamina and jumping ability are the vital ingredients for Aintree's spectacular. Form, therefore, is the key to the race despite its formidable reputation for thrills and spills. Animals carrying much above 11 st are at a serious disadvantage over such testing jumping country and an extreme distance. Conversely, minimum weight is 10 st. Few horses set to carry more than 7 lb over their long handicap weight (see specialist press) have the class to succeed.

Horses of all ages win, and advancing years have never prevented the right horse from claiming the prize. The betting market is the most consistent pointer of all. Despite the occasional winning outsider, well-backed horses, sometimes without obvious form claims, monopolise the record of results. Compare the opening, ante-post prices four or five weeks before with the prices available on the morning of the race to find out where the smart money has gone. No horse can win unless it completes the course, however, and finding the winner in a single selection is a difficult task.

The key race theory is not just hindsight. If you try it out, you will be amazed how often history repeats itself. There will, inevitably, be failures but the statistical record is there for those who wish to use it to their advantage.

45
THE BLUEPRINT METHOD

When winter comes, many punters turn to favourites as the likeliest source of a regular flow of winners. This is perfectly understandable. Despite the fact that National Hunt racing has become increasingly competitive in recent decades, jumping favourites retain a remarkably high level of consistency. However, one still has to pick the right favourites.

The problem has exercised some of the most ingenious minds in racing over the years, and a number of suggestions have been put forward for providing automatic selections. Below I show an analysis of some of the most sensible of these. In each case a one-year cycle of National Hunt racing has been used as a yardstick.

	Winning percentage	Average annual profit (+) or loss (−)
Longest distance chase of the day (including handicaps)	41.6%	+2 pts
Most valuable chase of the day (including handicaps)	41.2%	+5 pts
First non-handicap on the card (principal meeting)	38.6%	−4 pts
Last race on the card (principal meeting)	32.6%	−11 pts
Favourite quoted at the shortest price in the betting forecast of all favourites (all meetings)	74.1%	+10 pts
Favourite quoted at the second shortest price in the betting forecast of all favourites (all meetings)	52.5%	−1 pt

It can be seen that most of these methods are fundamentally sound. All of them embody some principle of selectivity but, to complete the statistical picture of National Hunt favourites, on the next page is another table. Here, whole categories of a particular race type are considered, with no attempt at discrimination at all.

	Winning percentage	Average annual profit (+) or loss (−)
All non-handicap chases	44.9%	−2 pts
All non-handicap hurdles	42.6%	−14 pts
Novice chases (non-handicaps)	45.1%	−1 pt
Novice hurdles (non-handicaps)	41.9%	−12 pts
Best race on the card (5th)	40.7%	+4 pts
Worst race on the card (6th)	34.9%	−15 pts

Of all the figures from these two tables, the 10 points profit produced by the shortest betting forecast favourite of the day is surely of great interest. Even more significant, perhaps, is the accompanying 74.1% strike rate.

It might be of value to readers to know exactly how this useful gain was generated. Therefore, here is the full record from the Ascot meeting of 22 November onwards when the jumping season of 2002–2003 finally got into full swing. The sequence closes at the end of the Cheltenham Festival week because immediately after that the number of National Hunt meetings drops off dramatically to make way for the Flat. From then on, there is not enough racing over jumps on a regular basis to make the shortest priced horse of the day an outstanding selection when compared with a reasonable number of other, possible bets from at least two jump meetings a day.

Throughout the series the same daily newspaper was used as the arbiter of selections. The level-stakes profit or loss for each selection to a £20 daily stake, and the running balance to date, are shown on the right.

Shortest priced betting forecast favourite of the day
(22 November 2002 to 16 March 2003)

Date	Horse	Result	Profit (+) or loss (−) on day	Overall profit (+) or loss (−)
22 Nov	BARACOUDA	Won 2–5	+£8.00	+£8.00
23 Nov	BEST MATE	Won 8–15	+£10.67	+£18.67
24 Nov	FIREBALL MCNAMARA	Lost	−£20.00	−£1.33
25 Nov	BALLYCASSIDY	Lost	−£20.00	−£21.33
26 Nov	VOL SOLITAIRE	Won 6–5	+£24.00	+£2.67
27 Nov	NO NEED FOR ALARM	Won 2–5	+£8.00	+£10.67
28 Nov	THE BAJAN BANDIT	Won 1–4	+£5.00	+£15.67
29 Nov	RHINESTONE COWBOY	Won 30–100	+£6.00	+£21.67
30 Nov	TEES COMPONENTS	Won 4–7	+£11.43	+£33.10
2 Dec	TELEMOSS	Won 4–11	+£7.27	+£40.37
3 Dec	FREE RETURN	Won 4–1	+£80.00	+£120.37
4 Dec	IBAL	Won 4–5	+£16.00	+£136.37
5 Dec	HERSOV	Won 4–6	+£13.33	+£149.70
6 Dec	VALLEY HENRY	Won 8–13	+£12.31	+£162.01
7 Dec	SKIPPERS CLEUCH	Won 1–2	+£10.00	+£172.01
9 Dec	BYRON LAMB	Won 4–9	+£8.89	+£180.90
10 Dec	BROCTON MIST	Lost	−£20.00	+£160.90
11 Dec	TIME N TIDE	NR		
12 Dec	NICK THE JEWEL	Won 8–11	+£14.55	+£175.45
13 Dec	RHINESTONE COWBOY	Won 2–11	+£3.64	+£179.09
14 Dec	ROSE D'APRIL	Lost	−£20.00	+£159.09
16 Dec	TEES COMPONENTS	Lost	−£20.00	+£139.09
17 Dec	MOORE'S LAW	Won 2–5	+£8.00	+£147.09
18 Dec	JOSS NAYLOR	Won 1–2	+£10.00	+£157.09
19 Dec	BEWLEYS HOTELS	NR		
20 Dec	BARACOUDA	Lost	−£20.00	+£137.09
21 Dec	TRABOLGAN	Lost	−£20.00	+£117.09
26 Dec	BLUE RIDE	Won 2–5	+£8.00	+£125.09
27 Dec	ASADOR	Lost	−£20.00	+£105.09
28 Dec	IL CAVALIERE	Won 4–7	+£11.43	+£116.52
31 Dec	GOLDEN ALPHA	Lost	−£20.00	+£96.52
1 Jan	TARXIEN	Lost	−£20.00	+£76.52
2 Jan	TO THE FUTURE	Won 7–4	+£35.00	+£111.52
3 Jan	INCA TRAIL	Won 1–4	+£5.00	+£116.52
4 Jan	NO NEED FOR ALARM	NR		
6 Jan	TAMANGO	Lost	−£20.00	+£96.52
13 Jan	NO COLLUSION	Lost	−£20.00	+£76.52
14 Jan	CHOPNEYEV	Won 1–3	+£6.67	+£83.19
15 Jan	TELEMOSS	Won 2–5	+£8.00	+£91.19
16 Jan	OUR VIC	Won 1–3	+£6.67	+£97.86
17 Jan	GLENMOSS TARA	Won 8–13	+£12.31	+£110.17
18 Jan	EDREDON BLEU	Won 1–3	+£6.67	+£116.84
20 Jan	MAJED	NR		
21 Jan	WOULD YOU BELIEVE	NR		

Date	Horse	Result	Profit (+) or loss (–) on day	Overall profit (+) or loss (–)
22 Jan	JOLY BEY	Won 4–7	+£11.43	+£128.27
23 Jan	MONTALCINO	Lost	–£20.00	+£108.27
24 Jan	ISIO	Won 4–11	+£7.27	+£115.54
25 Jan	DOBBIESGARDENWORLD	Lost	–£20.00	+£95.54
27 Jan	ONE KNIGHT	Won 1–2	+£10.00	+£105.54
28 Jan	ROVERETTO	Won 1–3	+£6.67	+£112.21
29 Jan	TANA RIVER	Won 2–7	+£5.71	+£117.92
30 Jan	MR WOODENTOP	NR		
31 Jan	ENITSAG	NR		
1 Feb	ROOSTER BOOSTER	Won 2–7	+£5.71	+£123.63
3 Feb	HANSBURY	Lost	–£20.00	+£103.63
4 Feb	EARTH MOVER	Won 4–6	+£13.33	+£116.96
5 Feb	FIRST LOVE	NR		
6 Feb	SUPREME PRINCE	Won 2–5	+£8.00	+£124.96
7 Feb	ENITSAG	Won 2–7	+£5.71	+£130.67
8 Feb	MAN MURPHY	Won 1–3	+£6.67	+£137.34
10 Feb	AVITTA	Lost	–£20.00	+£117.34
11 Feb	TACTFUL REMARK	Lost	–£20.00	+£97.34
12 Feb	LAST OPTION	Lost	–£20.00	+£77.34
13 Feb	OVER THE STORM	Lost	–£20.00	+£57.34
14 Feb	JOLY BEY	Won 4–6	+£13.33	+£70.67
15 Feb	AZERTYUIOP	Won 1–3	+£6.67	+£77.34
17 Feb	TORDUFF EXPRESS	Won 4–9	+£8.89	+£86.23
21 Feb	DEANO'S BEANO	Won evens	+£20.00	+£106.23
22 Feb	ISIO	Won 4–11	+£7.27	+£113.50
23 Feb	ENITSAG	Lost	–£20.00	+£93.50
24 Feb	INDALO	Won 2–5	+£8.00	+£101.50
25 Feb	PALARSHAN	Won 8–13	+£12.31	+£113.81
26 Feb	JOLY BEY	Won 2–7	+£5.71	+£119.52
27 Feb	DEEP SUNSET	Won 5–6	+£16.67	+£136.19
28 Feb	IRIS ROYAL	Won 1–7	+£2.86	+£139.05
1 Mar	VOL SOLITAIRE	Won 4–11	+£7.27	+£146.32
2 Mar	NAS NA RIOGH	Won 1–8	+£2.50	+£148.82
3 Mar	ROSARIAN	Won 1–5	+£4.00	+£152.82
4 Mar	LINUS	Won 4–11	+£7.27	+£160.09
5 Mar	PENNY PICTURES	Won 1–5	+£4.00	+£164.09
6 Mar	NEWS MAKER	Won 30–100	+£6.00	+£170.09
7 Mar	THE RILE	Won 2–5	+£8.00	+£178.09
8 Mar	THE LYME VOLUNTEER	NR		
10 Mar	BUCKBY LANE	Won 1–4	+£5.00	+£183.09
11 Mar	THE FRENCH FURZE	Won 2–7	+£5.71	+£188.80
12 Mar	INDEED	Lost	–£20.00	+£168.80
13 Mar	FRED'S IN THE KNOW	Won 4–9	+£8.89	+£177.69
14 Mar	CHIEF WITNESS	Won 4–11	+£7.27	+£184.96
15 Mar	TARASCO	Won 2–5	+£8.00	+192.96
16 Mar	FAIT LE JOJO	Won 30–100	+£6.00	+£198.96

The first thing to note about the final gain of £198.96 is that, whatever the doubters say, profits are possible from racing, and without using complex methods of selection or staking. A daily stake of £20 and a profit of 10 times that over the whole of the winter may not seem a wonderful scenario to those who dream of riches from the sport, but to the realist the above sequence is highly encouraging. Furthermore, there is every reason to believe that a similar final outcome is readily achievable in the future from the winter part of the jumping season, which constitutes the National Hunt season 'proper'.

Secondly, the winning percentage of no less than 74.1% is nothing short of magnificent, as anyone who knows racing as a betting medium intimately will testify. With a maximum losing run of only four during the entire series of bets, there is an obvious case for the use of a well-conceived staking plan as a means of enhancing the profit from level stakes. Provided one is not too ambitious in the type of plan adopted, it should be possible to convert the basic gain into an even better one without increasing the level of risk to the backer in any really significant way.

For the benefit of any reader interested in developing their betting along these lines, here are the rules of staking on a daily selection chosen in the way recommended.

LEVEL STAKES ENHANCEMENT BY STAKING ON A SERIES OF COUPS

Within the sequence of bets as a whole, each coup is entirely separate. When a profit is shown on a coup, however small, that coup ends and a new one is started immediately.

The stakes for the opening bets in each coup are as follows:

> 1st Bet 3 pts   2nd Bet 2 pts   3rd Bet 1 pt
> 4th Bet 4 pts   5th Bet 5 pts

After the 5th Bet, an increase of 1 pt is made after each loser.

During some coups the returns from a successful bet will not be large enough to show an overall profit on the coup. The coup is continued, but a set of special rules are applied after a winner:

1 If a winner at odds-on is backed, and the coup is still showing an overall loss, the stake for the next bet remains the same.

2 If a winner from evens up to 6–4 inclusive is backed, and the coup is still in deficit overall, the current stake is reduced by 1 pt, but is never reduced to below 5 pts.

3 If a winner is backed at over 6–4 up to 2–1 inclusive, and the coup is still losing overall, the stake is decreased by 2 pts, but is never reduced below 5 pts.

4 If a winner is backed at over 2–1, and the coup is still showing a loss, the stake is reduced by 3 pts, but never goes below 5 pts.

Rules 1, 2, 3 and 4 come into force from the sixth bet in a coup on.

Therefore, if the 5 pt 5th Bet is a winner and the coup is showing an overall loss, the stake remains at 5 pts, below which it cannot now fall. If the sixth or any later bet is a winner, and the coup is still in deficit, Rules 1–4 are then applied, but the maximum reduction allowed is one which does not let the stake drop below 5 pts.

No matter how many bets are needed to achieve a profit, the coup continues with stakes adjustments after losers and winners. The opening bet on a new coup once a profit has been realised is always the 3 pts laid down above as the 1st Bet.

The great advantage of a staking plan like this is that, provided it is worked on a selection system where the yield of winners is known to be very high, it is virtually impossible to come out much worse than at level stakes. If all goes well, there is every chance of an enhanced profit, provided the rules are strictly adhered to in every circumstance. Discipline and the self-control to do exactly what the formula prescribes at all times are necessary prerequisites for anyone who uses this form of staking.

Here is the plan in action on the above sequence of bets recorded during the winter of 2002–2003.

Coup No.	Bet	Stake	Result	Loss	Profit	Overall profit (+) or loss (−)
1	1st	£3	Won 2–5		£1.20	+£1.20
2	1st	£3	Won 8–15		£1.60	+£2.80
3	1st	£3	Lost	£3.00		
	2nd	£2	Lost	£2.00		
	3rd	£1	Won 6–5		£1.20	
	4th	£4	Won 2–5		£1.60	
	5th	£5	Won 1–4		£1.25	
	6th	£5	Won 30–100		£1.50	
				£5.00	£5.55	+£3.35
4	1st	£3	Won 4–7		£1.71	+£5.06
5	1st	£3	Won 4–11		£1.09	+£6.15
6	1st	£3	Won 4–1		£12.00	+£18.15
7	1st	£3	Won 4–5		£2.40	+£20.55
8	1st	£3	Won 4–6		£2.00	+£22.55
9	1st	£3	Won 8–13		£1.85	+£24.40
10	1st	£3	Won 1–2		£1.50	+£25.90
11	1st	£3	Won 4–9		£1.33	+£27.23
12	1st	£3	Lost	£3.00		
	2nd	£2	Won 8–11		£1.45	
	3rd	£1	Won 2–11		£0.18	
	4th	£4	Lost	£4.00		
	5th	£5	Lost	£5.00		
	6th	£6	Won 2–5		£2.40	
	7th	£6	Won 1–2		£3.00	
	8th	£6	Lost	£6.00		
	9th	£7	Lost	£7.00		
	10th	£8	Won 2–5		£3.20	
	11th	£8	Lost	£8.00		
	12th	£9	Won 4–7		£5.14	
	13th	£9	Lost	£9.00		
	14th	£10	Lost	£10.00		
	15th	£11	Won 7–4		£19.25	
	16th	£9	Won 1–4		£2.25	
	17th	£9	Lost	£9.00		
	18th	£10	Lost	£10.00		
	19th	£11	Won 1–3		£3.67	
	20th	£11	Won 2–5		£4.40	
	21st	£11	Won 1–3		£3.67	
	22nd	£11	Won 8–13		£6.77	
	23rd	£11	Won 1–3		£3.67	
	24th	£11	Won 4–7		£6.29	
	25th	£11	Lost	£11.00		

Coup No.	Bet	Stake	Result	Loss	Profit	Overall profit (+) or loss (−)
	26th	£12	Won 4–11		£4.36	
	27th	£12	Lost	£12.00		
	28th	£13	Won 1–2		£6.50	
	29th	£13	Won 1–3		£4.33	
	30th	£13	Won 2–7		£3.71	
	31st	£13	Won 2–7		£3.71	
	32nd	£13	Lost	£13.00		
	33rd	£14	Won 4–6		£9.33	
	34th	£14	Won 2–5		£5.60	
	35th	£14	Won 2–7		£4.00	
	36th	£14	Won 1–3		£4.67	
				£107.00	£111.55	+£31.78
13	1st	£3	Lost	£3.00		
	2nd	£2	Lost	£2.00		
	3rd	£1	Lost	£1.00		
	4th	£4	Lost	£4.00		
	5th	£5	Won 4–6		£3.33	
	6th	£5	Won 1–3		£1.67	
	7th	£5	Won 4–9		£2.22	
	8th	£5	Won evens		£5.00	
				£10.00	£12.22	+£34.00
14	1st	£3	Won 4–11		£1.09	+£35.09
15	1st	£3	Lost	£3.00		
	2nd	£2	Won 2–5		£0.80	
	3rd	£1	Won 8–13		£0.62	
	4th	£4	Won 2–7		£1.14	
	5th	£5	Won 5–6		£4.17	
				£3.00	£6.73	+£38.82
16	1st	£3	Won 1–7		£0.43	+£39.25
17	1st	£3	Won 4–11		£1.09	+£40.34
18	1st	£3	Won 1–8		£0.38	+£40.72
19	1st	£3	Won 1–5		£0.60	+£41.32
20	1st	£3	Won 4–11		£1.09	+£42.41
21	1st	£3	Won 1–5		£0.60	+£43.01
22	1st	£3	Won 30–100		£0.90	+£43.91
23	1st	£3	Won 2–5		£1.20	+£45.11
24	1st	£3	Won 1–4		£0.75	+£45.86
25	1st	£3	Won 2–7		£0.86	+£46.72
26	1st	£3	Lost	£3.00		
	2nd	£2	Won 4–9		£0.89	
	3rd	£1	Won 4–11		£0.36	
	4th	£4	Won 2–5		£1.60	
	5th	£5	Won 30–100		£1.50	
				£3.00	£4.35	+£48.07

Comparisons are difficult between level stakes and plans where the stakes vary, but if 1 point is counted as the opening stake of £3, the middle amount in the basic first to fifth bet sequence, then it could be said that now the profit in points is £48.07 ÷ 3 = 16 points, compared with the level-stakes profit of £198.96 ÷ £20 = 10 points. This enhanced profitability would not seem much to a backer using an opening stake of just £3, but for a substantial backer betting on short-priced favourites according to this automatic system of selection and staking, it represents a big difference.

However, not everyone is comfortable with betting at long odds-on most of the time. There are those whose natural inclination is to look for horses at better prices. This type of favourite backer should refer back to the two BLUEPRINT tables at the beginning of this chapter and aim to be more selective in finding market leaders to back. In addition, there are a number of factors whose worth cannot be demonstrated in statistical terms, but which long experience has shown must cut out many poor bets. Combined with the full analysis of jumping favourites in the BLUEPRINT tables, they can only help to increase the ratio of winners to losers.

1   Back only favourites that were first or second last time out. There are plenty of false favourites, even over jumps. This rule ensures backing animals with a basic form qualification that many market leaders do not have. Certainly a wager on a favourite that did not reach the first four in its previous race must have a huge question mark against it.

2   If you decide to back a favourite in a handicap, stick to small fields. I would make it an absolute rule not to bet in a handicap with more than 10 runners. 'The bigger the field, the bigger the certainty' is perhaps the silliest of all racing maxims. Even in non-handicaps the backer's chances are increased mathematically in small fields.

3   Most bets should be on horses running within 14 days of their previous run. As many as 51.2 per cent of all winners over jumps had this qualification in a survey of 500 races specially

undertaken to establish the statistical facts about recent form. Conversely, only 10.5 per cent of winners had been off the track for 29 or more days. Even if the '14-day rule' is not strictly kept, one must avoid any runner which has not had a public outing for over a couple of months.

4 Long periods of wet weather and the resulting heavy going up and down the country always see the strike rate of even the most successful types of favourite fall dramatically. Year after year, for example, January is a month when the percentage of winning favourites drops because rain and snow turn the ground into a quagmire. The backer's remedy is simple: either do not bet at all during such wet spells, or at the very least keep stakes down to an absolute minimum. No one makes the punter bet, not even the bookmakers, and readers would be wise to exercise their option in this respect when conditions are so obviously against them.

For someone who is really prepared to specialise, there is a great deal to be said for concentrating on favourites in certain types of race and, in the main, for disregarding others.

For example, National Hunt Flat races are hopeless for favourites. So many 'bumpers' are won by horses which have never seen a racecourse, that form in public seldom leads to the right conclusion about the result. Hunter chasers which appear on our National Hunt courses soon after the New Year are much less reliable from a form point of view than was even the case only a few years ago, probably due to greater competition. Point-to-point form is a closed book to most punters and does not translate well to racing under rules. Once again, the backer who studiously avoids these events will probably not be out of pocket in the long run. Even novice hurdle favourites are not the bread-and-butter events they used to be for followers of the market choice.

By contrast, novice chases and maiden hurdles are two sorts of race at the lower end of the sport in which demonstrably superior form over rivals is usually confirmed by results. At the other end of the class spectrum, graded hurdle races slightly more than graded chases are fundamentally sound propositions for the discriminating backer and student of form in general.

Personally, I am impressed by the high percentage of winning favourites in novice chases nowadays. Quite obviously there has been an important change on the jumping scene in this respect. There was a time when novice hurdles, not chases, were the best betting medium for followers of short-priced horses. However, the introduction of a system of penalties has made it much more difficult for a good novice hurdler to run up a string of consecutive victories, and the winning percentage of favourites has declined as a result.

Horses in their first chasing season, on the other hand, appear to be much better schooled these days. Though the traditional wisdom that it is risky to back unexposed animals over fences remains an important caveat when assessing the form of individual horses, the **overall** percentage of winning favourites and the **overall** record of only a tiny loss at level stakes in a season seems to belie the old notions about novice chases.

Here are the top 10 courses for novice chase favourites. Moving outside this select list is of course perfectly permissible, but as an additional pointer it is useful to know that a selection has the statistical record on its side.

TOP 10 COURSES FOR NOVICE CHASE FAVOURITES

1	Newcastle	61.0%
2	Fakenham	50.0%
3	Wincanton	50.0%
4	Leicester	49.3%
5	Folkestone	49.0%
6	Fontwell	48.6%
7	Uttoxeter	47.9%
8	Haydock Park	47.6%
9	Sedgefield	47.5%
10	Plumpton	44.2%

Novice chases are seldom very competitive, and if a favourite at fair odds-against can be found that ran first or second last time out and which is trained by one of the dozen or so leading National Hunt trainers, then that is definitely something to bet on. But if on a given day there is no horse which fulfils these conditions, then the BLUEPRINT should be used to select an outstanding prospect in another category of race. Everything depends on what material is available at the time. Sometimes it is not possible to find even one favourite which can be backed with real confidence. In that case, do not bet. In other words, discriminating betting pays; betting for betting's sake most certainly does not.

Yet if conditions are right, it might suit the temperament of some readers to back a number of favourites on the same day. This can be done in such a way that it is not necessary to insist on horses starting at odds-against, which some backers tend to do. Even a majority of odds-on chances can be made to aggregate to returns that amount to a significant profit. And it is on Saturdays, when at least three meetings are on offer at the height of the jumping season, that a multiple bet on favourites chosen on form alone, without too much respect to potential starting price, can pay off.

Forget the daily nap selection for the moment, and consider what can be done with doubles on four, five or even six horses on one day. Forget, too, those optimistic trebles and accumulators which most backers append to their bets on a plural number of horses. Doubles, and doubles alone, can be a short cut to consistent profitability from National Hunt favourites. This can even be achieved with just a little better than average strike rate from horses whose odds are generally considered too short for anything but the most substantial backer.

Consider the following series of wagers taken from my own recent Betting Book.

First, a bet on five horses on 28 December 2002 in which success, judged by the number of winners and losers, was only partial:

> FIRST LOVE Lost
> IL CAVALIERE Won 4–7
> KORELO Won 4–7
> SIMPLY SUPREME Won 2–5
> TONOCO Won 5–2
> 10 × £1 doubles

Total stake: £10

Return: £22.76

Profit: £12.76

Thus, while the same outlay in five £2 singles would not have produced a return that is worthwhile in most people's eyes, the situation is transformed by the use of doubles. One loser, only one winner at odds-against and as many as three at short odds-on have yielded a gain in excess of 125 per cent on outlay. Nor was it particularly difficult to pick out the selections for the day. All that was needed was the flexible application of the principles of the BLUEPRINT, mixed with a little common sense.

What if the loser had won? In fact there is no need to indulge in what-might-have-been, for later in the same season, on 1 March, all five selections did go in one Saturday with the aid of the same prescription of BLUEPRINT form and simple logic.

ALAM Won 1–2

COVENT GARDEN Won 5–2

FAR PAVILIONS Won evens

HASTY PRINCE Won 11–10

VOL SOLITAIRE Won 4–11

10 × £1 doubles

Total stake: £10

Return: £42.33

Profit: £32.33

This example is most definitely not intended as an invitation to readers to lay out their hard-earned cash on trebles, fourfolds and a fivetimer. Of course, the return would have been a great deal higher, but that is not the point. Five winners, three at unexceptional prices, and two at much poorer odds, returned a profit of more than triple the stake just by concentrating on doubles. Why risk sacrificing profitability of this order for the sake of hopeful accumulators which will succeed only very occasionally, when a more modest bet on doubles will still put the backer well in pocket? Losers in racing are commonplace; winning Canadians, or Super Yankees as multiple bets on five selections are sometimes called, are rare indeed, even on favourites.

A much more likely scenario is set out below. It was my Saturday bet for 7 December 2002.

COURAGE UNDER FIRE Lost
GUNNER WELBURN Won 11–4
LE ROI MIGUEL Lost
SKIPPERS CLEUCH Won 1–2
TARDAR Won 11–8
10 × £1 doubles
Total stake: £10
Return: £18.13
Profit: £8.13

Now the benefits of a doubles-alone bet on a number of horses becomes really apparent. Two losers, one winner at a very short price and two at odds-against that represent typical fare for the favourite backer, and the bet as a whole still managed to produce a reasonable profit. There could be no better illustration of the usefulness of the doubles concept for National Hunt favourites than this straightforward little bet.

Finally, an example of what happens when things go badly wrong, as they must from time to time. The date was 29 March 2003.

CANADIANE Won 15–8
DEL TROTTER Lost
MONTREAL Won 8–15
THOUTMOSIS Lost
TURN OF PHRASE Lost
10 × £1 doubles
Total stake: £10
Return: £4.41
Loss: £5.59

Three losers out of five, yet one horse at reasonable odds for a favourite, plus an odds-on chance, shows a loss of only just over half the stake. Even on a losing day, the doubles backer can come out with a return that, far from being a disheartening loss, is sufficient to underline the merits of this style of betting.

Some people look down on those who habitually back favourites. Favourite bets are viewed as routine wagers which need little ingenuity or inspiration. In short, they are boring. It is hoped the foregoing pages will have convinced readers, if convincing they needed, that well-chosen bets on winter favourites, whether in doubles, or as more substantial stakes on nap selections, far from being dull, can be the road to profit. And in my experience, there is nothing dull or boring about a profit from backing plenty of winners.

46
The VALUE FOR MONEY Jumping System

Racing systems are usually based on either favourites or outsiders. In a favourites system the backer hopes that a high percentage of winners will yield enough gains to offset the cost of losers. Thus if 100 horses are backed at an average price of 6–4, something over 40 must win for the backer to break even. A greater number of winners produce a profit. How much profit will depend on how many more than 40 per cent eventually win.

In an outsiders' system on the other hand, the calculation is, of necessity, less precise. The backer now chooses horses likely to go off at a much wider range of prices which together represent 'long odds', knowing full well that racing being the sport it is, most of them will be beaten. The hope here is that just a few outsiders will win to pay for the losers and still produce a profit. Typical of this sort of system is the old favourite of choosing 12 handicappers to follow at the beginning of the season and backing them through thick and thin for the rest of the year. If the horses selected fulfil expectations, a win or two for all, or nearly all, of them when starting at much better than average odds will cancel out the inevitable losers and produce an overall surplus from all the bets made during the season. There are other examples of systems for outsiders, but the '12 to follow' method exemplifies the principle underlying most of them.

Which is the better way to bet? Part of the answer to this question is that it is very much a matter of the individual punter's temperament. Some people need the reassurance of a reasonably steady flow of winners regardless of starting prices. Others are more sanguine and are able to bide their time until the big winners materialise.

Another approach is to deliberately choose a method of selection that is likely to throw up a varied mixture of horses in terms of starting prices, perhaps from odds-on chances through the middle order of the betting right up to the outsider category of runner. In my experience such methods are almost by definition unreliable and should be avoided. They cannot really be based on any consistent, logical principle of form, and the chaotic nature of selections must be reflected in a ragbag of results.

There is, however, a fourth way, and this is to deliberately target horses in the middle range of the betting market. That is the idea incorporated in the VALUE FOR MONEY system explained in this chapter. As we saw in Part 1, surveys by various authorities reveal that purely random betting on horses in this middle range will lose more than backing favourites at random, but a lot less than will be lost by focusing only on longshots. However, this is not the whole story.

If the random principle is replaced by logical form criteria, there is every chance that random losses from medium-priced horses can be converted into a sound overall gain. Suppose, by way of example, the backer finds a series of horses all starting at 4–1. Only one winner in four (i.e. 25 per cent) is needed to break even, and an average of between one and two winners in four will yield a profit that would certainly be acceptable over a period of time. Such a theoretical target does not seem unreasonable in practice, given the use of methods of selection designed to single out only quality choices with a well-above average chance of succeeding. Or put another way, if medium-priced horses can be found with form credentials at least as good as runners at shorter prices, then the former must represent 'value for money' and offer real potential for worthwhile profits.

The complete VALUE FOR MONEY formula uses a set of criteria that will guarantee such form credentials and apply them in races where the middle rank in the betting is known to do well. Therefore, there will be little prospect of very short-priced favourites or big outsiders spoiling the party.

The VALUE FOR MONEY rules are as follows:

1   Bet only in handicap chases of nine or fewer runners.

2   To qualify for a bet, a horse must have run in a chase last time out within the previous 50 days.

3   Only horses which were second last time out can qualify for a bet.

4   The horse must be clear top-rated in the race ratings of the newspaper used for betting purposes.

5   The horse must be second or third favourite in the betting
    forecast of the same newspaper. Joint or co-third favourites can
    qualify.

    For many busy punters, use of a betting forecast will be
    regrettably unavoidable to establish qualifiers. For those who
    have access to racecourse prices just before the 'off', however, the
    actual market on the race would indicate a favourite to be
    excluded or a second or third favourite which might qualify for
    a bet.

6   There is a 1-point stake on all qualifiers. The system is not
    suitable for use with an automatic staking plan, although it
    would be reasonable to increase the level of staking gradually if
    the overall level-stakes profit is consistently mounting.

Personally, I use Formcast, who provides the 'spot' horse in the
Daily Mail, and who is surely the leader among Fleet Street
journalists at work in the field of private handicapping. A
preference for a different handicapper or some other race ratings in
another newspaper is the reader's prerogative.

Here is the complete record of the plan for the winter jumping
season of 2002–2003:

Date	Horse	Result
20 Nov	HURRICANE LAMP	Won 9–2
25 Nov	TROOPER	Lost
26 Nov	MIGHTY FINE	Won 7–2
27 Nov	RIGADOON	Lost
30 Nov	KIT SMARTIE	Won 7–2
2 Dec	FAVOURED OPTION	Lost
11 Dec	RIVER STYX	NR
20 Dec	SAINT ROMBLE	Won 3–1
27 Dec	CATCHATAN	Won 11–8
28 Dec	TONOCO	Won 5–2
13 Jan	SIR NORMAN	Lost
14 Jan	CRESSWELL QUAY	Won 3–1
16 Jan	CIMARRON COVE	Lost
28 Jan	ASPARAGUS	Lost

Date	Horse	Result
30 Jan	MASTER OF ILLUSION	Lost
31 Jan	SUPER NOMAD	NR
8 Feb	TRIBAL RUN	Lost
11 Feb	CAITRONA'S CHOICE	Lost
28 Feb	REACH THE CLOUDS	Lost
7 Mar	ATHNOWEN	Lost
17 Mar	SUPREME BREEZE	Lost
19 Mar	ROMANTIC HERO	Won 7–2
24 Mar	HARIK	Won 7–2
28 Mar	QUARTERSTAFF	Won 11–4
29 Mar	CANADIANE	Won 15–8

Winners: 11

Losers: 12

Winning percentage: 47.8%

Profit at 1-point level stakes: 21 points

Percentage profit on outlay: 91.3%

Despite a losing run of no less than eight from the middle of the sequence, 21 points for the winter season is still a very sound return, at least for anyone with a realistic view of what is possible from betting on horses using a sound system, and who does not expect a fortune for a pound or two.

In order to achieve these kinds of result, it is important to follow the above rules on a consistent basis and to stick to the same race ratings throughout. The five selection factors combined in the rules together provide a rock-solid foundation for finding winners from one area of the odds range in a particular kind of race. As we have seen in Part 1, in the section on instant handicapping for jumps, handicap chases are ideal material for finding the sort of winner defined in, and envisaged by, the formula.

Seconds last time out have a good strike rate in this type of race and, unlike winners of their previous outing, do not suffer sharp increases in weight as a consequence of their prominent run. Concentrating on the two most likely alternatives to the favourite pinpoints horses in the right price range, and favourites do relatively badly in handicap chases with fields even as small as those with less than 10 runners (21.7 per cent in the 2002–2003 season).

Obviously, from such a tight set of rules, there will not be many qualifiers in a season. The logic behind the plan is to target winners which are known to match a distinct profile in terms of form and price. By aiming to single out a particular type of form horse in a particular type of race, while deliberately excluding the favourite, it may be possible in the future, as in previous years, to amass enough winning points to produce a profit in the long term. Patience, however, will be needed, both in waiting for qualifiers to emerge and in greeting losers as well as winners with equanimity. Readers who are temperamentally suited to playing a waiting game may find this system well worthwhile.

47
THE MULTI-LINK STAKING FORMULA

Although assured of plenty of winners, the confirmed favourite backer faces the constant problem of converting short-priced successes into a worthwhile profit. The MULTI-LINK method of staking is one of the best systems ever devised for solving the difficulty.

Stakes are on single daily selections but the formula links up a series of doubles spread over several days in order to make the very best use of those winners that are backed. Moreover, the maximum number of points at risk in any one week is known in advance. It is always 15.

The 15 points which cover one bet a day for a full six-day week are divided up as follows:

$$5 \quad 4 \quad 3 \quad 2 \quad 1 \quad 0$$

These basic daily units increase according to winners backed but, if the first five bets lose, then no double has materialised, so there would be no bet on Saturday.

On Monday the bet is always five points. After each winner combine the odds (3–1 = 3 + 1 = 4, 6–4 = 1½ + 1 = 2½, 4–7 = ⁴⁄₇ + 1 = 1⁴⁄₇ i.e. 1.57, and so on). Now add the resultant figure to each of the basic units for the remaining days including Saturday.

As an example, suppose the first bet wins at 3–1. Then the remaining bets for the week would each be increased by four points (3 + 1) to get:

4	3	2	1	0
4	4	4	4	4
8	7	6	5	4

The second and third bets lost but on Thursday there is a 2–1 winner. As a result the stakes for Friday and Saturday become:

5	4
3	3
8	7

Friday's selection is a loser but on Saturday a winner is backed at 6–4, so the stakes and results for the six-day cycle have been:

Stakes:	5	8	7	6	8	7		
Results:	3–1	L	L	2–1	L	6–4		
Gains:	15			12		10½	=	37½ pts
Losses:		8	7		8		=	23 pts
						Overall profit	=	14½ pts

Now if the 15 points had been invested at level stakes of 2½ points for each of the six days, the profit on this sequence would have amounted to only 8¾ points.

In other words, provided one can be reasonably confident of picking around 50 per cent winning favourites each week, then the MULTI-LINK formula should increase gains when compared with level-stakes betting on the same sequence.

However, as with practically everything connected with betting on horses, there are drawbacks. It is only fair to admit that the formula loses against level stakes if:

a) only one winner in a week is backed – the principle of linked doubles to boost profits fails to operate;
b) two or even three winners at very short odds, all odds-on or close to it are backed – level stakes do better by a slight margin.

In all other cases the formula scores and often quite handsomely.

If habitually backing a lot of horses at odds-on, the method of betting in separate coups given as part of the National Hunt BLUEPRINT is preferable to the MULTI-LINK. The first works best on strings of near-consecutive winners, only realistically possible with very short-priced favourites. MULTI-LINK, on the other hand, should be used for selections at the kind of prices shown in our examples, even if the strike rate of winners is sacrificed, at least in part, to find horses at reasonable odds.

For example, examine this sequence of bets. Prices are far from exceptional, but most are at odds against. That is enough to produce a healthy plus in favour of the MULTI-LINK formula over level-stakes betting:

	Basic Units			
Monday	5			
Tuesday	4			
Wednesday	3	$+3\frac{1}{2}$	=	£6.50
Thursday	2	$+3\frac{1}{2} + 2\frac{3}{4}$	=	£8.25
Friday	1	$+3\frac{1}{2} + 2\frac{3}{4}$	=	£7.25
Saturday	0	$+3\frac{1}{2} + 2\frac{3}{4} + 1\frac{8}{13}$	=	£7.87

	Stakes	Result	Profit or loss
Monday	£5.00	Lost	−£5.00
Tuesday	£4.00	Won 5–2	+£10.00
Wednesday	£6.50	Won 7–4	+£11.38
Thursday	£8.25	Lost	−£8.25
Friday	£7.25	Won 8–13	+£4.50
Saturday	£7.87	Won 5–4	+£9.84

'MULTI-LINK' profit = £22.47

Level-stakes (£2.50) profit = £10.31

The MULTI-LINK Formula was originally conceived as a series of double events arising from a single daily selection from Monday to Saturday. However, if it is felt that on a particular day there is no worthwhile wager, the system can still be used. Provided it is applied to six consecutive selections on different days, the mathematical symmetry of the formula is retained. If the preference is not to bet every day, it is simpler to think of it in terms of six bets and not in terms of days of the week, thus:

Bet 1	Bet 2	Bet 3	Bet 4	Bet 5	Bet 6
5	4	3	2	1	0

This might represent a series of wagers spread as follows:

Bet 1	Bet 2	Bet 3
Monday	Wednesday	Friday
5	4	3

Bet 4	Bet 5	Bet 6
Saturday	Tuesday	Thursday
2	1	0

Moreover, if departing in this way from the strict Monday-to-Saturday rota, there is no need to miss a good wager on the sixth day should the first five in the series prove unsuccessful. Suppose Bets 1 to 5 lost in the above example. In that event the selection for Thursday could become Bet 1 with a 5-point stake in a new series of six bets.

This method of numbering the bets 1 to 6, rather than labelling them Monday to Saturday, can also be used to accommodate Sunday racing, where Sunday would be the first bet in a new sequence if six bets had been made in the week so far, from Monday onwards. It could also be some other number in the sequence if not betting every day. The important thing is to calculate stakes from a rota comprising bets 1 to 6, whatever days of the week they happen to fall on.

In the case of a mathematical formula of this kind a great deal depends on prices in relation to the number of winners and losers. But if you are the kind of backer who finds it relatively easy to pick out one good thing a day, then MULTI-LINK is for you. You need to avoid strings of odds-on chances for the formula to do its work but it will always increase profits compared with level stakes on a turnover of winners at reasonable prices.

48
THE COUNTERPOISE PLAN

In most staking plans the backer is required to increase stakes on a series of losers. An eventual winner, it is hoped, will pay off losses to date and still yield a profit. Frequently, however, too long a losing run and a winner at too short a price combine to defeat the idea. The sequence reaches the point where the chance of recovering losses, still less of showing a gain, finally disappears. With the COUNTERPOISE method – a unique way of betting from Monday to Saturday – stakes gradually diminish while prices increase. In this way it overcomes the fundamental deficiencies of the usual type of staking formula.

The plan works like this. Choose one horse each day of the racing week. Selections should be based on sound form principles but the deciding factor in arriving at a final choice is the probable starting price. On Monday and Tuesday look for a 2–1 shot. For the next two days aim to find winners around 4–1. Bets for Friday and Saturday are chosen from horses priced at about 6–1. The price requirements for particular days apply irrespective of the number of winners and losers backed.

Stakes are regulated in the following way:

Monday	2–1	3 pts
Tuesday	2–1	3 pts
Wednesday	4–1	1½ pts
Thursday	4–1	1½ pts
Friday	6–1	1 pt
Saturday	6–1	1 pt

Now one might well ask: why not begin by trying to pick a winner at 6–1? The answer is quite simply that it is easier to find one at 2–1. Obviously it is desirable to win as early in the week as possible. In the event of failure, one is faced with the choice of increasing stakes or selecting a better-priced winner. The pitfalls inherent in rising stake progressions have already been outlined. It must be far safer in the long term to try for winners at better prices. Now if things can be so arranged mathematically that stakes can actually be reduced without sacrificing the chance of a profit, then so much the better. This is exactly what the COUNTERPOISE method does.

Beginning with a 6–1 selection, one might as well try to find one every day. Rather this plan aims at finding easy winners first so that there is cash in hand for later bets on horses at longer odds. The mathematics of the formula are such that one is quite justified in reducing stakes as the week advances, whether one has won or lost earlier in the week. More gains are wanted after a win but not at the risk of dissipating existing profits. Because it reduces stakes on longer-priced selections, the formula achieves this double objective. On the other hand, an early loss means that one is looking to limit losses. Again the plan does the trick – stakes are diminishing and yet a winner or winners at good prices could still pull the fat out of the fire.

A mathematical arrangement of prices and stakes, however sound, cannot produce profits out of thin air. Winners still have to be backed. Given the ability to find some winners, the mathematics of the plan enable calculations to be made in advance as to how much can be won or lost. With just one winner from six bets the maximum loss on the week will be 4 points and possibly less. Two winners, a reasonable expectation for the average competent backer, will provide an overall gain of between 3 and 7 points, depending on which horses actually win. Three winners guarantee a profit of at least 10½ points and possibly a good deal more. Four or more winners must yield a handsome return.

The one problem is being dependent on a betting forecast for the purpose of determining the daily selections. Fluctuations inevitably arise from market operations on the racecourse, so that betting-forecast predictions seldom correspond exactly to actual returned starting prices. In fact this is not too serious a drawback. One may just as well gain as lose from this and in the long run things should even themselves out. The basic soundness of the formula will do the rest.

Finally, it is necessary to say a word about methods of selection. Since the largest stakes go on to the 2–1 chances, special care must be exercised in choosing them. Here the search is for out-and-out form horses but at the same time avoiding the apparent good things which will start at really short prices close to odds-on. For the 4–1 selections it is necessary to concentrate on second favourites with sound form in small fields where the favourite is quoted at upwards of 2–1 and so is not greatly fancied. The best way of singling out a 6–1 shot worth backing is to make a list of all horses in the right price category. Examine each in the light of recent form; winning or good placed form in similar company as revealed by a comparison of race values or grade will lead to some live candidates.

So the COUNTERPOISE method offers backers plenty of scope for making their own judgements. It is rigid in terms of selections being governed by the likely starting price but it is possible that a lot of backers who frequently find themselves spoilt for choice on a busy day's racing may well benefit from this discipline.

A mathematical plan is not an automatic road to racing riches but faulty staking is probably the biggest single reason why most backers lose. A reasonable aptitude for picking winners means the COUNTERPOISE method will help to maximise successes.

49
THE 19 WAYS TO WIN DOUBLES FORMULA

A lot of backers achieve consistent results without ever managing to turn them into overall profit. They follow racing closely, know the form book well and can pick out two or three sound wagers each day that are certain to go close at decent prices. Yet in the long run they lose – too many near misses, good seconds and thirds eat into the gains from winners. If the reader falls into this category of punter, then the 19 WAYS TO WIN formula is one to consider.

The trick is to link up one horse from one race with two from another in singles and each-way doubles. Suppose you select Horse A as a banker for the first race and decide on Horse B and Horse C for the second leg. The full bet is written as follows:

Race 1	Race 2
1 pt win A	½ pt win B
	½ pt win C

1 pt each-way double A and B
1 pt each-way double A and C

For a 6-point stake this series of bets offers no less than 19 chances of a return. The possible combinations are set out in full below.

1   A wins and B wins.   C places
    Result: 2 win singles, 1 win double, 2 place doubles.

2   A wins and C wins.   B places
    Result: 2 win singles, 1 win double, 2 place doubles.

3   A wins and B wins.   C loses
    Result: 2 win singles, 1 win double, 1 place double.

4   A wins and C wins.   B loses
    Result: 2 win singles, 1 win double, 1 place double.

5   A wins and B places.   C places
    Result: 1 win single, 2 place doubles.

6   A wins and B places.   C loses
    Result: 1 win single, 1 place double.

7   A wins and C places.   B loses
    Result: 1 win single, 1 place double.

8   A wins and B loses.   C loses
    Result: 1 win single.

9   B wins and A places.   C places
    Result: 1 win single, 2 place doubles.

10 B wins and A places.   C loses
    Result: 1 win single, 1 place double.

11 B wins and C places.   A loses
    Result: 1 win single.

12 B wins and A loses.   C loses
    Result: 1 win single.

13 C wins and A places.   B places
    Result: 1 win single, 2 place doubles.

14 C wins and A places.   B loses
    Result: 1 win single, 1 place double.

15 C wins and B places.   A loses
    Result: 1 win single.

16 C wins and A loses.   B loses
    Result: 1 win single.

17 A places and B places.   C places
    Result: 2 place doubles.

18 A places and B places.   C loses
    Result: 1 place double.

19 A places and C places.   B loses
    Result: 1 place double.

Each-way doubles are definitely value bets for the careful punter. The 19 WAYS TO WIN system with its clever combination of win singles and each-way doubles on three horses has tremendous scope. Many of the winning permutations will produce a really good gain on the day. Other patterns of results will recover some or all of the stake. Thus there is plenty of insurance against those all-too-frequent near misses that usually mean total failure. There are even two chances of finding the winner in one race with very little wastage of stakes.

Since place betting at fractions of win odds is involved, a lot depends on prices. Clearly short-priced favourites should be avoided and while the banker should be an obvious form horse at fair odds, it is often worth taking a chance with a selection at a really good price as a danger to the first choice in the second leg. In the hands of a skilled punter who knows the form and can pick out value-for-money wagers in the right races, this staking formula is in a class of its own.

50
THE WEEKENDER

For the most part the treble chance mentality is absent among followers of horse racing. Few punters seriously expect to make a fortune, even a small one, from the sport. In fact the majority do not try. By and large they look for small regular gains from their betting while hoping for an occasional nice touch measured in tens, not thousands, of pounds to make the whole thing worthwhile.

Yet there is absolutely no reason why multiple cumulative wagers should not be used to aim for a jackpot payout. If these can be arranged so that the prospect of smaller wins on a regular basis is retained, then such a bet must represent a really attractive proposition. The WEEKENDER goes a long way towards achieving this dual aim.

Saturday always sees a lot of racing up and down the country with plenty of opportunities to sort out an above-average number of good bets. The WEEKENDER requires six selections. Since the system is made up of doubles, trebles and accumulators, it is not necessary to have a series of rank outsiders to produce the big win that is its ultimate goal. A judicious mixture of well-backed form horses with one or two at longer prices will do very nicely. This should not be too much of a problem. There are lots of ways of finding winners at all kinds of odds outlined in this volume.

Having chosen six horses in different races, number them 1 to 6 as in the example below. The system depends on a set of firm guarantees, so this order, once decided upon, must be adhered to throughout when writing the full bet.

    1 Chesterfield
    2 No Tricks
    3 Gala Day
    4 Extra Strain
    5 Marcus Superbus
    6 Directory

The sequence of doubles, trebles and accumulators which makes up the WEEKENDER is as follows:

Doubles
1 and 3   1 and 6   2 and 4   2 and 5   3 and 6   4 and 5
Trebles
1, 2 and 5   1, 3 and 5   1, 4 and 6
2, 3 and 4   2, 3 and 6   4, 5 and 6
Accumulators
1, 2, 3 and 4   1, 2, 5 and 6
3, 4, 5 and 6   1, 2, 3, 4, 5 and 6

So in our example the whole bet would be:

Doubles	**Trebles**	**Accumulators**
Chesterfield	Chesterfield	Chesterfield
Gala Day	No Tricks	No Tricks
————	Marcus Superbus	Gala Day
Chesterfield	————	Extra Strain
Directory	Chesterfield	————
————	Gala Day	Chesterfield
No Tricks	Marcus Superbus	No Tricks
Extra Strain	————	Marcus Superbus
————	Chesterfield	Directory
No Tricks	Extra Strain	————
Marcus Superbus	Directory	Gala Day
————	————	Extra Strain
Gala Day	No Tricks	Marcus Superbus
Directory	Gala Day	Directory
————	Extra Strain	————
Extra Strain	————	Chesterfield
Marcus Superbus	No Tricks	No Tricks
————	Gala Day	Gala Day
	Directory	Extra Strain
	————	Marcus Superbus
	Extra Strain	Directory
	Marcus Superbus	————
	Directory	
	————	

Each group of wagers has a definite guarantee. Two winners may produce a winning double; three guarantee it. Similarly, a treble is certain with four winners and a possibility with only three. Five successes mean you must land a four-horse accumulator, although only four can do the trick. Multiple winners, therefore, can add up to an impressive array of doubles, trebles and four-timers and, if all the selections win, every one of the 16 separate bets, including the six-timer, must score.

In other words, the WEEKENDER method is a balanced wager that can be used for a weekly tilt at a gigantic payout without sacrificing the possibility of regular small-scale profits. For the small backer there is every prospect of plenty of bread and butter. There might be quite a wait for the honey, but the chance of it is always there.

PART 3

Making a 'Backer's Book'

How to beat the bookmakers at their own game

Introduction

Most people who know something about racing are aware that bookmakers bet to figures even if they may be rather vague about the precise *modus operandi*. They could also be perhaps more than just a bit hazy about the mathematics of odds and chances in their own betting. Yet a common dream among racing folk of all sorts is that they might be able to counteract the layers' advantage by some figure system of their own if only they had the necessary mathematical expertise.

Is it ever possible to beat the 'book' by mathematical means? The answer is a definite 'no' if mathematics alone are used, for the edge built into the odds offered by any competent racecourse bookmaker can never be completely eroded, no matter how the backer juggles with stakes. The same applies to the odds received from a race meeting via satellite into betting shops, as well as the final starting price returns formulated by independent Press representatives working in the Ring. The truth is that the bookmakers' method is just about foolproof, certainly over a reasonable period of time and at least in dealing with the totality of punters who bet with one bookmaking firm or another.

Nevertheless, the individual backer can also adopt a mathematical approach to enhance the prospect of a credit balance, both on single races and on a lot of races spread over several days, weeks or even months. Provided sound methods of selection are employed that regularly throw up a healthy supply of winners, regulation of stakes in relation to the odds by mathematical prescription can go a long way towards wresting the initiative from the bookmaker.

In fact there is a way by which punters may win through manipulating stakes and odds so as to make a 'backer's book'. This method is an attempt to beat the bookmakers at their own game by using, in a slightly different way, the system that they themselves use.

Before explaining in detail how to go about this, it is necessary to understand how racecourse bookmakers conduct their business, for the prices they show on their boards before each race are much more than a series of educated guesses. Their reading of form comes into it, together with any knowledge they have about the home form of horses but the range of odds in the context of a whole race is in fact calculated by mathematical principles. This ensures that the odds are definitely and decisively to their own advantage and contrary to that of punters. The basis of these calculations and in fact the basis of all professional bookmaking operations is the following table of odds converted to percentage probabilities. Note that the conversions in this table are to one place after the decimal point. This is sufficiently accurate for normal bookmaking requirements and, as we shall see, for backers too.

51
TABLE OF ODDS AND PERCENTAGES

Odds	Percentage probability	Odds	Percentage probability	Odds	Percentage probability
1–5	83.3	5–4	44.4	9–1	10.0
2–9	81.8	11–8	42.1	19–2	9.5
1–4	80.0	6–4	40.0	10–1	9.1
2–7	77.8	13–8	38.1	11–1	8.3
30–100	76.9	7–4	36.4	12–1	7.7
1–3	75.0	15–8	34.8	13–1	7.1
4–11	73.3	2–1	33.3	14–1	6.7
2–5	71.4	85–40	32.0	15–1	6.3
40–95	70.4	9–4	30.8	16–1	5.9
4–9	69.2	95–40	29.6	18–1	5.3
40–85	68.0	5–2	28.6	20–1	4.8
1–2	66.7	11–4	26.7	22–1	4.3
8–15	65.2	3–1	25.0	25–1	3.8
4–7	63.6	100–30	23.1	28–1	3.4
8–13	61.9	7–2	22.2	30–1	3.2
4–6	60.0	4–1	20.0	33–1	2.9
8–11	57.9	9–2	18.2	35–1	2.8
4–5	55.6	5–1	16.7	40–1	2.4
5–6	54.5	11–2	15.4	50–1	2.0
10–11	52.4	6–1	14.3	66–1	1.5
20–21	51.2	13–2	13.3	100–1	1.0
Evens	50.0	7–1	12.5	150–1	0.7
21–20	48.8	15–2	11.8	200–1	0.5
11–10	47.6	8–1	11.1	250–1	0.4
6–5	45.5	17–2	10.5	500–1	0.2

At first sight all this may look unfathomable but it is really very simple. A look at the table gives the obvious example that a horse quoted at evens can be said to have a 50 per cent chance of winning. Two horses both priced at evens add up to a probability of 100 per cent and would make a 'round' book in a two-horse race. Again, the probability for a 6–4 shot is 40 per cent, whereas 4–1 represents a 20 per cent chance. One horse at the former and three at the latter would also constitute a perfectly 'round' book of 100 per cent in a four-horse contest.

52
BOOKMAKING

A knowledge of the percentages in the table are second nature to
the bookmakers, for their livings depend on it. In the hectic few
minutes before the start of a race, as money flows in from the
punters, each layer may not worry greatly about the fractions, but
each one knows that the percentages for the odds offered about all
the runners must together remain above an aggregate of 100 to give
a viable trading margin. When this is the case, and it nearly always
is, except on those rare occasions when some bookmakers are
prepared to bet a point or two below 100 to attract business in a
highly competitive market, the book is said to be 'over-round'.

In the unlikely event of the aggregated percentages for the
prices on a race in any one book dropping below 100, the layer is
betting 'under-round' or 'over-broke'. In this case, or more likely by
taking the best of the prices from several competing bookmakers,
the alert backer could, by simply staking the percentage of the odds
obtainable about each runner converted to pounds, or sums in
exact proportion, back every horse in the race and be sure of a
profit.

However, most of the time backers must face an 'over-round'
book. Here is an example drawn from the starting price returns on
a recent 2000 Guineas at Newmarket:

2000 GUINEAS STAKES. NEWMARKET. 1M.

	Odds converted to probability	True odds	True probability of winning $(100 \div 19 + 1)$
4–1 HOLD THAT TIGER	20.0%	19–1	5%
9–2 LATEEN SAILS	18.2%	19–1	5%
9–2 REFUSE TO BEND	18.2%	19–1	5%
7–1 TOMAHAWK	12.5%	19–1	5%
7–1 TOUT SEUL	12.5%	19–1	5%
9–1 MUQBIL	10.0%	19–1	5%
14–1 SONGLARK	6.7%	19–1	5%
16–1 AUDIENCE	5.9%	19–1	5%
20–1 HURRICANE ALAN	4.8%	19–1	5%
20–1 INDIAN HAVEN	4.8%	19–1	5%
33–1 ZAFEEN	2.9%	19–1	5%
50–1 SATURN	2.0%	19–1	5%
66–1 LUNDY'S LANE	1.5%	19–1	5%
66–1 MISTER LINKS	1.5%	19–1	5%
100–1 CHECKIT	1.0%	19–1	5%
100–1 MONSIEUR BOND	1.0%	19–1	5%
100–1 NORSE DANCER	1.0%	19–1	5%
100–1 ROCKETS 'N' ROLLERS	1.0%	19–1	5%
200–1 JAY GEE'S CHOICE	0.5%	19–1	5%
200–1 TIZZY MAY	0.5%	19–1	5%
	126.5%		100%

Thus, the over-round here is 26.5 per cent. Therefore, in the theoretical event of one bookmaker's clients staking according to the percentages, they will stake 126.5 units, but, whatever horse wins, the bookmaker has to return only 100 units.

If the theory were possible to translate into practice and a total of £1,265 is bet in line with the percentages, £100 would go on, say, Muqbil which would cost the bookmaker a payout of £100 × 9 + £100 = £1,000 and produce a gain of £265 had it won. If £182 is invested on the actual winner of the race, Refuse to Bend at 9–2, the bookmaker returns £1,000 (actually £1,001 due to the rounding up of the probability percentage) and keeps £265. In this way there is always that amount of profit for the layer whatever the result.

This, in essence, is the system of the racecourse bookmaker and that is why, in theory, the bookmaker should win. In reality, it is a practical impossibility that a group of clients patronising one firm will actually bet so conveniently for both the bookmaker and the theory.

To understand why the theory still works well in practice for the bookmaker in most real cases, the following table should be examined. It shows the advantage or otherwise to the layer when the probability percentages for the odds on offer are compared with the true mathematical probability of each horse winning.

2000 GUINEAS STAKES. NEWMARKET. 1M.

		Odds converted to probability	True proba- bility	Book- maker's advantage	Backer's advantage
4–1	HOLD THAT TIGER	20.0%	5%	15.0%	
9–2	LATEEN SAILS	18.2%	5%	13.2%	
9–2	REFUSE TO BEND	18.2%	5%	13.2%	
7–1	TOMAHAWK	12.5%	5%	7.5%	
7–1	TOUT SEUL	12.5%	5%	7.5%	
9–1	MUQBIL	10.0%	5%	5.0%	
14–1	SONGLARK	6.7%	5%	1.7%	
16–1	AUDIENCE	5.9%	5%	0.9%	
20–1	HURRICANE ALAN	4.8%	5%		0.2%
20–1	INDIAN HAVEN	4.8%	5%		0.2%
33–1	ZAFEEN	2.9%	5%		2.1%
50–1	SATURN	2.0%	5%		3.0%
66–1	LUNDY'S LANE	1.5%	5%		3.5%
66–1	MISTER LINKS	1.5%	5%		3.5%
100–1	CHECKIT	1.0%	5%		4.0%
100–1	MONSIEUR BOND	1.0%	5%		4.0%
100–1	NORSE DANCER	1.0%	5%		4.0%
100–1	ROCKETS 'N' ROLLERS	1.0%	5%		4.0%
200–1	JAY GEE'S CHOICE	0.5%	5%		4.5%
200–1	TIZZY MAY	0.5%	5%		4.5%
		126.5%	100%	64.0%	37.5%
		−100.0%		−37.5%	
		26.5%		26.5%	

The reason why the bookmaker wins in the end should now be obvious. In this example, for the first eight horses in the betting, that is all the really fancied horses and the only ones that have a realistic chance on form except possibly the two at 20–1, the layer offers below the true odds in every single case. The 0.2 per cent chance in the backer's favour for Hurricane Alan and Indian Haven represents a slight chink in the bookmaker's armour which is rather unusual. In the main, however, every horse with real potential is running for the 'book' and against the backer in terms of the lion's share of probability. The backer is left with only a series of small advantages for Hurricane Alan and Indian Haven and the 'rags' of the race.

It is simply not true, however, that the bookmakers cannot lose. If most of the money on a race is for the favourite, as it usually is, they will lose on that race when the favourite wins. The only defence if it is considered a 'good thing' is to shorten it up and lengthen the odds about the remainder of the runners in the hope of diverting cash away from the 'jolly'. That way the layers can reduce their liabilities about the favourite, but there are times when they must pay up, hopefully with a smile. On the other hand, the fact that beaten favourites outnumber winning favourites in the ratio of about 65 to 35 means that on a typical day most bookmakers win on balance and go home with a sound profit for their endeavours.

53
THE 'BACKER'S BOOK'

How does this short course on bookmaking help the backer? The answer is that the backer can learn much from the bookmaker, for while bookmakers are never guilty of constructing a 'book' in a way that leaves them vulnerable over time, punters by contrast frequently fall prey to faulty staking in their attempts to relieve the layers of their money.

EXAMPLE 1

The 2003 race for the Sunderlands Imperial Cup, a big handicap hurdle run over 2m ½f at Sandown in early March, featured a favourite, Korelo, with sound prospects, representing as it did the Pipe/McCoy combination of champion National Hunt trainer and champion jockey. Although Korelo opened at only 2–1 on the course and eventually started at 9–4, there was plenty of 5–2 in the betting offices on the morning of the event, and the horse also touched that price in the pre-race betting exchanges in the afternoon.

But there were plenty of others with chances among the 17-runner field: Dancing Bay at 10–1, Mister McGoldrick (16–1) and Lawz which started at 33–1, having been 40–1 in places, were three others with good form last time out from powerful stables that make a habit of winning races like the Imperial Cup.

Suppose it was decided to back these four horses. This gave four chances to win, not one, and has already reduced the bookmaker's favourable position to some extent. But to press home the potential advantage, stakes must be arranged correctly. Let us assume that £25–£10 was obtained about Korelo by telephone in the morning and that bets of £10 each were placed on the other three fancies in a betting shop, taking the prices available just before the 'off'. The resulting wager is a completely unbalanced series of bets.

Bet	Odds	Horse	Return on win	Gain/loss on total outlay
£10	5–2	KORELO	£35.00	–£5.00
£10	10–1	DANCING BAY	£110.00	+£70.00
£10	16–1	MISTER McGOLDRICK	£170.00	+£130.00
£10	33–1	LAWZ	£340.00	+£300.00

£40 outlay

There is a wide discrepancy between the potential profit from a victory for Dancing Bay when compared with the possible gains from the two longer priced horses, themselves showing a difference of £170 between each other, but if Korelo wins, as was the case, there is actually a small loss on the race. Despite finding the winner, a stake of £40 returned only £35. Regularly confronted with this sort of bet from their clients, the bookmakers are laughing all the way to the bank.

An extreme example, perhaps, but it is far better on a set of horses and prices like this to adjust stakes using the table of odds and percentages, thus acting like a bookmaker in reverse.

Total stake £40 on horses at 5–2 (28.6%), 10–1 (9.1%), 16–1 (5.9%), 33–1 (2.9%).
Backer's percentage of the 'book': 46.5 per cent.

Stakes on each horse (to the nearest 5p or 10p):

KORELO $£40 \times \dfrac{28.6}{46.5}$ at 5–2 = £24.60

DANCING BAY $£40 \times \dfrac{9.1}{46.5}$ at 10–1 = £7.80

MISTER McGOLDRICK $£40 \times \dfrac{5.9}{46.5}$ at 16–1 = £5.10

LAWZ $£40 \times \dfrac{2.9}{46.5}$ at 33–1 = £2.50

Bet	Odds	Horse	Return on win
£24.60	5–2	KORELO	£86.10
£7.80	10–1	DANCING BAY	£85.80
£5.10	16–1	MISTER McGOLDRICK	£86.70
£2.50	33–1	LAWZ	£85.00

Outlay £40.00

Profit if any horse wins: £86 minus £40 = £46 (to the nearest £).

Here the total stake on the four horses is split up in such a way as to return the same amount whichever horse wins (allowing for the difference in pence occasioned by rounding up or down decimals in the table of odds and percentages). Now the advantage of making a 'backer's book' becomes apparent. In this second wager, Korelo is a winner in the 'book', not a loser as previously. The punter has taken 46.5 per cent of the chances in the race, leaving the bookmaker with 53.5 per cent, but the backer's margin is not 46.5 per cent. It is in fact $£^{46}/_{40} \times 100 = 115$ per cent. This surely is a very acceptable profit. It is not possible to have nearly every horse in the race on the backer's side, in the same way that the bookmaker, accepting a large liability on the favourite, contrives to have the whole field without the favourite running for a conventional layer's 'book'. Nevertheless by adjusting stakes to the odds in a similar manner to the bookmakers adjusting their odds to the stakes bet by their clients, a punter can have a significant number of horses in a race and still retain the prospect of a worthwhile win.

54
OPPOSING WEAK FAVOURITES

This method of 'making a book against the book' need not be confined to just handicaps where better prices are usually on offer. It can also be worked successfully on non-handicaps where the winners will probably come from the fancied horses starting at comparatively short odds.

EXAMPLE I

This was the case with the 2000 Guineas of 2003 at Newmarket. We have already noted in the KEY RACES method that the Classic seldom goes to a horse outside the first five or six in the betting and that nearly all winners won their previous race. We have also used the 2003 renewal itself to illustrate how the bookmakers skilfully arrange percentages converted to odds in their own favour and to the punters' detriment. Yet this very race also provides an excellent example of how the backer can 'make a book against the book' and utilise the bookmakers' own system of betting to get the better of them.

If this strategy is combined with the KEY RACES recommendation, the following simple analysis would have been the first stage in attaining this desirable objective.

2000 GUINEAS. MAY 2003. FIRST SIX IN THE BETTING.

Position last time out		Starting Price
3rd	HOLD THAT TIGER (opened 7–2, then 9–2)	4–1
Won	LATEEN SAILS (opened 11–2, 6–1 in places)	9–2
Won	REFUSE TO BEND (4–1 before 5–1)	9–2
4th	TOMAHAWK (from 8–1)	7–1
Won	TOUT SEUL (8–1 to 9–1 before down to 7–1)	7–1
Won	MUQBIL (opened 10–1 before touching 11–1)	9–1

Hold That Tiger was definitely a weak favourite. He was extremely easy in the market on the race throughout the day, having been best-priced at no more than 5–2 in the morning, before drifting out to 9–2 and then settling at 4–1 before the 'off'. His form was good but not outstanding in such a high-class field. He had been third in the Breeders' Cup juvenile race in the US the previous autumn. It could be argued that his position at the head of the betting was really due to his status as Ballydoyle's first string. Moreover, the Irish stable was also running Tomahawk, which did not suggest confidence on the part of connections. It seemed reasonable to follow the market and oppose the drifting favourite.

Tomahawk, too, looked highly suspect. The colt had been rejected by stable jockey Mick Kinane in favour of Hold That Tiger, and was only Ballydoyle's number two. He had been beaten last time out, having finished fourth of six in a sprint finish for a Group Three race over a mile at Longchamp in April. Before that, he had again been beaten, this time finishing a length and a quarter behind the winner, Tout Seul, one of his leading rivals today, in the Dewhurst Stakes at the back end of the previous season. It does not always pay to do the obvious in racing, far from it, but surely Tomahawk could be left out of the calculations.

Muqbil was a borderline case. He had won his only start as a three-year-old in the Greenham Stakes at Newbury, but in his final race of the previous year had surprisingly been beaten by Governor Brown, hanging badly in a small field for the 7f Somerville Tattersall Stakes. Governor Brown was definitely not top class.

If Muqbil was omitted, that left Lateen Sails, Refuse To Bend and Tout Seul. In a positive sense all had first-rate form and it was virtually impossible to choose between them with any degree of confidence. The solution was to back all three.

This time, a level-stakes bet on each of them would have shown a profit if any of them had won. If Tout Seul came out on top, the gain would be 5 clear points; if either Lateen Sails or Refuse To Bend were successful, a much less remunerative 2½-point gain would have been the outcome. However, this is still an unbalanced wager, although here the spread between prices is not great. From an equal division of the total stake the punter gains least from the shortest-priced horses. Yet these are precisely the selections likely to win most often over a period of time.

The 'backer's book', illustrated in the last section, is a much better wager. The calculations are shown below. For the sake of argument, starting prices are taken as their basis. To get away from an aggregate of £10 per horse in our examples, this time £50 is spread among bets on the three selected runners.

Total stake £50 on horses at 9–2 (18.2%), 9–2 (18.2%), 7–1 (12.5%). Backer's percentage of the 'book': 48.9 per cent.

The stake on each horse (to the nearest 5p or 10p) would be:

LATEEN SAILS $£50 \times \dfrac{18.2}{48.9}$ at 9–2 = £18.60

REFUSE TO BEND $£50 \times \dfrac{18.2}{48.9}$ at 9–2 = £18.60

TOUT SEUL $£50 \times \dfrac{12.5}{48.9}$ at 7–1 = £12.80

This would give the following situation:

Bet	Odds	Horse	Return on win
£18.60	9–2	LATEEN SAILS	£102.30
£18.60	9–2	REFUSE TO BEND	£102.30
£12.80	7–1	TOUT SEUL	£102.40

£50.00 outlay

Profit if any horse wins: £52 (to the nearest £).

Thus the punter has obtained just over evens by opposing the favourite and making some eminently logical deductions about other fancied runners. What would have been the result, however, if Muqbil had not been excluded? The backer would be in a worse position of course, but by how much? Would the profit from a bet on four, not three, market leaders have been worthwhile?

Here are the calculations:

Total stake £50 on horses at 9–2 (18.2%), 9–2 (18.2%), 7–1 (12.5%), 9–1 (10.0%).
Backer's percentage of the 'book': 58.9 per cent.

Stake on each horse (to the nearest 5p or 10p):

LATEEN SAILS $£50 \times \dfrac{18.2}{58.9}$ at 9–2 = £15.45

REFUSE TO BEND $£50 \times \dfrac{18.2}{58.9}$ at 9–2 = £15.45

TOUT SEUL $£50 \times \dfrac{12.5}{58.9}$ at 7–1 = £10.60

MUQBIL $£50 \times \dfrac{10.0}{58.9}$ at 9–1 = £8.50

Betting on four horses led to the following situation:

Bet	Odds	Horse	Return on win
£15.45	9–2	LATEEN SAILS	£85.00
£15.45	9–2	REFUSE TO BEND	£85.00
£10.60	7–1	TOUT SEUL	£84.80
£8.50	9–1	MUQBIL	£85.00

£50.00 outlay

Profit if any horse wins: £35 (to the nearest £).

Now the backer is betting at odds-on, but by no means prohibitive odds-on. Odds of 7–10 might well suit a professional punter, but probably not someone betting in smaller sums.

In the event, of course, Refuse to Bend won and Muqbil finished down the field. The 'pro' might have considered the extra insurance on Muqbil worthwhile, but both 'pro' and amateur punter alike ought to have been well satisfied with the return from the three most likely candidates, Lateen Sails, Refuse to Bend and Tout Seul.

Conclusion: In fact it is in betting against weak favourites that some modern professionals make the most effective use of the 'backer's book'. Despite vastly improved Press coverage of the sport in the present era, there are still enough false favourites in racing to make this a paying strategy. Not even every horse starting at odds-on has a genuinely odds-on chance. An intimate knowledge of the form book will reveal to the trained eye lots of examples of races in which the bookmakers ask for odds about a favourite which in reality may very well not win.

In weak betting markets at small meetings this is a regular occurrence. The backer who can knock out an odds-on favourite and find the winner of the race from two or three opponents in a small field, adjusting stakes in the manner recommended, is very close to being a bookmaker. Both the bookmaker and the professional backer want the 'jolly' beaten for the same reason. Selectivity is essential for the latter who must choose races in which to bet with the utmost care, but given the necessary skill, winning becomes nothing more than a matter of technique.

EXAMPLE 2

A 2m 4½f novice chase at Bangor on Saturday, 12 October 2002.

There were five runners in the race, two of which, Glenfarclas Boy and Tigerburningbright, were clearly 'rags'. Priced at 20–1 and 33–1 respectively, they could be ignored for serious betting purposes.

The favourite was Gentle Rivage at around evens, but never at odds-on, and a glance at the form book would have immediately sounded a warning note about its chance of winning. To begin with, the horse had been off the course for no less than 245 days. Clearly, its fitness would have to be taken on trust, not a wise thing to do when such a niggardly price was on offer. That run had been at Haydock in February 2002, where in a Class D novice chase, Gentle Rivage had finished last of four over 2m 6f behind Historg, having started the outsider of the party. On its previous start, at Towcester, it had likewise been the complete outsider, this time in a field of six. The race was much better class, but Gentle Rivage had fallen at the seventh fence. Prior to that it had also fallen in a race at Newbury at the end of November 2001. But earlier in November, almost 11 months before today's race at Bangor, it had actually plodded on to be second in a Class A Grade 2 novice event at Chepstow.

Here at last was some kind of reason why Gentle Rivage was being made favourite. On the surface, a second in a race with that status should have been good enough to guarantee a sound run today. However, a closer inspection of the form revealed that the horse had been beaten nine lengths by Gola Cher and since two of the better of the six runners had both fallen, in fact Gentle Rivage had only managed to finish in front of two horses of little account.

Even if one took the second in a Class A Grade 2 race at its face value, which would have been a very foolish thing to do, the horse's record in subsequent races was lamentable. Two falls followed by a last of four as the outsider of the field in the same class as today's race gave no encouragement to believe that this 'dodgy' jumper was capable of reproducing even the somewhat tarnished Chepstow form, the more so as the length of the horse's absence from the racecourse raised serious doubts about its fitness. This was a false favourite if ever there was one.

What of the opposition, apart from the two rags? Well, both second and third favourites were from high-profile yards, neither of which is given to carrying passengers in their crowded boxes.

Rainbow Dance, the second favourite, had a real chance. Priced at about 7–4, this was its first run over fences, but in its previous race, a Class C handicap hurdle over 2m 4f at Worcester in June, it had won well by $3\frac{1}{2}$ lengths. In the section on novice chases in this book (see Criterion 20) we noted that the time to bet on a good hurdler in novice chases is sometimes first time over the bigger fences, if only because reasonable odds are likely to be obtainable. The 7–4 was not exactly 'reasonable', suggesting that in its case, Rainbow Dance was to some extent 'expected'. Provided the horse had been well schooled over fences, and it almost goes without saying that it would have been, there was every reason to believe that, in contrast to the favourite, Rainbow Dance would run extremely well.

On offer at a best price of 13–2, Miss Knight's horse, Keep Smiling, was similarly inexperienced over fences. Eighteen days before, the horse had started at 2–1 against in a Class F Maiden Chase at Fontwell, but it had taken too keen a hold from the 'off' and had fallen at the second fence. Having only run in novice hurdles previously, clearly it was a chaser in the making. Today it was actually raised in class despite its fall, and improvement could surely be anticipated. Although the horse did not have good form in the book like Rainbow Dance, Keep Smiling was at the start of a career over fences and might give the rest of today's field something to think about, even if it did not win.

In a classic case of a race where making a 'book' against the weak favourite would very likely pay off, the shrewd punter might have struck two bets as follows:

Total stake £50 on two horses, one at 7–4 (36.4%) and one at 13–2 (13.3%).
Backer's percentage of the 'book': 49.7 per cent.

Stake on each horse (to the nearest 10p):

RAINBOW DANCE $\quad$ £50 $\times \dfrac{36.4}{49.7}$ at 7–4 = £36.60

KEEP SMILING $\quad$ £50 $\times \dfrac{13.3}{49.7}$ at 13–2 = £13.40

Betting on two horses had the following result:

Bet	Odds	Horse	Return on win
£36.60	7–4	RAINBOW DANCE	£100.65
£13.40	13–2	KEEP SMILING	£100.50
£50.00 outlay			

Profit if either horse wins: £50 (to the nearest £).

In the actual race Miss Knight's potential chaser Keep Smiling beat the good ex-hurdler trained by Jonjo O'Neill, Rainbow Dance. The margin was five lengths. Gentle Rivage finished a remote third, 25 lengths behind the second horse, having made an error at the fourth fence and blundering badly at the sixth, after which it was never in the race.

This was a clear vindication of how an astute reading of the form book, aided by making a 'book' in the way recommended, can put money in the clever backer's pocket. The luxury of backing two of the three fancied horses in the race was made possible by the system of regulating stakes according to percentages, which puts the punter on level terms with the bookmaker. The fact that the favourite here was highly unlikely to win on its past record did the rest.

Conclusion: Races like this do not occur every day, but there are still plenty of them over a season, particularly in jump races. You can always make a mistake and see the favourite romp home with the horses you have backed trailing in its wake, but the clever punter with an expert knowledge of the form book and the ability to read the signs correctly should get it right most of the time. There are no certainties in racing form, but surely the sport offers no more straightforward way of making money than the above race and others like it.

55
BIG HANDICAPS

There is one other kind of race in which skilled operators can win consistently by making their own 'book'. This method too is by no means infallible, but a little flair in working the bet can land some really nice coups.

At regular intervals throughout the Flat season, bookmakers are happy to offer ante-post prices for big handicaps. There are also a number of races of this kind during the National Hunt season, beginning with the Gold Cup Handicap Chase at Cheltenham in November.

The trick in taking a good profit from these races is to time one's bets correctly, for the market on a big handicap generally goes through a number of stages.

When the prices from the layers first appear, some time before the race, betting is a lottery. Final running plans are not known, and only someone genuinely 'in the know' can avoid backing non-runners. Ante-post betting is a risky and unrewarding business for the ordinary punter, as we shall see below.

After the five-day declaration stage a much clearer picture emerges and a realistic set of prices becomes available. At this point the backer should go carefully through all the form and make a note of all those horses which have a sound chance of winning. This group should be rather larger than the intended final bet to be struck when the backer has arrived at definite conclusions about prospects. The draw and the way the bookmakers price up the race just after the overnight declaration is known will quite possibly cause some modification of original ideas.

Eve-of-race bets are not ante-post, but on a 'non-runner, no bet' basis. It is at this point that a final list of candidates for the big race should be settled on and all bets struck. Do not wait until the next day. That will be the morning of the race and whatever value is left from the overnight prices framed at about midday on the previous day will go in the betting exchanges once the bookmakers start taking bets from the 'early birds'. There is no need to worry, however. Backers' bets are 'on' immediately after the 'overnight' when in possession of all the facts such as the draw and non-runners. The prices obtained are fixed.

The final stage in the market is betting on the course in the time leading up to the 'off'. Here again there may be another shrinkage in value for the odds about a few horses as the bookmakers assess their final liabilities. But again this does not affect bets already laid. Value has already been obtained and, if a horse does not come under starting orders for any reason, your money is returned.

Exceptional value from the very best of the odds requires bets to be made immediately after the five-day declaration is announced. Most connections will not have paid the final forfeit if they do not really intend to run their horse, so the small gamble of backing an occasional non-runner is more than offset by the opportunity to obtain much better prices. Horses to avoid are those with a light weight which may not get into the race if all the higher-weighted horses stand their ground. These can always be backed later if and when their participation becomes certain. Also, if the draw is likely to have a big effect on the race, it is wise to wait for the overnight declaration before making a commitment. These considerations apart, a wager struck just after the five-day stage may provide 'tasty' prices about some horses whose odds may gradually shrink, although of course there is absolutely no guarantee of a big reduction in the odds, and in fact many prices do not change between the five-day and overnight declaration stages.

EXAMPLE

A recent running of the Royal Hunt Cup over the straight mile at Ascot will highlight the most important points about making a 'backer's book' in big handicaps.

On the left in the table opposite are the opening prices offered by one big bookmaker the day after an important forfeit stage for the race at the end of May 2003. These prices represent the first publicly advertised ante-post 'book' for the event. On the right are the prices for the Royal Ascot feature, offered by the same bookmaker, as they stood after the overnight declaration and the draw was known on the late morning of the day before the race, due to be run on Wednesday, 18 June 2003.

Royal Hunt Cup. Ascot. 1m.

Opening ante-post prices		Prices after overnight declaration, the morning before the race
10–1	FUNFAIR	5–1
12–1	GREEN LINE	Non-runner
14–1	MORAHIB	14–1
16–1	AKSHAR	Non-runner
16–1	COLISAY	12–1
16–1	DEMONSTRATE	Non-runner
16–1	EVEREST	Non-runner
16–1	MYSTIC MAN	Non-runner
16–1	NORTON	20–1
16–1	SELECTIVE	12–1
20–1	BONECRUSHER	Non-runner
20–1	CAMP COMMANDER	16–1
20–1	DUKE OF MODENA	25–1
20–1	FAITHFUL WARRIOR	25–1
20–1	GOBLET OF FIRE	Non-runner
20–1	ISLAND LIGHT	Non-runner
20–1	ONE MORE ROUND	Non-runner
20–1	PABLO	Non-runner
20–1	SAHAAT	33–1
20–1	SERIEUX	33–1
20–1	SMIRK	Non-runner
20–1	SURPRISE ENCOUNTER	25–1
20–1	WITH REASON	Non-runner
20–1	ZONERGEM	20–1
25–1	ADIEMUS	Non-runner
25–1	AVORADO	Non-runner
25–1	CAT'S WHISKERS	Non-runner
25–1	CHIVALRY	Non-runner
25–1	HALLION	12–1
25–1	ILE MICHER	Non-runner
25–1	LADY BEAR	Non-runner
25–1	MACADAMIA	11–1
25–1	PENTECOST	25–1

Opening ante-post prices		Prices after overnight declaration, the morning before the race
25–1	PERFECT STORM	25–1
25–1	PRIZE TIME	Non-runner
25–1	SAMHARI	Non-runner
Not originally quoted		
	ATLANTIC ACE	33–1
	COMMANDING	33–1
	COURAGEOUS DUKE	33–1
	GRYFFINDOR	Not quoted
	HALAWELLFIN HALA	33–1
	INTERNATIONALGUEST	Not quoted
	MY RAGGEDY MAN	33–1
	NASHAAB	20–1
	RAPSCALLION	Not quoted
	RYME INTRINSECA	Not quoted
	SHOT TO FAME	33–1
	TOUGH LOVE	25–1
	UNSHAKABLE	25–1
	WING COMMANDER	25–1
	WINNING VENTURE	33–1
	ZUCCHERO	Not quoted

There are two significant points to note here for those tempted to indulge in ante-post betting. In the first place, just a cursory glance at the above demonstrates quite clearly the very real danger of backing eventual non-runners. Of the first ten in the original betting, only five horses took their place in the actual field for the race. The rest were automatic losers for anyone who backed them ante-post. Also, it is clear that in many cases one may gain little or nothing in terms of better odds to justify the risk of betting ante-post. Backers of Morahib, Norton, Duke of Modena and Faithful Warrior, just to mention horses well to the fore in the betting, were either no better off or actually worse off by taking the ante-post price very early on rather than waiting for the odds after the overnight declaration. The actual starting prices for the race confirmed this lack of advantage from ante-post with these four examples, as well as with a number of other horses in the race, especially among the extreme outsiders.

There can be no doubt that the best time to bet on these big handicaps is shortly after the overnight declaration stage. Bets made then are on a 'non-runner, no bet' basis, so the risks attendant upon betting at ante-post are avoided. One knows the draw for starting positions and may be able to make important inferences from it. And, as we shall see, by betting at this point, one may well do better than the starting price which is finally returned after the morning and afternoon markets on race day have firmed up the bookmakers' liabilities for the event.

The comparison between the initial ante-post 'book' on a big handicap and the prices on offer around midday the day before the race should be no mere academic exercise, however. The comparison can be used with great effect to discover which horses have been best backed over an extended period. Indeed, this is a technique every serious backer ought to employ for big handicaps before getting financially involved in such difficult races to unravel by form alone.

Therefore, by looking down both sets of prices for this Royal Hunt Cup, it is apparent that two horses have attracted most attention from backers. Hallion, which has dropped from 25–1 to 12–1, is one candidate that must have attracted a great deal of money. Macadamia (25–1 to 11–1) has likewise been the subject of sustained interest, backed up by hard cash.

The influence of the draw in big fields on the straight course at Ascot seems to vary from year to year, but at this particular Royal Ascot in 2003 there were no prizes for realising that horses drawn farthest from the stands rail were at a considerable disadvantage. In fact, it was not unreasonable to say that any animal drawn 20 or over could, to all intents and purposes, be ignored. Hallion was drawn 18, not ideal but at least likely to enable it to race with the favoured stands-side runners in the 32-strong field. Macadamia had drawn six, which was more or less perfect. This filly would be racing with the favoured half of the field, but was not so close to the rails as to run the risk of getting cut off behind a wall of horses, which might be the fate of any very low-drawn runner lacking the pace to hold its place among the almost inevitable bunching right next to the fence.

Hallion and Macadamia were definitely worth including in a bet on the race.

Of the remainder of the field, the ante-post market indicated that only the favourite, Funfair, had attracted serious money, having opened at 10–1 at the end of May and standing at half those odds the day before the race. However, Funfair had drawn number 26 of the 32 possibles. In the opinion of most professionals, Funfair would have needed to be a superhorse to win from that position. Good handicapper though he undoubtedly is, it was reasonable to take a chance and exclude the horse from bets on the race, even though the public, ignoring the draw, continued to back him so that he actually went off the 4–1 favourite.

To complete the short list of probables for making a 'backer's book' on the Hunt Cup, one might have studied very closely the Victoria Cup at Ascot earlier in the season. Though run over a furlong less, but on the same course, this race has been a significant trial for the Hunt Cup for a number of years, as was noted in the KEY RACES chapter of this manual. In 2003, three candidates which ran in the Victoria Cup all appeared to have definite chances in the Royal Hunt Cup. Camp Commander had actually won the Victoria Cup, and had been backed from 20–1 to 16–1 for the Hunt Cup. Selective had finished a close second to it and had likewise dropped four points in the ante-post market, from 16–1 down to 12–1. Pentecost, the winner of the Britannia Handicap as a three-year-old in 2002, looked a likely outsider at 25–1, having finished in mid-division in the Victoria Cup, its only outing of the 2003 season so far. Also, all three horses had been favoured by apparently reasonable draws: Camp Commander (10), Selective (14) and Pentecost (2). These three runners, along with Hallion and Macadamia, would make up a strong 'book' on the Royal Hunt Cup.

Before showing in full the necessary calculations, the technique for which readers will be familiar with by now, a final comparison between the odds on offer the day prior to the race and the eventual starting price is most instructive. This information is set out below.

	Price after overnight declaration	Starting Price
HALLION	12–1	14–1
MACADAMIA	11–1	8–1
CAMP COMMANDER	16–1	11–1
SELECTIVE	12–1	10–1
PENTECOST	25–1	25–1

Therefore, in three of the five cases, striking a bet on the previous morning on a 'non-runner, no bet' basis would have considerably improved the backer's position overall on the five-horse 'book'. True, Hallion had drifted a couple of points and Pentecost was steady at 25–1, but on balance there is no doubt that the odds available shortly after the overnight declaration are the ones to take.

The 'backer's book' on the 2003 Royal Hunt Cup would have been calculated as follows:

Horse	Odds	Percentage
HALLION	12–1	7.7%
MACADAMIA	11–1	8.3%
CAMP COMMANDER	16–1	5.9%
SELECTIVE	12–1	7.7%
PENTECOST	25–1	3.8%

Backer's percentage of the 'book': 33.4%

Stake on the race: £50

Bets on each horse:

Calculation	Horse	Odds	Stake	Win returns
$£50 \times \dfrac{7.7}{33.4}$	HALLION	12–1	£11.50	£149.50

$£50 \times \dfrac{8.3}{33.4}$ MACADAMIA   11–1   £12.45   £149.40

$£50 \times \dfrac{5.9}{33.4}$ CAMP COMMANDER 16–1   £8.85   £150.45

$£50 \times \dfrac{7.7}{33.4}$ SELECTIVE   12–1   £11.50   £149.50

$£50 \times \dfrac{3.8}{33.4}$ PENTECOST   25–1   £5.70   £148.20
                                                  £50.00

Profit if any of the five wins: £99 (approx).

Thus backing the winner, Macadamia, made a profit of around £99, the maker of the 'backer's book' having enjoyed the luxury of staking on no less than five horses for the same gain. The recommended technique got the punter the best of the odds and enhanced profitability beyond what would have been possible at starting price, all without the risk of dangerous ante-post betting. The ante-post market had been used to indicate the eventual winner as one possible to back among several, but risky bets at ante-post had been scrupulously avoided.

This Royal Hunt Cup was not absolutely typical, in that the market finally settled at 4–1 the field, whereas in some of the season's other big handicaps, betting can start as high as 10–1 the field. This will reduce the percentage of the 'book' needed to cover four, five or even six likely candidates, since the odds for horses other than the market leader will be proportionately longer, leading to enhanced profitability from a winning selection.

Conclusion: No matter how many horses in a race are backed, the winner still has to be found, and there will be times when it will escape even the widest net made possible by making a 'backer's book'. Nevertheless, even the greatest pessimist would probably agree that betting in the way recommended in the preceding pages makes life easier in the hazardous business of backing horses. Over a period of time, judicious use of a 'backer's book' ought to result in a winning betting ledger.

PART 4

Betting Exchanges

56
GAMBLING ON THE INTERNET

Betting exchanges, the new century's gift to the sport of horse racing from a gambling point of view, are in the vanguard of changes in the betting industry. This manual would not be complete without at least an introduction to the new facilities. The following survey goes some way beyond a mere explanation, however, and attempts to highlight the advantages and draw attention to the pitfalls for the unwary in the new ways to bet. What follows will, hopefully, be of assistance to all readers, whether they already have a betting-exchange account, are considering opening one, or have not so far investigated the possibilities of the exchanges.

THE MATCHING PRINCIPLE

Before becoming involved in a betting exchange, it is absolutely vital to get clear in one's own mind exactly how bets work and what one's liabilities are. All the exchanges and in particular the biggest, Betfair, offer a range of bets on many sports and financial markets, but the betting dealt with in this section will be straightforward bets on horse racing only.

With apologies to those readers who are already experienced betting-exchange hands, here are the various scenarios for horse racing bets expressed in the simplest possible, non-computerised form. On the internet screen itself the options are shown as keys with prices and amounts of money on them, and actual bets are made through the PC using a keyboard and mouse.

Offers

It is important to realise that all bets are with other customers of the exchange, not with the exchange operators themselves. Commission is paid to the exchange on winnings, not losses, at a rate of between two and five per cent depending on the customer's betting turnover. The higher the winning turnover, the less one pays in percentage terms.

The principal offers, with an example, are:

Conventional punter	Via the internet or telephone you offer to BACK Russian Rhythm to WIN at odds of 10 (9–1) to a stake of £100.
Conventional bookmaker	One or more customers of the exchange accept your offer and LAY Russian Rhythm to LOSE at 10 (9–1) to a stake of £100.

OR

Conventional bookmaker	One or more customers of the exchange accept your offer and LAY Russian Rhythm to LOSE at 10 (9–1), but only to a stake of £50.
Conventional punter	If you allow the original offer to stand, the exchange will attempt automatically or by telephone, depending on what service you are using, to accommodate you with another punter or punters for the remaining £50 with which you have offered to BACK Russian Rhythm to WIN at odds of 10 (9–1).

Conventional bookmaker	You offer to LAY Russian Rhythm to LOSE to a stake of £100 at 10 (9–1).
Conventional punter	One or more customers of the exchange accept your offer and BACK Russian Rhythm to WIN at 10 (9–1) to the whole of your £100 stake.

OR

Conventional punter	One or more customers of the exchange accept your offer and BACK Russian Rhythm to WIN at 10 (9–1), but only to a stake of £50.
Conventional bookmaker	If you allow the original offer to stand, the exchange will try to accommodate you with another punter or punters for the remaining £50 with which you have offered to LAY Russian Rhythm to LOSE at 10 (9–1).

Acceptances

The exact reverse now applies where you are the acceptor:

Conventional punter	One or more punters via the internet or telephone have offered to BACK Russian Rhythm at 10 (9–1) to WIN to a stake of £100.
Conventional bookmaker	You accept the offer and LAY Russian Rhythm to LOSE a stake of £100 at 10 (9–1).
OR	
Conventional bookmaker	You accept the offer and LAY Russian Rhythm to LOSE, but only to a stake of £50 at 10 (9–1).
Conventional punter	The betting exchange will attempt to accommodate the person or persons who made the offer to BACK Russian Rhythm at 10 (9–1) for the balance of £50, unless the offer is cancelled in the interim.

Conventional bookmaker	One or more customers of the exchange have offered to LAY Russian Rhythm to LOSE at 10 (9–1) to a £100 stake.
Conventional punter	You accept the offer and BACK Russian Rhythm to WIN at 10 (9–1) to a stake of £100.
OR	
Conventional punter	You accept £50 of the offer and BACK Russian Rhythm to WIN at 10 (9–1) for that amount.
Conventional bookmaker	The betting exchange will attempt to find one or more customers to accept the offer to LAY Russian Rhythm to LOSE at 10 (9–1) for the outstanding £50, assuming the original offer is allowed to stand.

This, in the most straightforward terms, with all complications and nuances omitted, is how bets are offered and accepted on the exchanges. Before actually making a bet on an exchange, of course, it will be necessary to get the relevant screen up on the computer and relate this very simplified summary to the actual mechanics and phraseology used for betting. It will pay readers to understand these fully and, if they are not sure about any point, to seek explanation from an exchange operator. Do not be afraid to ask.

Below are guidelines for each of the various betting options, with some recommendations about what to do and what not to do in order to make the best of the opportunities offered by betting exchanges.

Be warned, however. If you are a newcomer to the exchanges, you will be dealing immediately with clients who are already adept at making bets in the new way. Caution must be the watchword until you are completely confident about operating a PC to make bets, and until you fully understand the nature of the bets and the financial implications of them. Betting on the telephone, which on Betfair requires a minimum stake of £50, as opposed to the £2 minimum on the internet, there is a set procedure for making bets and if you make an obvious mistake which reveals that you do not fully understand what you are about, the exchange operator will no doubt guide you. However, he or she cannot be expected to offer advice about the wisdom or otherwise of a bet.

BACKING HORSES TO WIN

Betfair claim in their promotional literature that the odds obtained via their exchange are, on average, some 20 per cent better than from conventional bookmakers. At the present time at least, this is certainly true, but apart from a better return overall, there are cases almost every week of astronomical odds being matched among those who play the horses using their facility. A few examples from 2003 will serve to illustrate the point.

Monty's Pass, the eventual winner of the Grand National, was easily matched at 160 (159–1) when the market on the race opened in February; the most that could be obtained from the bookmakers at that time was around 50–1. Hold That Tiger and Six Perfections, the bookmakers' short-priced favourites for the 2000 Guineas and 1000 Guineas respectively, were freely available at 34 (33–1) and 21 (20–1) very early in the evolution of the Betfair ante-post markets for the Newmarket Classics. As for the eventual winner of the 1000 Guineas, Russian Rhythm, Sir Michael Stoute's filly, was pushed out to 13–2 by the bookmakers in the days leading up to the

Sunday Classic after unfavourable remarks by Sir Michael about the filly's lack of readiness to compete in the race. So seriously did backers take Sir Michael's comments that Russian Rhythm drifted again on the afternoon of the contest to start at a price of no less than 12–1. That would have been a remarkable price for an animal with such obvious form claims before the advent of the betting exchanges, yet 25 (24–1) was readily matched on Betfair during the preceding Wednesday.

Nor is it just on candidates for big races in their ante-post markets that Betfair are able to facilitate such astonishing prices for their clients. Take, for example, Yaheska who won a small handicap at Bath at 50–1 on the Saturday before Royal Ascot: 500 (499–1) was matched for one lucky Betfair backer, albeit to a relatively small stake.

It may surprise some readers, but huge odds like this are not isolated instances. There are examples every week, though even on Betfair, one is unlikely to get a price well in excess of conventional odds to a very large stake. On the other hand, there is no lack of liquidity generally in the Betfair markets. Hawk Wing, the stunning winner of the Lockinge Stakes at Newbury, was matched at around 1.64 (64–100 or about 6–4 on in traditional odds) to the tune of £2.2m on Betfair when the horse reappeared in the Queen Anne Stakes at Royal Ascot. These odds were available when Hawk Wing was 7–4 on with racecourse bookmakers before the horse drifted very slightly with them to go off at an official starting price of 13–8 on. The point here is that any attempt to get such huge sums of money on the horse with conventional bookmakers, even in a racecourse market as strong as Royal Ascot, would have resulted in a very severe contraction in the odds about the horse.

The reason why large odds well in excess of the racecourse prices are sometimes available on the exchanges is due to the fact that a betting exchange is not organised in the same way as a conventional bookmaker's 'book'. Although they reserve the right to refuse any bet, bookmakers must offer a price for each horse in a race, and do so in such a way that the total percentage of all their odds are well in excess of 100. This excess, as we saw in Chapter 52, represents their theoretical profit. For a bookmaker to lay the kind of huge prices to be had from time to time on the exchanges would make a nonsense of this system, throwing the 'book' seriously out of balance. On a betting exchange there is no such constraint. If a punter is prepared to lay odds way above the prevailing, conventional rate, a betting exchange's matching facility means that there is every chance of those odds being matched by other punters at least to some of the amount of stake required, depending on the bet.

Yet big odds, excessively big odds, can be a snare and a delusion for the ordinary punter who bets as a pastime. For the question that anyone should always ask is why is someone on a betting exchange prepared to lay odds significantly over the current, general rate emanating from the racecourse ring? Why, for instance, is someone willing to lay a horse to lose at 11 (10–1) when only 6 (5–1) is available anywhere else? Market forces in an independent arena, and the lack of over-round, are surely not sufficient by themselves to account for it, at least all of the time.

Betting exchanges, the biggest innovation in racing for decades, are very probably here to stay. Yet doubts have been expressed, and in the short period of their existence the greatest potential problem with the new facilities has been perceived to be one of regulation. For years now it has been an article of faith among punters, traditional bookmakers and the racing authorities alike that it is in the best interests of all concerned that betting should be monitored by the Jockey Club and their inspectors with the object of keeping the sport as clean as possible. Yet it was only on 15 June 2003 that Betfair signed a memorandum of understanding with the Jockey Club to the effect that they would in future cooperate on suspicious incidents where 'unusual' betting patterns might be involved. Shortly afterwards it was reported in the press that a blacksmith working for a northern stable had successfully laid three of his employer's runners to lose large amounts at inflated prices.

There is definitely an important lesson here for anyone considering transferring their betting allegiance from a conventional bookmaker to a betting exchange. Big odds are all very well, but someone who avails themselves of this presumed advantage immediately exposes themselves to exploitation by anyone who is better informed about a given animal's well-being (or lack of it) than they are. Even without skulduggery, the average punter betting on an exchange is in a gambling jungle, where rival punters may be racing professionals who could be in a position to take advantage of privileged information. The exchange, as an absolute rule, will not divulge the identities of persons who are laying or backing horses with it to other punters who are on the opposite side of a match, or for that matter to anyone else. And, unlike the stock exchange, for example, there is no legislation or regulation about insider trading. Conventional bookmakers are excluded from betting on the exchanges by the organisers, but racing insiders are not. The ordinary readers of the present book, who bet as a pastime and are not professionally engaged in the racing industry, should ask themselves whether they believe they can come out on top in such an environment. They should certainly be suspicious of any offer to bet at way above the current odds where significant sums of money in stakes are involved.

One final point, amid all this talk of inflated odds, is that there is no guarantee that a better price will automatically be obtainable on an exchange than from a conventional bookmaker. Here one should, as far as possible, shop around. A home PC is needed to bet on an exchange, unless the telephone service is used, which requires far bigger stakes than the internet, but there are other sources of information about prices that should bear on one's betting decisions. The teletext service on mainstream television is one, and the betting shows from the course in betting shops are another. To get the best available prices needs access to more than one source of information and, for the ordinary person who is not professionally involved in backing horses, this may be difficult to achieve, certainly as a matter of routine. As for anyone betting on the racecourse, access to betting-exchange information is not too hard to acquire, since mobile phones are allowed in the betting rings, although betting from a PC on the track without an associate poses obvious problems. For home punters without a PC, the introduction by Betfair of a limited teletext information service on Channel 4 from August 2003 was a step in the right direction.

LAYING HORSES TO LOSE

Most readers of this book probably back a lot of losers. Everyone does, no matter how many winners are also backed to offset this unfortunate fact of life. It may be tempting to believe, therefore, that laying horses to lose will be a lot more profitable than trying to back winners. However, when horses are laid to lose on a betting exchange, layers must not fool themselves into believing that they are behaving like a bookmaker, with all the attendant, presumed advantages that this entails. In fact they are doing no such thing. They are betting without the over-round that is the conventional bookmaker's protection and theoretical profit margin, and they have no way of manipulating the odds for the whole field in their own favour as bookmakers contrive to do and often succeed in doing. This is true even if several horses in the same race are laid to lose on a betting exchange. Indeed, far from being protected by the over-round for at least a marginal profit, layers on the exchanges must pay commission to the exchange operator each time they make a successful bet.

In fact, laying horses to lose on the new facilities might be a dangerous and costly business. Here is an extreme example, but one which makes the general point very effectively.

It is taken from Betfair's market on the Epsom Derby of 2003. One of their clients was fortunate enough to back trainer David Elsworth's 2000 Guineas third, Norse Dancer, at 980 (979–1) for the Epsom Classic. The same punter even succeeded in obtaining a match for a place bet at the fantastic odds of 660 (659–1). The bet was made some days before the colt was supplemented for the big race, since it was not originally an entry. The person who laid Norse Dancer to lose at those odds must have been completely confident that the horse would not in fact be supplemented at the five-day acceptance stage.

Yet the colt was indeed supplemented for the race at that point, at a cost of many thousands to its owners. Here again the question of insider trading rears its ugly head. For it is clearly possible that the backer was acting on information known only to a few people, and certainly not to the layer. Either that, or the backer had made a very good guess, and the layer, equally ignorant of the true position, had taken the opposite, mistaken view.

In the event, the layer, though losing the first round in the battle, came out on top, for Norse Dancer, though supplemented, did not win the Derby and did not even reach a place. He did, however, make a tardy start, then trailed the field into Tattenham Corner, before finishing like an express train to run through beaten horses to finish fourth, one place short of what was required for the place bet at 660 to succeed.

The layer had won the bet and had a very lucky escape, but this case does illustrate the dangers of laying horses at huge odds when not in possession of all the facts. If a horse is laid to lose, there is always a possibility that the punter who backs the horse knows more than the layer does.

On the other hand, if information comes into your possession that, say, a horse in a small race is well short of peak fitness, and this knowledge is not in the public domain, there is no ethic in the exchanges betting jungle that says you should not yourself take advantage of the information and lay the horse to lose at odds to tempt the unwary to whatever stake you feel comfortable with. This may not be fair, but the horse could still win, which makes it a legal bet in the world of the new exchanges. On balance, however, given its lack of fitness, it is more likely to lose and you have taken advantage of knowledge not shared by those who back the horse.

Thus, the facility to lay horses means that in all but the biggest races where everything about the well-being of leading candidates is extensively reported in the press, success or failure can be as much about correct information as opinion. The person who is in possession of very accurate knowledge about a horse or group of horses can make money from the fact. If readers of this book are betting on opinion alone, they should realise that however good they believe their judgement to be, they are likely to come up against people whose judgement may be the equal of theirs, or superior to it, or, worse, who may have privileged information not known to the public. There may be plenty of other 'opinion' betters on the exchanges – not everyone is 'in the know', far from it – but they are still at risk from the punter who does have inside knowledge.

LAYING AN ORDER ON THE SYSTEM

If you decide to accept the price about your selection currently on the system, but want to stake more than the amount the screen tells you is available at the odds when you are making the bet, you can leave an order for the outstanding amount through your computer, or by telephone if you are betting in this way.

Also, if you do not like the odds which are currently available, you can leave an order to bet at a higher price. Thus, if you want to back a horse to win at 4 and only 3 is on offer, you can leave an order specifying these odds and the maximum amount you are prepared to bet. Similarly, you can request better odds as a layer. So, if you want to lay a horse at shorter odds than those currently available, you can leave an order for that price, together with the amount you are willing to stake.

This is all very well, but you can easily miss a winning bet in this way, certainly as a backer. In the betting office or on the racecourse, you might prefer 3–1, or even 4–1, but knowing you are being fanciful, you are likely to accept 2–1 if that is the best offer available. You might not have got the odds which would have made the bet a much better bet, but you will probably make the bet anyway, and if the horse wins, you are 'on'. The problem with the order facility on the betting exchanges is that it tends to make for unrealistic expectations of an individual bet and of betting in general.

It would be wrong to underestimate this point, for there is a real danger here that some backers, especially those conscious of the concept of 'value' in betting, may be too fastidious for their own good in the light of the order facility. A winner at 3 is not as good as the same horse winning at 4, but it is still a great deal better than no bet at all at 3 if the horse wins. If one operates a rigid 'value' system whereby only a horse available at a 'value' price can be backed, fair enough. The iron self-discipline required to bet in this way is made far easier to impose on oneself through the existence of the order facility. Ultimately, however, some backers, not possessed of such single-mindedness, would find themselves missing out on winners just because the price was not quite right, if they got into the way of predetermining acceptable odds about all or most of their bets. One wonders, too, how long the rigid adherent of 'value' would persevere in this approach, faced with a long string of winning selections which have gone unbacked.

BACKING AND LAYING THE SAME HORSE

We have seen that laying horses to lose on a betting exchange is not the same as being a bookmaker, contrary to what some people might believe, but in one respect, namely the opportunity to back and lay the same horse, the punter can operate just like a bookmaker in one of the peripheral manoeuvres of the latter's trade.

Racecourse bookmakers make most of their money from laying horses to punters who are trying to back the winner of a race, but sometimes the bookmaker can also turn punter when prices and movements in the betting market allow. Betting-exchange punters can imitate this manoeuvre.

Consider the example below, where the same horse is backed by a punter on a betting exchange both to win and to lose the race in which it is running.

£50 to win at 3 (2–1).	Return, if win: £150.
	Profit, if win: £100.
	Loss, if lose: £50
£50 to lose at 2 (evens).	Return, if lose: £100.
	Profit, if lose: £50.
	Loss, if win: £50.

What has happened here is that the horse in question has shortened on the exchange from 3 to 2. By betting in the way shown, the alert punter can have it both ways to show a profit overall should the horse win, or to retrieve all the stakes if the horse is beaten.

If the horse is successful, a profit of £100 is produced by backing it to win, but this is offset by the £50 given up in laying the horse to lose that amount. So a net profit of £50 is made. If the horse loses, the punter gains £50 from laying it to lose which offsets the loss from backing it to win. In one circumstance the punter wins less commision, in the other the punter breaks even, but pays a small amount of commission on the successful lay. In neither eventuality can the punter lose, apart from paying a little commission in one outcome.

Of course, for the bet to work in the punter's favour and produce the win/no-lose situation, the odds for a win must shorten significantly, but the beauty of the wager is that one does not have to lay the horse to lose unless the no-lose overall scenario occurs in the shape of a significant reduction in the odds. Even if the horse does not shorten in price, the punter is left with a bet on a horse to win which, if he or she knows their business, is a reasonable bet at odds at least commensurate with the horse's chance.

Moreover, the betting exchanges do not exist in a vacuum. It is perfectly possible to back the horse to win with a conventional bookmaker at the longer price, and lay the horse to lose on a betting exchange at a shorter price.

Bookmakers who lay horses to lose large amounts in the racecourse betting ring get plenty of opportunities to take advantage in this way of the odds shortening about a horse. In the financial world the difference in prices between markets, which makes this kind of trading possible, is known as arbitrage, and professional dealers in financial markets are paid by merchant banks and the like to make money for their employers by taking advantage of these no-lose situations. The advent of betting exchanges for horse racing has seen the appearance of similar traders, working independently, who are willing to bet on the arbitrage between an exchange's backing and laying markets, or, as we have seen, on the same kind of arbitrage between the traditional market on horse racing run by bookmakers and the facility to lay horses to lose on the betting exchanges.

Take, for example, the colt Audience, which was the medium of a big gamble for the 2000 Guineas of 2003. In the ante-post market for the race on the exchanges the horse was very easy to back at around 70 (69–1) early in April. It was then announced that Audience would be the mount of champion jockey, Kieron Fallon, at Newmarket. This was enough to precipitate a general, public gamble on the horse. Anyone in a position to know before the public that Fallon would ride, or even someone who reads the newspapers and realised that the horse was bound to shorten in price because of the announcement, could have made a killing in the exchanges by reacting quickly to the situation.

A professional trader, or an inspired amateur, might have struck the following wagers:

AUDIENCE backed to win at 70 to a £100 stake (in early April)
AUDIENCE backed to lose at 16 to a £100 stake (in late April)

Thus, if Audience had eventually won the 2000 Guineas, the punter would have a return of £7,000 and a profit of £6,900 less commission from the win bet, less the £100 lost in laying the horse to lose, for a net profit of £6,800 less commission. If, as actually happened, Audience lost, a profit of £1,500 (£100 × 16 – £100) less commission would accrue from laying the horse to lose, but this would be reduced by the £100 staked on the horse to win. Thus a profit of £1,400 less commission is forthcoming as a result of Audience being beaten. So in one outcome the punter wins £6,900 less commission; in the other the gain is £1,400 before commission.

Audience had not been a top-class two-year-old. His form was well below the standard required to win the 2000 Guineas, and he would have had to have made dramatic improvement on what he had achieved so far to have a realistic chance of winning, even with the assistance of Fallon in the saddle. If the trader were confident that Audience would lose, having made the bets only because of the arbitrage situation, profits could have been enhanced by changing the stakes so that the punter becomes a bigger layer of the horse to lose:

£100 AUDIENCE to win at 70
£7,000 less £100 stake, less £400 laid to lose
= £6,500 profit less commission if Audience wins

£400 AUDIENCE to lose at 16
£6,400 less £400 stake, less £100 backed to win
= £5,900 profit less commission if Audience loses

Obviously, considerable prescience would be needed to pull off a spectacular coup like the one above, but the example given is nevertheless illustrative of the different perspectives on backing horses that exchanges bring within the bounds of possibility. What has now come into being is a significantly different way of looking at betting on racing as a means to financial gain.

That said, however, it is the opinion of this writer that laying horses to lose is not what the sport of racing from a betting, or from any other point of view for that matter, is all about. The fun of horse racing as a punter lies in backing a winner. Success brings not only some financial reward but the reflected glory of winning a race shared with the owner, trainer and jockey of the horse in question. Horse racing is about winning, not losing, and anyone who successfully picks a loser, having laid it to lose, may feel a certain financial satisfaction, but surely would not derive much joy from the accomplishment. The feel-good factor must be pretty small.

Nor is picking horses to lose quite as easy as it may seem. Suppose one lays a series of horses to lose, all of which are a 6 (5–1). If a single horse wins in a series of six, all that one will have achieved is to break even. Put another way, one needs to be right and pick six horses which lose before there is the certainty of a profit from the series as a whole. Being wrong more than once in six bets produces a loss overall. If one is wrong twice in that period, for example, there is a deficit of no less than six points. Looking at things like this, it becomes clear that laying horses to lose is, in fact, no picnic.

One of the most prominent of the late nineteenth-century bookmakers who was in business in a big way on the racecourse at a time when the modern arrangements for backing horses (long before betting exchanges) were just emerging, had, what he claimed, was an infallible way of making money. The trick lay in a simple game of spinning a coin for heads or tails where the odds are exactly even for both contestants. The bookmaker claimed that he would take money off any man at the game, *provided his opponent, and not he (the bookmaker), made the choice between heads or tails*. The bookmaker won a fortune from the mistakes of others, and was never short of hopeful gamblers willing to take him on on these terms.

It would seem that the bookmaker, who certainly knew his business as well as any of his contemporaries, judged by his success as a 'leviathan of the Ring', was exploiting a fundamental truth about human beings, namely that if they have a straight option in choosing between two outcomes, one right and one wrong, with exactly the same probability of occurring, more often that not they will choose the wrong one. Thus, when it comes to gambling, it is better to be passive than active. The person who accepts bets from fallible human beings has a better chance of coming out on the right side than those who have to make choices. This fallibility may explain, at least in part, why trying to pick out winners from a number of races each day is so difficult, but the opposite scenario of picking horses to lose must surely be affected by it too. Whereas bookmakers, in the passive role, make their money from people choosing losers, the punter who, in the active role, attempts to do likewise, may fall into the trap so successfully exploited by the bookmaker with his game of 'heads or tails'. It is surely much harder from a financial viewpoint for a punter to actively choose a horse to lose, then lay it, than for a conventional bookmaker to be passive and accept bets from others.

It is certainly no easier to be right in laying horses to lose rather than backing them to win. There may be people who can take pleasure in the joyless business of trying to single out horses to get beaten but, mathematical trading apart, there may well be much less profit in it than one might anticipate and certainly much less fun.

BETTING IN RUNNING

On the new betting exchanges it is even possible to bet while a race is being run, where the opportunity of betting at almost unlimited odds right down to the minimum 1.01 (100–1 on) exists. This used to be the preserve of bookmakers and a few insiders in Tattersall's Ring on the racecourse, but with the advent of exchanges, anyone who is prepared to back their judgement on the outcome of a race while it is in progress can watch the race on television and have their bets matched by the exchange in real time on the computer with other punters who wish to stake on their opinion. There is also an obvious arbitrage between the pre-race and in-running markets on a race, and very skilful traders can take advantage of it.

Such betting is really outside the scope of this manual. It is one more instance of how betting exchanges have widened the possibilities of horse racing for those who wish to bet on it. Betfair describe their in-running market as being among the 'advanced uses of Betfair'. In the opinion of the author, it is not suitable for those who wish to back horses for pleasure and possibly some profit, and have bought this manual for that reason.

CONCLUSION

It is to be hoped that this ultra-cautious writer has not been over-vigilant in stressing some of the dangers inherent in the new exchanges. Thousands of ordinary punters have switched to the exchanges and are being rewarded by better odds, for the moment at least. This is surely the way to view what has been described as a revolution in betting. If a 4–1 chance with a bookmaker can be backed at 5.5 (9–2) or 6 (5–1) on an exchange, it would be foolish to ignore this opportunity. Those who have a home computer or wish to participate by telephone, and have the time to devote to their betting, should open an account, even if they only have occasion to use it infrequently. But it is the advice of this book to most of its readers that they should not get involved in astronomical odds beyond what seems reasonable, attempted clever coups and 'advanced' markets – at least until they are fully conversant with every aspect of the new facilities. Even then, it is a distinct possibility that, rather like someone who wishes to play cards for money, they will pay to learn.

Better odds than conventional prices from bookmakers are the big selling point of the exchanges, but despite this perhaps it is fair to wonder whether the bookmaking fraternity will not eventually find ways of competing successfully with the betting exchanges which, themselves the product of new technology, may also evolve further in the long run. No one really knows what the future holds for bookmakers, the betting exchanges and punters alike.

Finally, here are two pieces of advice for betting on the exchanges as they operate at present. Both recommendations are aimed at those who have mastered the basics and now feel they are at the stage where they might be able to exploit situations which involve very long odds when compared with the sort of prices to which years of dealing with conventional bookmakers have accustomed them. This advice is offered without forgetting the caveats set out in the preceding pages about the dangers lying in wait on the exchanges for the inexperienced or unwary punter.

First, never bet at very long odds-on as a backer. By definition there will be very little profit from wagers in the order of 1.02 (50–1 on), 1.10 (10–1 on) and so on, even though plenty of punters regularly indulge in this way in some of the betting-exchange markets. Such bets can and do lose of course. In the world of horse racing there are no certainties in so far as the results of races are concerned. Events repeatedly demonstrate this fact, whatever the long odds-on. Do not try to 'buy money'. Conversely, as a layer, never offer huge odds-against. It is so easy to be caught out.

The second piece of advice, and the other side of the coin, is that with an outcome about which you are really confident, you have nothing to lose by attempting to get matched at spectacular odds. We have said that those who consistently leave orders for fanciful prices as a matter of routine may well be heading for disappointment over a period of time. However, there may be special situations where you are genuinely confident that you will be proved right. These may be exceptional cases calling for a different ordering strategy. Suppose, for example, you have reason to really fancy a horse to win a small race with a very poor field quoted at 33–1 or 40–1 with a bookmaker. There are examples each week of bets on such horses currently being matched at 300 to 400 on the exchanges. It is difficult to comprehend the logic of those who lay bets like these, but lay them they do. There is no reason why you, too, should not leave a request on an exchange website for odds way above what seems reasonable. Even if you are not matched in full at the specified price, you might still eventually find a taker or takers at lesser odds which nevertheless represent a real bargain bet. Failing that, as the time for the race approaches, you may have to accept a much lower price, but at least you will have given yourself the chance of finding a match far in excess of the conventional rate, bets which other punters are at present managing to secure on the exchanges.

There is always a chance, therefore, that if you take the part of optimistic odds-maker, you too will find a match or near-match with someone out there who has an opposite view and who will lay an irrational price, however illogical it may seem. So there is a sound case for sometimes asking for excessive odds as a backer.

However, as we have seen earlier in this chapter, accepting unsolicited offers of gigantic odds may have hidden dangers.

All in all, one word sums up what is needed in approaching betting exchanges, and that word is 'caution'. On the other hand, to exploit to the full the new opportunities they undoubtedly present, at least for the time being, it may be necessary to throw caution to the winds on occasion. As with conventional betting, success is most likely to come to the person who is most adept at the difficult art of risk management, and who is able to combine caution with a speculative approach in such a way that some of the risks accepted pay off in a big way.

PART 5

Racecourse Guide

A track-by-track guide to the most significant betting trends at all courses in Britain

Flat Courses

Ascot

Right-handed. A 1m 6f galloping, triangular course with a stiff 2½f uphill run-in. There is a straight mile with slight undulations.

Grade: A

Effect of the draw: Apart from the undesirability of being drawn in the middle, away from the pace on either side, there was a time when the draw in big fields on the straight course tended not to matter too much, winners and placers coming from either side. In recent years, however, a huge bias has developed in favour of low-drawn horses on fast ground. A high draw and a position on the far side have been the kiss of death. Softer ground might make a difference, for the track drains poorly and unevenly, depending on how much rain has fallen. Check the prevailing bias at the current meeting when such conditions prevail. The draw has little influence on the round course.

Success rate of all favourites: 24.3 per cent.

Favourites' success in two-year-old stakes: 35.5 per cent.

Most significant form: (1st, 2nd, 3rd, 4th last time out) from Sandown. At the Royal meeting, horses that were first or second last time out at Epsom, Newbury, Sandown or York have an excellent record. The Flat season falls into two unequal halves – before Royal Ascot and after. Do not be mesmerised by Royal Ascot form. It is suspect for the future. In the short term in particular, animals which have had a hard race at Ascot in mid-June may take a long time to recover from their exertions.

Trainer tip: M. Johnston's northern stable is very prominent, with a big level-stakes profit from all types of runner. S. bin Suroor's two-year-olds and three-year-olds in stakes races are frequent winners for Frankie Dettori.

N.B. From 2005, Ascot will undergo extensive alterations which are likely to render some of the statistics in the above section no longer valid.

AYR

Left-handed. This galloping, oval track is just over 1m 4f in length with a 4f run-in. In addition there is a straight 6f.

Grade: D

C (Western meeting, September)

Effect of the draw: In large fields over 7f and a mile, low numbers are favoured, especially on soft going. Over 5f and 6f the stands rail is generally favoured. So when the stalls are on the stands side, high numbers should have the best of it on the straight course in races such as the Silver and Ayr Gold Cups, particularly if the ground is good or fast, although very soft ground could reverse this trend. On the infrequent occasions when the stalls are placed on the far side, low numbers may be better. However, it pays to check out races on the straight course from early in a meeting to establish the prevailing bias, because results do not always conform to preconceived ideas of the draw's precise effect.

Success rates of all favourites: 30.3 per cent.

Favourites' success in two-year-old stakes: 36.2 per cent.

Most significant form: (1st, 2nd, 3rd, 4th last time out) from York.

Trainer tip: For many years B.W. Hills has been leading trainer, despite the distance his horses have to travel. His high winning percentage does not stem from masses of runners, and it is usually the stable's less glamorous inmates which are cleverly placed to win.

BATH

Left-handed. This is a kidney-shaped, turning course of just over 1m 4f, with an uphill run-in of 4f. Races over the 5f 11yd and 5f 161yd distances are run from a chute. Galloping horses are favoured but form from the course often fails to stand up elsewhere.

Grade: D

Effect of the draw: Low numbers are favoured in races of 1m 5yd, but the bias in their favour in sprints is not as pronounced as is sometimes claimed, except in very big fields.

Success rate of all favourites: 31.2 per cent.

Favourites' success in two-year-old stakes: 32.1 per cent.

Most significant form: (1st, 2nd, 3rd, 4th last time out) from Salisbury.

Trainer tip: Mrs A.J. Perrett is worth following. Her record in three-year-old maiden and other stakes races is particularly sound.

BEVERLEY

Right-handed. At 1m 3f, this oval, undulating course has an uphill 2½f run-in. The 5f course is on the climb all the way and is especially severe. The downhill run to the straight on the round course can unbalance some horses. Course specialists should be followed.

Grade: D

Effect of the draw: High numbers are dominant in 5f, 7f 100yd and 1m 100yd races, one of the strongest biases in the entire country, for there is a pronounced dog-leg just after the round course meets the straight 5f. However, when the going is very soft or heavy, horses drawn low in large fields can sometimes gain an important advantage by racing up the stands rail, but this should not be counted on. It is often the explanation, however, when the high numbers do not dominate as most punters expect to happen in any circumstance.

Success rate of all favourites: 29.8 per cent.

Favourites' success in two-year-old stakes: 45.4 per cent.

Most significant form: (1st, 2nd, 3rd, 4th last time out) from Beverley itself.

Trainer tip: E.A.L. Dunlop likes to run his two-year-olds at Beverley. They often win.

BRIGHTON

Left-handed. A 1m 4f undulating horseshoe, there is a steep downhill run from half a mile out which lasts for 2f. The actual run-in is 3½f. This sharp track is totally unsuited to galloping types. At summer-holiday meetings the ground can become bone hard, favouring top weights. Course specialists do well but the form is suspect for other courses.

Grade: D

Effect of the draw: Low numbers have some advantage in sprints and races up to 7f 214yd, although high numbers should not be ruled out because of their draw alone. When the ground comes up soft, however, fields usually cross over to race up the stands' rail. This can give those drawn high a decisive edge.

Success rate of all favourites: 33.2 per cent.

Favourites' success in two-year-old stakes: 44.4 per cent.

Most significant form: (1st, 2nd, 3rd, 4th last time out) from Brighton itself. Brighton is on the summer-holiday circuit, and horses running within seven days of a win on one of the small, southern tracks often 'go in' again.

Trainer tip: Both Sir M. Prescott and J.L. Dunlop place their runners exceptionally well here. The former has a higher winning percentage, but the latter is currently ahead in terms of profitability at level stakes.

CARLISLE

Right-handed. A 1m 5f undulating, pear-shaped course with easy turns. Strong, long-striding gallopers are favoured by the long run from the start of the final bend 5f out. The 5f 207yd course starts from a chute. There is a stiff 3½f uphill finish.

Grade: E

Effect of the draw: High numbers are supposed to have an advantage over sprint distances, but it would be wrong to make too much of this. Very soft ground, on the other hand, definitely favours low numbers over 5–6f.

Success rate of all favourites: 27 per cent.

Favourites' success in two-year-old stakes: 40.5 per cent.

Most significant form: (1st, 2nd, 3rd, 4th last time out) from northern tracks in two-year-old races over the minimum trip. Because Carlisle is a fundamentally fair but testing track, betting coups on juveniles are often engineered by small, local trainers whose owners like to bet.

Trainer tip: K.R. Burke's runners should be noted. His senior handicappers and two-year-olds do best.

CATTERICK

Left-handed. This is a sharp, undulating oval course of not much more than 1m 1f with a downhill run into a 3f straight. The track is dog-legged. Quick starters have a big advantage in races up to 7f.

Grade: E

Effect of the draw: On soft ground high numbers are definitely best in races over 5f but, on fast ground, this slight advantage may be reversed in favour of those drawn low. On the round course, over 5f 212yd and 7f, low-drawn horses have a significant edge. A slow start, however, can cancel out any draw advantage in races over a short trip.

Success rate of all favourites: 34.7 per cent.

Favourites' success in two-year-old stakes: 44.1 per cent.

Most significant form: (1st, 2nd, 3rd, 4th last time out) from Catterick itself. Horses which have led all the way to win on this and other northern tracks frequently stage a repeat performance.

Trainer tip: B. Hills is a potent force in weight-for-age and stakes races, but his handicappers do not always run well, despite short prices. The relatively few raiders from P. Cole's southern yard have notched up a 40 per cent strike rate.

CHEPSTOW

Left-handed. A 2m oval course, it is undulating with two sharp turns and a straight run-in of 5f. The straight mile (1m 14yd) is on an extension to the round course.

Grade: D

Effect of the draw: High numbers used to be regarded as favoured on the straight course but, to all intents and purposes, the draw has no influence on results nowadays.

Success rate of all favourites: 28.6 per cent.

Favourites' success in two-year-old stakes: 39.4 per cent.

Most significant form: (1st, 2nd, 3rd, 4th last time out) from Chepstow itself.

Trainer tip: Two-year-olds and three-year-olds trained by Sir M. Stoute are well worth backing in non-handicap races. E.A.L. Dunlop has recently been developing a liking for the track, which might become a pronounced trend.

CHESTER

Left-handed. This is a very tight, flat, circular course of slightly more than 1m. The track turns all the way, which favours handy sorts, though long-striding gallopers can overcome the conformation of the course over long distances, especially on soft ground. Sprints are on the round course. Run-in of barely 2f.

Grade: C

      B (May meeting)

Effect of the draw: Low numbers have a big advantage in races of less than a mile, provided the horse starts quickly enough to get a good position. Soft ground makes the bias even greater.

Success rate of all favourites: 34.2 per cent.

Favourites' success in two-year-old stakes: 49.2 per cent.

Most significant form: (1st, 2nd, 3rd, 4th last time out) from Newmarket. In the spring, horses which ran well at the Craven meeting at Headquarters but which bypassed the Guineas festival often turn up at a nice price at the big May meeting on the Roodeye. Newmarket form is worth following closely later on in the season. Form from Chester, however, needs treating with caution, especially from handicaps. Chester is such a unique venue that a good run there is not necessarily duplicated on more conventional courses.

Trainer tip: Sir M. Stoute averages one winner in four at the Roodeye and his handicap record is far superior to that of any other handler. Also, J.H.M. Gosden's three-year-olds excel here, with a one-in-three success rate. Look out for them in maiden races and handicaps confined to that age group.

DONCASTER

Left-handed. This flat, galloping conical-shaped course of some 2m has a long 4½f run-in that can find out a horse just lacking in stamina for the trip. There is also a straight mile but races of 1m are run on the straight extension and also on the round course.

Grade: C
> A (St Leger meeting, September)
> B (first March and late October meetings)

Effect of the draw: The draw is always an issue for the Spring Mile and Lincoln Handicap when low numbers should dominate if the going is on the soft side. In other ground conditions, study early results from the meeting to detect any prevailing bias on the straight track. Low numbers have some advantage on the round course, but only in big fields.

Success rate of all favourites: 35 per cent.

Favourites' success in two-year-old stakes: 44.8 per cent.

Most significant form: (1st, 2nd, 3rd, 4th last time out) from Newmarket and York. The first 10 home in the Lincoln Handicap might well be followed until 30 June with a stop-at-a-win policy, a system which has produced some very fine results down the years. In other years, though, it can come badly unstuck, usually due to too much clashing among qualifiers competing for the same big prizes. Winners at the big September meeting in the stakes races for two-year-olds are nearly always among the very best of their generation. They should be carefully watched as three-year-olds.

Trainer tip: Although he has plenty of runners here, B.W. Hills still shows a big profit on Town Moor. There is no more skilled trainer at landing a handicap coup with a horse whose form is only partly exposed. Also, Doncaster has long been a happy hunting ground for the cream of the Newmarket stables. Godolphin's record in stakes races, either for two-year-olds or older horses, is outstanding but S. bin Surror's occasional tilts at handicaps usually go astray. H. Cecil's maidens and occasional handicap runners could pay to follow throughout the year.

EPSOM

Left-handed. A 1½m switchback course shaped like a horseshoe. Straight 5f is downhill for 4f with a sharp rise to the post; it is the fastest sprint strip in the world.

Grade: B

A (Derby meeting)

Effect of the draw: Low numbers are at an advantage on the round course except on soft ground when the runners tend to tack over to the stands' rail to get the higher, better ground. The traditional advantage to high numbers over 5f is easily nullified by a fast break from the stalls.

Success rate of all favourites: 27.2 per cent.

Favourites' success in two-year-old stakes: 47.6 per cent.

Most significant form: (1st, 2nd, 3rd, 4th last time out) from Goodwood.

Trainer tip: Epsom trainers do not do as well as they might at their home track. It would be unusual if the Derby meeting passed without at least one winner from M. Johnston's powerful Middleham yard.

FOLKESTONE

Right-handed. This is a 1m 3f pear-shaped, undulating course with tight bends and a run-in of 2½f. There is also a straight 6f course. Small, handy horses are favoured.

Grade: E

Effect of the draw: There is a strong bias in favour of high-drawn horses over 5f and 6f on any ground, especially when the field is likely to split into two. Heavy ground tends to magnify the bias. High numbers are also at an advantage on the round course.

Success rate of all favourites: 30 per cent.

Favourites' success in two-year-old stakes: 30.9 per cent.

Most significant form: (1st, 2nd, 3rd, 4th last time out) from Newmarket. Plenty of horses without recent form to speak of win here, but those which ran well at Headquarters on a recent outing appreciate the drop in class.

Trainer tip: Mrs A.J. Perrett is a prominent player. S.C. Williams enjoys a lot of success with two-year-olds.

GOODWOOD

Mainly right-handed together with a straight 6f. The very fast 5f section is downhill much of the journey. The right-handed loop for races from 7f to 1m 6f joins the straight course for a long run-in of 4f. Distance races start the reverse way up the straight and turn left-handed into the loop. This is one of the few top tracks in the country with a bias against galloping horses, due to the tight turns.

Grade: A

Effect of the draw: Over 7f and 1m high numbers do best though in soft ground the jockeys usually prefer to challenge up the stands rail, thus cancelling out the bias from the stalls. The vital edge that favoured high-drawn horses on the straight course in races such as the Stewards' Cup has reasserted itself in recent years, certainly on good or fast ground. Any deviation from this pronounced bias when the ground becomes soft or heavy should be revealed fairly quickly by monitoring results from the sprint track.

Success rate of all favourites: 30.2 per cent.

Favourites' success in two-year-old stakes: 42.6 per cent.

Most significant form: (1st, 2nd, 3rd, 4th last time out) from all the top courses, but good form from Newmarket stands up best of all. Two-year-old form in all races, including nurseries, works out extremely well. When the ground rides very fast at the 'Glorious' meeting, following first and second favourites from the top yards in every kind of race can reap a handsome reward. The winner and placed horses from the Stewards' Cup generally pay to follow for the rest of the season. Unlike Royal Ascot, the form at the fashionable July/August meeting can be relied upon in the weeks that follow.

Trainer tip: At Glorious Goodwood in July, M. Johnston usually sends a large raiding party. Several winners during the week is frequently the result. Handicappers alone should show a profit over the five days, whatever the fate of the better-class horses. J.H.M. Gosden is consistently successful here throughout the season.

HAMILTON PARK

Right-handed. Straight 6f 5yd course. Races from 1m 65yd up to 1m 5f 9yd start in reverse direction and are run round a pear-shaped loop which rejoins the straight course for a 5f run-in with a stiff uphill finish that dips 3f out. The ground can become bottomless in the dip during spells of wet weather. This unique course is sharp, but galloping types are not necessarily inconvenienced.

Grade: E

Effect of the draw: High numbers are much the best in all races up to 1m 65yd. In soft ground or worse, conditions that often prevail, low-drawn horses have virtually no chance in sprints. The racecourse executive has recently announced that the stalls will always be placed on the stands side except when the ground is heavy. This confirmation of what has been the status quo for some time is unlikely to alter the very strong bias against low-drawn horses on the course.

Success rate of all favourites: 30.9 per cent.

Favourites' success in two-year-old stakes: 44.1 per cent.

Most significant form: Despite the low grade of racing here, or perhaps because of it, many runners are sent from the south. Quite a few are beaten at short odds. In fact, a well-known trainer, now sadly deceased, once remarked: 'If you want to get a good horse beaten, take it to Hamilton.'

Trainer tip: This is a favourite venue for M.R. Channon. His two-year-olds are much more reliable than they used to be. They currently win one in every two races they contest.

HAYDOCK PARK

Left-handed. This is a flat, oval track of 1m 5f with a 4½f run-in which climbs slightly throughout. There is also a straight 6f. The course is a very fair test which favours neither galloping nor handy types.

Grade: B

Effect of the draw: Low numbers do slightly better on the round course in races of 7f 30yd and 1m 30yd but in soft ground most races finish on the stands side, thus rendering the low-draw advantage ineffective. In sprints the recent tendency to place the stalls in the centre rather than on the stands side, and a more active watering policy, have done much to nullify the time-honoured bias in favour of high numbers.

Success rate of all favourites: 31.3 per cent.

Favourites' success in two-year-old stakes: 35.5 per cent.

Most significant form: (1st, 2nd, 3rd, 4th last time out) from all the classier courses, but York is the best single indicator of a good run here. Winners of the best races at Haydock often go on to even better things.

Trainer tip: M.A. Jarvis's Newmarket stable has a consistently high return from only an average number of runners.

KEMPTON PARK

Right-handed. This is a sharp 1m 5f triangular, flat track with a straight course for 5f–6f races which bisects the main circuit. The Jubilee course for 7f up to 1m 2f races joins this at the beginning of the run-in which is about 3½f in length.

Grade: B

Effect of the draw: In races of 5f or 6f low numbers are clearly best in soft ground when the stalls are positioned on the stands side. When the stalls are on the opposite side of the track, high numbers are best, as they are when a big field is likely to spread right across the course. Fast ground renders the bias much less significant. Although high numbers ought, in theory, to be favoured on the turning 7f and 8f, there is little in the records to support this view.

Success rate of all favourites: 29.9 per cent.

Favourites' success in two-year-old stakes: 43.4 per cent.

Most significant form: (1st, 2nd, 3rd, 4th last time out) from Goodwood and Kempton itself.

Trainer tip: J.R. Fanshawe and Mrs A.J. Perrett are two trainers whose runners should be examined very closely. The Perrett three-year-olds in stakes races are worthy of special note.

LEICESTER

Right-handed. A 2m oval course with a run-in of about 5f. Straight course of 1m 8yd, downhill to halfway, then uphill for 2f, finishing on the level.

Grade: C

Effect of the draw: Sometimes prevailing local conditions produce a bias at a particular meeting, but no hard-and-fast rules can be applied over a period of time.

Success rate of all favourites: 30 per cent.

Favourites' success in two-year-old stakes: 42.6 per cent.

Most significant form: (1st, 2nd, 3rd, 4th last time out) from Doncaster.

Trainer tip: Sir M. Stoute has recorded spectacular percentages in stakes races at the Midlands course. There is every reason to think that the trend will continue.

LINGFIELD PARK (TURF)

Left-handed. A sharp, triangular course of nearly 1½m with a run-in of 4f, the course rises to the farthest point from the stands then descends into a tight home bend. Horses need to be handy and adaptable. There is a straight 7f 140yd extension to the main circuit which is downhill for most of the way. Course specialists do well, and it is regarded as an excellent trial ground for Epsom, being a similar track.

Grade: C

Effect of the draw: It is impossible to extract from the statistics any bias that consistently applies from meeting to meeting. Lingfield's watering policies have much to do with this.

Success rate of all favourites: 33.5 per cent.

Favourites' success in two-year-old stakes: 40.1 per cent.

Most significant form: (1st, 2nd, 3rd, 4th last time out). Despite the dissimilarities between the two tracks, Newmarket form is best of all.

Trainer tip: J.L. Dunlop is always a force to be reckoned with in Group and Listed races here.

LINGFIELD PARK (ALL-WEATHER)

Left-handed. The very sharp polytrack, only 1½m in circumference, is inside the turf course. There is a short run-in of about 2f. A chute provides a 1m 4f and 1m 5f start. Held-up horses seem most favoured with the advent of the polytrack.

Grade: E (but form from the polytrack is not reliable on grass)

Effect of the draw: The new polytrack is much fairer than the equitrack it has replaced.

Success rate of all favourites: 35 per cent.

Favourites' success in two-year-old stakes: 44 per cent.

Trainer tip: None of the all-weather specialists stand out, but G. Butler, who is better known for his turf exploits, has a one-in-four strike rate with his dual-purpose runners.

MUSSELBURGH (EDINBURGH)

Right-handed. A 1m 2f oval track with tight bends and a run-in of 4f together with a straight 5f. Galloping types are at a disadvantage.

Grade: E

Effect of the draw: Over 7f 15yd and 1m 16yd high numbers have the advantage. Low numbers are best over 5f when the stalls are on the stands side.

Success rate of all favourites: 32.6 per cent.

Favourites' success in two-year-old stakes: 42.4 per cent.

Most significant form: (1st, 2nd, 3rd, 4th last time out) from Redcar and Musselburgh itself.

Trainer tip: Sir Mark Prescott often goes for a 'touch' at the

Edinburgh course, while another Newmarket trainer, M.L.W. Bell, currently boasts a winning percentage of over 40.

NEWBURY

Left-handed. This is a 1m 7f oval, galloping track with easy turns and a 5f straight. On the round course, races over 7f 64yd and 1m 7yd start from a chute. There is an extension to the main circuit to form a slightly undulating straight mile.

Grade: A

Effect of the draw: When the ground is soft or worse, high numbers are favoured, both on the straight and round courses. When it rides fast, however, low numbers are much the best over the round 7f and 8f track.

Success rate of all favourites: 25.6 per cent.

Favourites' success in two-year-old stakes: 37.1 per cent.

Most significant form: (1st, 2nd, 3rd, 4th last time out) from Newmarket.

Trainer tip: One would not naturally associate M. Johnston with the Berkshire course, but in fact horses from his Middleham yard have completely outshone the locals. All types of race come alike to the Johnston winner machine. Of the locals, J.H.M. Gosden's classy stable has easily the best record.

NEWCASTLE

Left-handed. This is a galloping, triangular circuit of 1m 6f with a stiff uphill 4f run-in. The straight course is 1m 8yd long. The track is exceptionally testing on soft ground.

Grade: C

Effect of the draw: On most ground, low numbers have an edge on the straight course. The swing to high numbers being favoured when racing is up the stands rail now only seems to apply if the going is lightning fast and the stalls are on the stands side.

Success rate of all favourites: 28.1 per cent.

Favourites' success in two-year-old stakes: 25.9 per cent.

Most significant form: (1st, 2nd, 3rd, 4th last time out) from Haydock, and from Beverley for outsiders.

Trainer tip: M.L.W. Bell has taken over from H. Cecil as the Newmarket trainer to follow at Gosforth Park, though runners from the latter's Warren Place stable should still command the utmost respect.

NEWMARKET (ROWLEY MILE COURSE)

Right-handed. A long straight stretch, beginning at the 2m 2f start, which is out of view of the stands, turns into the exceptionally wide home straight, 10f 'Across the Flat' to an uphill finish from the 'Dip' 1½f out. Galloping types are obviously in their element.

Grade: A

Effect of the draw: There is no bias in most races, although in very big fields when the stalls are stretched right across the course, a middle to high number is a distinct advantage.

Success rate of all favourites: 31.3 per cent.

Favourites' success in two-year-old stakes: 41.8 per cent.

Most significant form: As befits the headquarters of racing, Newmarket is very cosmopolitan in terms of the form of competing horses, but Yorkshire stables should be noted for an occasional handicap raid. The booking of a top jockey from the south is often a big clue about an impending coup. Apart from that, Newmarket's handicaps are a nightmare. The relatively high winning percentage in two-year-old non-handicaps could be the backer's salvation.

Trainer tip: J.H.M. Gosden is the trainer to follow at Headquarters, despite the move to Manton.

NEWMARKET (JULY COURSE)

Right-handed. There is a long straight stretch from the 2m 24yd start, which turns almost at right angles into the straight Bunbury Mile. The course undulates slightly until it begins to climb to the winning post 1f out. Absolutely fair test which again favours the long-striding animal.

Grade: A

Effect of the draw: None. The course is only used in the summer months when the going is nearly always fast. The rarity of cut in the ground, however, produces no bias.

Success rate of all favourites: 29.9 per cent.

Favourites' success in two-year-old stakes: 43.3 per cent.

Most significant form: (1st, 2nd, 3rd, 4th last time out) from Ascot. Yorkshire trainers specialise in handicap coups on this course as well as on the Rowley Mile.

Trainer tip: Sir M. Prescott's operation usually hits peak form just as racing moves from the Rowley Mile to the July Course. Take note of his runners there during the later summer months. E.J. Alston is a Lancashire trainer who likes to land a gamble in handicaps.

NOTTINGHAM

Left-handed. This is a 1m 4f oval course with easy turns and a 4½f straight. There is also a straight 6f 15yd track as an extension to the circuit. The whole arena is exceptionally flat.

Grade: D

Effect of the draw: At Nottingham the stalls are usually placed on the stands side, which gives an edge to high-drawn horses, especially on soft going. When the stalls are occasionally positioned on the far side, low numbers are best, though it would be wrong to make too much of this. Low numbers, however, are definitely at an advantage in big fields on the turning course.

Success rate of all favourites: 32 per cent.

Favourites' success in two-year-old stakes: 46.9 per cent.

Trainer tip: J.H.M. Gosden is the trainer to note here, especially in non-handicaps. The Manton trainer likes to place good two-year-olds at the Colwick Park venue. They often go on to much better things.

PONTEFRACT

Left-handed. A pear-shaped course of about 2m, it is almost all on the turn. The run-in is only 2f long and there is no straight course.

Grade: D

Effect of the draw: Low numbers have a distinct advantage in races up to 1m 4yd. On soft ground, however, the situation changes to the extent that high numbers are then much the best. If, however, the ground is so heavy that the stalls are moved to the outside of the course, the advantage of a high draw is cancelled out. A further factor confusing the picture is that any draw edge will be nullified by a slow start. Nevertheless, the astute punter can make money by mastering the ramifications of the draw at this quirky course.

Success rate of all favourites: 26.9 per cent.

Favourites' success in two-year-old stakes: 42.6 per cent.

Most significant form: Two-year-olds strong enough to win on the stiff sprint course often run well in better company in near-at-hand engagements.

Trainer tip: The stable of M.A. Jarvis has an outstanding strike rate if handicaps are ignored. M. Dods likes a tilt at the handicaps and sometimes comes up with a winner at a big price.

REDCAR

Left-handed. 1m 5f oval course with a 5f run-in and a straight mile. Though the course is narrow, galloping horses are not inconvenienced.

Grade: C

Effect of the draw: With the draw traditionally supposed to favour high numbers on the straight mile, this is confirmed when the stalls are placed nearest to the stands as they nearly always are. In very big fields, however, quite often a feature of Redcar cards, horses racing out wide in the centre of the course win their share. On the round course low numbers are favoured.

Success rate of all favourites: 29.2 per cent.

Favourites' success in two-year-old stakes: 35.5 per cent.

Most significant form: (1st, 2nd, 3rd, 4th last time out) from Thirsk for winning outsiders.

Trainer tip: C.A. Dwyer's runners are not all that frequent but may repay careful study. T.D. Easterby's strike rate goes up by leaps and bounds when K. Darley is in the plate.

RIPON

Right-handed. A 1m 5f undulating, oval circuit, this track has tight bends and a 5f run-in. The straight course is 6f long.

Grade: C

Effect of the draw: There is a slight advantage to high numbers on the round course over a mile. In sprints, although the stalls are usually on the stands side (low numbers), on fast ground high numbers are much favoured when the field is likely to split into two, enabling them to take a position on the far rail and cash in on a strip of quick ground over there. A middle draw is always a serious disadvantage. Low numbers in 5f–6f races seem best in small fields when the entire field races up the stands rail.

Success rate of all favourites: 31.7 per cent.

Favourites' success in two-year-old stakes: 42.2 per cent.

Most significant form: (1st, 2nd, 3rd, 4th last time out) from Doncaster.

Trainer tip: This is another northern course where J.L. Dunlop's two-year-olds are outstanding. Also, maidens and other non-handicap performers trained by B.W. Hills go in with pleasing regularity.

SALISBURY

Right-handed. The straight mile has a dog-leg 5f out and an uphill finish of 4f. Races of more than a mile on a loop which turns sharply right-handed into the straight course for a home run of 6½f. A compact course favouring handier types, though the straight mile suits all horses.

Grade: C

Effect of the draw: On fast ground, runners drawn high dominate on the straight mile. When the ground is soft, however, low numbers may have the call. On the turning course high numbers are best.

Success rate of all favourites: 32.9 per cent.

Favourites' success in two-year-old stakes: 40.8 per cent.

Most significant form: (1st, 2nd, 3rd, 4th last time out) from Goodwood and Windsor. Two-year-olds often go on to bigger successes at top meetings, making the course Grade B for juveniles.

Trainer tip: Local trainer R. Charlton dominates at this, his home course. Concentrate on his runners in stakes races.

SANDOWN PARK

Right-handed. A 1m 5f oval course with easy turns but a stiff run-in of just over 4f. The separate 5f course bisecting the main track is also uphill.

Grade: A

Effect of the draw: On the separate 5f course high numbers have a big advantage, particularly when there is a lot of 'give' in the ground and the stalls are on the far side. If the stalls are on the stands side, low numbers are better but only slightly. However, the ground gets progressively faster as the far rail is approached – high numbers may again assert if, in a biggish field, a horse can get across the course without being too far behind the leaders. As the ground gets softer, these trends are magnified proportionately. Over 7f 16yd and 1m 14yd high numbers are marginally superior.

Success rate of all favourites: 26.8 per cent.

Favourites' success in two-year-old stakes: 34.5 per cent.

Most significant form: (1st, 2nd, 3rd, 4th last time out) from Goodwood.

Trainer tip: Sir M. Stoute has a brilliant record with juveniles. P. Cole's record in three-year-old handicaps is currently second to none.

SOUTHWELL (ALL-WEATHER)

Left-handed. This is quite a sharp, true, oval course with a run-in of about 3f. The fibresand track is outside the grass course. Both courses have a straight 5f.

Grade: E (but form from the all-weather surface is not reliable on grass)

Effect of the draw: Except on the 5f straight course, low numbers are much the best. Anything drawn wide tends to lose ground on the bends.

Success rate of all favourites: 31.6 per cent.

Favourites' success in two-year-old stakes: 36 per cent.

Trainer tip: T.D. Barron makes a habit of coming up with long-priced winners.

THIRSK

Left-handed. A flat, oval 1m 2f track, there are sharp turns and a 4f run-in. The straight course is 6f long.

Grade: C

Effect of the draw: High numbers are definitely favoured in sprint races, except on soft or heavy ground. In big fields it is best to be drawn near the rail. Low numbers have the edge up to a mile on the turning course.

Success rate of all favourites: 34.7 per cent.

Favourites' success in two-year-old stakes: 35.2 per cent.

Most significant form: (1st, 2nd, 3rd, 4th last time out) from Doncaster.

Trainer tip: Sir M. Stoute does extremely well in 3-y-o stakes races. Even his runners in all-aged handicaps have a sound scoring rate.

WARWICK

Left-handed. A circular 1m 6f course with a 2½f run-in. The 5f track is dog-legged.

Grade: E

Effect of the draw: Low numbers do best on good or faster ground because the course's left-handed bends favour them. When the ground is really soft, on the other hand, high numbers are favoured in all events up to a mile as the ground up the stands rail is then much faster.

Success rate of all favourites: 31.1 per cent.

Favourites' success in two-year-old stakes: 44.6 per cent.

Most significant form: (1st, 2nd, 3rd, 4th last time out) from Wolverhampton. A fair effort at Warwick's all-weather neighbour is often the precursor of a winning run on a track which is of a similar grade, despite the difference in surface.

Trainer tip: Sir M. Stoute's runners currently win one in three. M.C. Pipe's 33 per cent success rate in staying handicaps is an interesting statistic.

WINDSOR

Right-handed. A very flat 1m 4f figure-of-eight track with sharp turns, it has a long run-in of 5f, giving the galloping types plenty of time to get balanced for the finish. The 5f 217yd track is not quite straight.

Grade: D

Effect of the draw: Sprinters drawn high are clearly best, but only if the ground is good or fast. Soft going favours low-drawn horses.

Success rate of all favourites: 27.9 per cent.

Favourites' success in two-year-old stakes: 32.7 per cent.

Most significant form: (1st, 2nd, 3rd, 4th last time out) from Windsor itself.

Trainer tip: Provided his two-year-olds are ignored, punters can cash in on Sir M. Stoute's penchant for winning at the Thameside course.

WOLVERHAMPTON (ALL-WEATHER)

Left-handed. This oval course is only 1m long and, with a straight of about 2f, it obviously has very sharp bends.

Grade: E (but form from the all-weather surface is not reliable on grass)

Effect of the draw: Horses which can come up the centre of the course have an advantage. Harrowing of the fibresand, however, often changes the bias. In general, a high draw is preferable, provided the horse can keep up with the pace, but a low draw tends to favour an animal which makes its run late in the race off the cambered bend.

Success rate of all favourites: 33.9 per cent.

Favourites' success in two-year-old stakes: 34.4 per cent.

Most significant form: (1st, 2nd, 3rd, 4th last time out) from Wolverhampton itself.

Trainer tip: All-weather specialist N.P. Littmoden regularly turns a profit here. Sir Mark Prescott sometimes slips in an unexposed, quality animal once the Turf season is well advanced, and his charges are just about to fire. Keep your eyes peeled for this unusual manoeuvre. It often signals a horse which may run up a sequence.

YARMOUTH

Left-handed. A 1m 5f oval circuit with a 5f run-in, the course is flat and favours big, long-striding horses. All races up to 1m are on the straight course.

Grade: C

Effect of the draw: Yarmouth has a policy of moving the stalls about. When the stalls are on the stands side, high numbers are best on the straight track. If the stalls are on the far side or in the centre, however, low numbers are preferred except in biggish fields when high-drawn horses may again be favoured. However, low numbers come into their own once more when the ground is generally soft in a very big field. A middle draw is nearly always fatal on soft ground in large fields. Low numbers have the edge over middle distances.

Success rate of all favourites: 32.4 per cent.

Favourites' success in two-year-old stakes: 39.5 per cent.

Most significant form: Top two-year-olds from the big Newmarket yards often make their debut here.

Trainer tip: J.L. Dunlop's juveniles can be relied upon to do at least as well as contenders from Newmarket.

YORK

Left-handed. This is a 2m horseshoe-shaped, galloping track with a 5f run-in. There is a straight 6f and a chute for races over 6f 214yd.

Grade: A

Effect of the draw: Low to middle numbers are best in all races up to 6f 214yd, especially on soft or even heavily watered ground. Races over a distance also favour low-drawn horses which can hold a position near the inside rail.

Success rate of all favourites: 27.7 per cent.

Favourites' success in two-year-old stakes: 38.2 per cent.

Most significant form: (1st, 2nd, 3rd, 4th last time out) from Newmarket. All the handicaps at York are exceptionally tricky because of the keenness of the competition there. The form from York, where the best horses from the north and the south meet, is very reliable. The May meeting in particular is one of the best guides to the near future in the racing calendar.

Trainer tip: S. bin Suroor's three-year-olds are outstanding in stakes races, but his two-year-olds are best watched.

National Hunt Courses

As with the Flat, all course gradings are unofficial. National Hunt Flat form is included in the winning percentages for all favourites but, because of the problems associated with races of this type, they are excluded from the recommendations for best and worst races for favourites. The latter are not based solely on winning percentages or the level-stakes profit or loss position. In all cases a recommendation has been arrived at by taking into account both these factors in relation to one another against the background of other relevant form factors. Similarly, the trainer tips are not necessarily for handlers with the highest strike rates or best profit figures. Other factors bearing on both the past and the future have been considered in framing them.

AINTREE

Grand National Course: Left-handed. This is a flat circuit of 2m 2f with 16 extremely stiff fences, despite repeated modifications. There is a long run-in of 494yd with an elbow.

Mildmay Course: Left-handed. A sharp, flat course of 1m 4f, the fences are only of average difficulty. There is a run-in of 260yd. Front runners are favoured.

Grade: A

Success rate of all favourites: 33.6 per cent.

Best races for favourites: Novice hurdles 45.1 per cent.

Worst races for favourites: Weight-for-age hurdles (excluding novice hurdles) 20 per cent.

Trainer tip: J.J. O'Neill shows a particular liking for the place. Trainer L. Lungo and jockey Tony Dobbin are also a combination to be feared in races below top-class.

ASCOT

Right-handed. This triangular course of 1m 6f is level and enables horses to gallop freely but is still testing, with very stiff fences. The uphill finish of 240yd adds to the difficulties.

Grade: A

Success rate of all favourites: 34.9 per cent.

Best races for favourites: Handicap chases 33.9 per cent.

Worst races for favourites: Handicap hurdles 20 per cent.

Most significant form: (1st, 2nd, 3rd, 4th last time out) from Cheltenham and Ascot itself.

Trainer tip: At a jumping venue which though in the top flight is not as competitive as it might be, M.C. Pipe dominates the winning percentages. Stable jockey Tony McCoy is usually in the plate for the winners.

N.B. From 2005, Ascot will undergo extensive alterations which are likely to render some of the information and statistics in this section no longer valid.

AYR

Left-handed. A 1m 4f fair, flat, galloping track. Fences slightly more severe than average, but there is no water jump. There is a run-in of 210yd.

Grade: C

  B (Scottish National meeting, April)

Success rate of all favourites: 41 per cent.

Best races for favourites: Handicap hurdles 48.1 per cent.

Worst races for favourites: Handicap chases 35.2 per cent.

Most significant form: Form from the Grand National meeting at Liverpool is untrustworthy at the big April meeting here. Results from Kelso are very instructive about more ordinary fare.

Trainer tip: F. Murphy does not have too many runners at the Scottish seaside track, but they are always worth a second look. A.C. Whillans has a good strike rate, and his charges show a profit over a period of time.

BANGOR-ON-DEE

Left-handed. A 1m 4f round, turning course with sharp bends. All hurdle races are run on the inside track of the circuit. The fences are of average difficulty. The run-in is a long 325yd. The track favours handy types and front runners. The ground can become very testing, making it foolhardy to support a horse whose fitness is in doubt.

Grade: E

Success rate of all favourites: 34 per cent.

Best races for favourites: Weight-for-age chases (excluding novice chases) 42.9 per cent.

Worst races for favourites: Weight-for-age hurdles (excluding novice hurdles) 15 per cent.

Most significant form: (1st, 2nd, 3rd, 4th last time out) from Stratford.

Trainer tip: J.J. O'Neill usually makes the journey from the Cotswolds pay. P.R. Webber's runners in novice hurdles and handicap chases are nearly always fit and fancied with a current strike rate of one in four.

CARLISLE

Right-handed. A 1m 5f stiff, undulating circuit with average-size fences. The severe, uphill run-in measures 300yd. Stamina is essential on a course that does not drain well in periods of very wet weather.

Grade: D

Success rate of all favourites: 36.8 per cent.

Best races for favourites: Novice hurdles 41.5 per cent.

Worst races for favourites: Novice chases 25.9 per cent.

Most significant form: (1st, 2nd, 3rd, 4th last time out) from Carlisle itself.

Trainer tip: Carlisle is a stiff jumping track and there is no finer trainer in the North of a stayer than Mrs M. Reveley. Her runners in races over the longer distances are consistently profitable.

CARTMEL

Left-handed. A sharp, undulating track of just over a mile with testing fences. The 800yd run-in is the longest in the country. Cartmel favours small, handy horses.

Grade: E

Success rate of all favourites: 30.5 per cent.

Best races for favourites: Weight-for-age hurdles (excluding novice hurdles) 47.4 per cent.

Worst races for favourites: Handicap chases 19 per cent.

Trainer tip: Even distant Cartmel is not too far for M.C. Pipe's runners to travel in search of prize money. His strike rate is currently down 10 per cent from three years ago, but it is still extremely high at around 40 per cent. P. Bowen and Mrs M. Reveley, too, both score frequently at the infrequent meetings on the track.

CATTERICK

Left-handed. A sharp, oval track of 1m 1f which is wider and not quite so tight as the Flat course. The fences are easy. There is a run-in of 240yd. Well-balanced front runners perform well.

Grade: D

Success rate of all favourites: 36.7 per cent.

Best races for favourites: Handicap chases 56.2 per cent.

Worst races for favourites: Handicap hurdles 20.6 per cent.

Most significant form: (1st, 2nd, 3rd, 4th last time out) from Catterick itself.

Trainer tip: R.A. Fahey trains nearby at Butterwick in North Yorkshire. His winning percentage is 26 at the time of writing and he will surely continue to show a level-stakes profit on his home ground.

CHELTENHAM

Left-handed. This is a 1m 4f oval track with extremely stiff fences. There is a testing, uphill run-in of just over 350yd on the Old Course. The New Course finish is half a furlong less at 237yd, again up the famous hill. Horses must stay every yard of the trip to score.

Grade: A (Old and New Courses)

Success rate of all favourites: 34.8 per cent.

Best races for favourites: Weight-for-age hurdles (excluding novice hurdles) 40 per cent.

Worst races for favourites: Handicap chases 25.8 per cent.

Most significant form: (1st, 2nd, 3rd, 4th last time out) from Kempton and Cheltenham itself. The first half-dozen home in the Gold Cup Handicap Chase in November are usually worth following for the rest of the season.

Trainer tip: The Festival apart, N.J. Henderson has become something of a course specialist.

CHEPSTOW

Left-handed. A 2m undulating, oval course with a very long straight. Fences are of above-average difficulty. The downhill run-in is 240yd long. The going is often very testing.

Grade: B

Success rate of all favourites: 35.5 per cent.

Best races for favourites: Weight-for-age hurdles (excluding novice hurdles) 51.3 per cent.

Worst races for favourites: Weight-for-age chases (excluding novice chases) 16.7 per cent.

Most significant form: (1st, 2nd, 3rd, 4th last time out) from Exeter and Chepstow itself.

Trainer tip: P.F. Nicholls is now a frequent visitor to the winner's enclosure at the Welsh course. Do not expect big prices about the roughly one in three horses that win, but when the occasional runner at a longer-than-usual price is included, the Somerset handler shows a very sound profit at level stakes.

DONCASTER

Left-handed. The flat, galloping track with easy bends inside the Flat course is 2m long. The fences are of moderate difficulty and there is a run-in of 250yd.

Grade: B

Success rate of all favourites: 34.1 per cent.

Best races for favourites: Novice hurdles 46 per cent.

Worst races for favourites: Handicap chases 31.9 per cent.

Most significant form: (1st, 2nd, 3rd, 4th last time out) from Wetherby.

Trainer tip: Both M.C. Pipe and N.J. Henderson currently have a 30 plus percentage here. Town Moor's wide, open spaces and easy fences are just the thing for some of the lesser lights in both stables.

EXETER

Right-handed. This is a hilly 2m course. The fences are slightly above average and the fairly stiff, uphill run-in is of 300yd.

Grade: D

Success rate of all favourites: 35.5 per cent.

Best races for favourites: Handicap hurdles 32.8 per cent.

Worst races for favourites: Handicap chases 29.7 per cent.

Most significant form: (1st, 2nd, 3rd, 4th last time out) from Exeter itself.

Trainer tip: This course used to be a Pipe/McCoy benefit, but of late the runners of P.J. Hobbs have stolen a march in all departments.

FAKENHAM

Left-handed. This almost square track of about 1m is sharp but the fences are easy. There is an uphill run-in of 200yd.

Grade: E

Success rate of all favourites: 36 per cent.

Best races for favourites: Novice chases 50 per cent.

Worst races for favourites: Handicap hurdles 25.4 per cent.

Trainer tip: N.J. Henderson is the big trainer to follow, but look out for the runners of Mrs P. Sly. The Newmarket trainer often produces a winning outsider here.

FOLKESTONE

Right-handed. This is an easy track of 1m 3f with easy fences and no complications. The run-in is about a furlong for chases, slightly more for hurdles.

Grade: D

Success rate of all favourites: 38.7 per cent.

Best races for favourites: Novice chases 49 per cent.

Worst races for favourites: Handicap hurdles 28.4 per cent.

Trainer tip: M.C. Pipe's percentage is outstanding at currently over 50, though prices will be short. N.J. Henderson also has an excellent strike rate, but for a 'touch' at a nice price take note of the runners of D.M. Grissell. The average starting price of his winners is over 10–1, so a little imagination will be needed to find them.

FONTWELL

Left-handed. The hurdle course is a tight oval of 1m round. The chase course is a figure-of-eight. The fences are moderate and the run-in is 230yd. The horses-for-courses theory works here.

Grade: D

Success rate of all favourites: 34.1 per cent.

Best races for favourites: Novice chases 48.6 per cent.

Worst races for favourites: Handicap hurdles 21.9 per cent.

Most significant form: (1st, 2nd, 3rd, 4th last time out) from Plumpton and Fontwell itself.

Trainer tip: P.F. Nicholls is way ahead of his contemporaries, with a winning percentage of around 35. His hurdlers are just as potent as his chasers.

HAYDOCK PARK

Left-handed. It is a 1m 5f flat, oval course with the hurdles track inside the chase course which, in turn, is inside the Flat circuit. The drop fences are very severe. There is a long run-in of 440yd. A fair but tough test.

Grade: A

Success rate of all favourites: 42.7 per cent.

Best races for favourites: Novice chases 47.6 per cent.

Worst races for favourites: Handicap chases 27.1 per cent.

Most significant form: (1st, 2nd, 3rd, 4th last time out) from Wetherby and Haydock itself.

Trainer tip: On a course which has always been good for fancied horses, Miss V. Williams does well, and Mrs S.J. Smith is not far behind her in percentage terms, usually at better prices.

HEREFORD

Right-handed. A 1m 4f square course with nine moderately difficult fences. A 300yd run-in from the final fence is slightly downhill. Despite the square shape, the circuit has easy turns. However, the home turn, which is on falling ground, is quite sharp. Speed is at a premium.

Grade: E

Success rate of all favourites: 38.3 per cent.

Best races for favourites: Novice hurdles 43.9 per cent.

Worst races for favourites: Weight-for-age chases (excluding novice chases) 25.3 per cent.

Most significant form: (1st, 2nd, 3rd, 4th last time out) from Hereford itself.

Trainer tip: N.J. Henderson's Lambourn yard produces many winners. Recently Miss H.C. Knight seems to have developed a liking for the track, a trend which may well continue.

HEXHAM

Left-handed. A 1m 4f undulating course. The fences are fairly easy. The home straight is on the climb with a run-in of 250yd, making this a testing track.

Grade: E

Success rate of all favourites: 35.1 per cent.

Best races for favourites: Novice hurdles 45.3 per cent.

Worst races for favourites: Handicap chases 18.8 per cent.

Most significant form: (1st, 2nd, 3rd, 4th last time out) from Carlisle.

Trainer tip: The quality of the racing is not great here and, with fields on the large side, finding winners is seldom easy. Fancied runners from the yard of N.G. Richards, however, may keep the punter on the right side.

HUNTINGDON

Right-handed. A flat, oval 1m 4f course. Some of the fences are of above-average difficulty, and there is a run-in of 200yd. The long-striding animal who can race up with the pace is admirably suited here.

Grade: C

Success rate of all favourites: 36.2 per cent.

Best races for favourites: Novice hurdles 42.2 per cent.

Worst races for favourites: Weight-for-age chases (excluding novice chases) 27.3 per cent.

Most significant form: (1st, 2nd, 3rd, 4th last time out) from Worcester.

Trainer tip: One name which consistently appears in the winning lists here is that of Ian Williams. He should continue to show a profit from runners which, though not as plentiful as from the bigger yards, are always tuned up to run really well.

KELSO

Left-handed. This is a tight, oval track with part of the hurdle course inside the main circuit of 1m 3f. The fences are of only average difficulty. Sharp turns disadvantage the galloping types. There is a long, stiff, uphill finish of 490yd from the final fence.

Grade: E

Success rate of all favourites: 40.1 per cent.

Best races for favourites: Novice hurdles 52.9 per cent.

Worst races for favourites: Handicap chases 28.2 per cent.

Most significant form: (1st, 2nd, 3rd, 4th last time out) from Ayr and Kelso itself.

Trainer tip: This is another course where N.G. Richards's runners should be closely monitored. L. Lungo has a one-in-four strike rate, only in part from horses with exposed, public form. Do not try to spot winning outsiders. There will be few clues in the form book.

KEMPTON

Right-handed. A flat, triangular circuit of 1m 5f. The fences are stiff. Short run-in of 175yd accentuates the fact that speedy types are much favoured.

Grade: A

Success rate of all favourites: 34 per cent.

Best races for favourites: Novice hurdles 41.7 per cent.

Worst races for favourites: Handicap hurdles 24.6 per cent.

Most significant form: (1st, 2nd, 3rd, 4th last time out) from Kempton itself.

Trainer tip: N.J. Henderson is especially fond of the metropolitan course if his percentage of winners is anything to go by. He sometimes has a field day here. Stable jockey Mick Fitzgerald usually gets it right if the yard has more than one in a race.

LEICESTER

Right-handed. This very undulating, sharp, oval course is 1m 6f long. The fences are quite demanding. There is a run-in of 250yd. This is a searching test and because the going can get very heavy in winter it adds to the rigours imposed by the course.

Grade: D

Success rate of all favourites: 36.4 per cent.

Best races for favourites: Novice chases 49.3 per cent.

Worst races for favourites: Weight-for-age chases (excluding novice chases) 24.7 per cent.

Trainer tip: C.J. Mann has a lot of winners from not too many runners. M.C. Pipe and N.J. Henderson are dominant among the big yards.

LINGFIELD PARK

Left-handed. A round track outside the Flat circuit measuring 1m 7f. The fences are of slightly above-average difficulty. A 200yd run-in. The course is one for well-balanced horses and course specialists.

Grade: C

Favourites: No recent statistics available.

Trainer tip: The ubiquitous M. Pipe is likely to remain the trainer to follow.

LUDLOW

Right-handed. A 1m 4f oval course. The fences are of moderate difficulty and there is a long run-in of 450yd. This flat track has sharp bends at the entrance and exit to the straight.

Grade: E

Success rate of all favourites: 39.6 per cent.

Best races for favourites: Novice hurdles 44 per cent.

Worst races for favourites: Handicap chases 27.3 per cent.

Most significant form: (1st, 2nd, 3rd, 4th last time out) from Hereford.

Trainer tip: N.J. Henderson's charges currently yield a win percentage close on 40. No other trainer can begin to match this.

MARKET RASEN

Right-handed. A 1m 2f oval course which is sharp and undulating. The fences are moderate in difficulty. The run-in is a furlong in length. Handy sorts are best, with horses up with the pace likely to score if good enough.

Grade: D

Success rate of all favourites: 34.1 per cent.

Best races for favourites: Novice hurdles 44.1 per cent.

Worst races for favourites: Handicap hurdles 25.5 per cent.

Most significant form: (1st, 2nd, 3rd, 4th last time out) from Market Rasen itself. The form works out badly at this 'farmers' meeting' where many of the lesser lights of the jumping game do not get too much competition from the top yards.

Trainer tip: The chasers of D.L. Williams usually repay an interest. Namesake Ian Williams has a good all-round record.

MUSSELBURGH (EDINBURGH)

Right-handed. A sharp 1m 2f oval course. The fences are easy but, positioned close together, they require accurate jumping around the tight, fast turns. The run-in is only 150yd long. Adaptable horses are obviously favoured.

Grade: E

Success rate of all favourites: 39.4 per cent.

Best races for favourites: Novice hurdles 52.1 per cent.

Worst races for favourites: Handicap chases 24.7 per cent.

Trainer tip: Look out for L. Lungo's runners when jockey Tony Dobbin is aboard. The trainer's strike rate shoots up in this circumstance.

NEWBURY

Left-handed. A level, galloping track. It is 1m 7f in length, lying inside the Flat circuit. The fences are severe and there is a run-in of 255yd. It makes for a fair test of a jumper but horses lacking in courage are soon found out.

Grade: A

Success rate of all favourites: 36.7 per cent.

Best races for favourites: Weight-for-age hurdles (excluding novice hurdles) 49 per cent.

Worst races for favourites: Handicap chases 27 per cent.

Most significant form: (1st, 2nd, 3rd, 4th last time out) from Cheltenham and Newbury itself.

Trainer tip: At the Berkshire course, N.J. Henderson again shows his liking for tracks in the London area. More than one winner in five is an excellent return for a level-stakes profit at such a competitive venue.

NEWCASTLE

Left-handed. This is a 1m 6f oval, galloping circuit with testing fences and a run-in of 220yd. The home straight is uphill.

Grade: B

Success rate of all favourites: 39.2 per cent.

Best races for favourites: Novice chases 61 per cent.

Worst races for favourites: Handicap hurdles 33 per cent.

Most significant form: (1st, 2nd, 3rd, 4th last time out) from Ayr.

Trainer tip: Over time, Mrs M. Reveley has built up a huge level-stakes gain at the track. There seems no reason why things should not go on as before.

NEWTON ABBOT

Left-handed. Another flat, oval course, it is only 1m 1f with tight bends. The fences are of moderate difficulty. The run-in is 300yd and the track is ideal for the quick, well-balanced runner.

Grade: C

Success rate of all favourites: 39.3 per cent.

Best races for favourites: Weight-for-age races over hurdles and fences (excluding novice races) 51.5 per cent combined.

Worst races for favourites: Handicap chases 30.6 per cent.

Most significant form: (1st, 2nd, 3rd, 4th last time out) from Newton Abbot itself. Winning favourites at short prices used to be a feature of most meetings, but of late the racing here has become much more competitive, and to some extent it has dried up as a source of favourite bankers, even in the summer months.

Trainer tip: West country trainer P.F. Nicholls is the man to be on here. His runners should continue to show a profit from level stakes.

PERTH

Right-handed. The flat circuit is just over 1m 2f in length. The fences are fairly easy. The run-in is 300yd in hurdle races and 450yd on the chase course. The bends are very tight and badly inconvenience the galloping type of animal.

Grade: E

Success rate of all favourites: 30.8 per cent.

Best races for favourites: Novice hurdles 40.9 per cent.

Worst races for favourites: Handicap chases 19 per cent.

Trainer tip: Now that J.J. O'Neill has moved south, F. Murphy is probably the most reliable trainer to watch closely at the Scone circuit. His 22 per cent strike rate and a current profit of nearer 40 than 30 points over three seasons are much the best figures. Two who frequently land a coup with a well-placed animal are J.S. Goldie and C. Grant.

PLUMPTON

Left-handed. A small, tight course of 1m 1f with sharp bends. The fences are fairly easy. The back straight is all downhill, but a stiff, uphill finish 200yd from the last bend makes this a difficult course to negotiate. It thus favours track specialists.

Grade: E

Success rate of all favourites: 36.6 per cent.

Best races for favourites: Novice hurdles 45.6 per cent.

Worst races for favourites: Handicap chases 25.7 per cent.

Most significant form: (1st, 2nd, 3rd, 4th last time out) from Plumpton itself.

Trainer tip: Of the top yards, P.F. Nicholls leads the way with one winner for every three runners. T.P. McGovern's hurdlers are definitely worth a second glance whenever one is down to run.

SANDOWN PARK

Right-handed. An oval course, it is about 1m 5f in length. The fences are quite severe and there is a testing uphill run-in of 300yd which favours front runners which see the trip out.

Grade: A

Success rate of all favourites: 38.8 per cent.

Best races for favourites: Hunter chases 63.2 per cent. Novice hurdles 53.7 per cent.

Worst races for favourites: Handicap hurdles 23.7 per cent.

Most significant form: (1st, 2nd, 3rd, 4th last time out) from Cheltenham.

Trainer tip: A quarter of N.J. Henderson's candidates run out winners. Since he is just as effective in handicaps as stakes races, that is sufficient to give a handsome profit to a level stake.

SEDGEFIELD

Left-handed. This is a sharp, oval track of 1m 2f with average fences. A 3f downhill run to the final obstacle is followed by a tough 200yd climb to the finishing post. It is another course where horses with winning form at the venue continue to do well.

Grade: E

Success rate of all favourites: 36.6 per cent.

Best races for favourites: Novice chases 47.5 per cent.

Worst races for favourites: Handicap hurdles 24.2 per cent. Weight-for-age hurdles 27.3 per cent.

Trainer tip: If you believe in 'trainers for courses', go for the runners of L. Lungo.

SOUTHWELL

Left-handed. The turf course inside the all-weather track is only 1m 1f in circumference. Fences are average. The run-in is 250yd long and the course is extremely tight, especially for chasers.

Grade: E

Success rate of all favourites: 36.2 per cent.

Best races for favourites: Novice hurdles 52.7 per cent.

Worst races for favourites: Handicap chases 27.5 per cent.

Most significant form: (1st, 2nd, 3rd, 4th last time out) from Market Rasen.

Trainer tip: Miss V. Williams has a really outstanding record from just the occasional runner. Her novices, under both codes, are particularly dangerous.

STRATFORD

Left-handed. This is a sharp, flat, triangular course of just over 1m 2f where the fences are moderate. The run-in is 200yd long.

Grade: C

Success rate of all favourites: 38.8 per cent.

Best races for favourites: Weight-for-age hurdles (excluding novice hurdles) 52.1 per cent.

Worst races for favourites: Handicap chases 27.6 per cent.

Most significant form: (1st, 2nd, 3rd, 4th last time out) from Worcester and Stratford itself.

Trainer tip: The Midlands track has been a ready source of winners for J.J. O'Neill since he moved to the Cotswolds.

TAUNTON

Right-handed. A flat, oval track of 1m 2f, cambered to offset the tightness of the bends, with an uphill run-in of 150yd. The ground tends to be very heavy in winter but can become extremely firm at either end of the National Hunt season.

Grade: E

Success rate of all favourites: 36.4 per cent.

Best races for favourites: Novice hurdles 46.4 per cent.

Worst races for favourites: Novice chases 30.2 per cent.

Most significant form: (1st, 2nd, 3rd, 4th last time out) from Wincanton and Taunton itself.

Trainer tip: While M. Pipe's runners should always command respect, K. Bishop should be noted for winners at better starting prices.

TOWCESTER

Right-handed. This 1m 6f undulating, square circuit is set out on the side of a hill. The first half is downhill before a long climb over the final 6f leads to a run-in of 200yd. Though the fences are no more than moderate, this is a severe test of a jumper.

Grade: D

Success rate of all favourites: 32.9 per cent.

Best races for favourites: Weight-for-age-hurdles (excluding novice hurdles) 47.4 per cent.

Worst races for favourites: Handicap chases 24.1 per cent.

Trainer tip: Watch out for Miss V. Williams's chasers both in novice events and handicaps. Her runners nearly always go off at a value price which accounts for the sound, if unspectacular, level-stakes profit from backing every horse she sends to Lord Hesketh's course at Easton Neston, south of Northampton.

UTTOXETER

Left-handed. This is an easy, galloping oval of 1m 2f with average fences. The level run-in is only 170yd long. Front runners do well in hurdle races.

Grade: D

Success rate of all favourites: 41.9 per cent.

Best races for favourites: Novice chases 47.9 per cent.

Worst races for favourites: Weight-for-age hurdles (excluding novice hurdles) 16.7 per cent.

Trainer tip: P.F. Nicholls now has a strike rate of nearly 30 per cent around here.

WARWICK

Left-handed. A circular course of just over 1m 5f, with quite sharp bends. The fences are on the stiff side. The run-in is 240yd long.

Grade: C

Success rate of all favourites: 33.8 per cent.

Best races for favourites: Novice hurdles 36.1 per cent.

Worst races for favourites: Handicap chases 22.9 per cent.

Trainer tip: This is another course where the rise of P.F. Nicholls has taken him to the top of the trainer statistics. His chasers in particular are dominant here, with nearly 70 per cent successful in races for novices, and the handicappers winning one in four. C.J. Mann is also very successful at the Midlands track, his victories coming from every type of race.

WETHERBY

Left-handed. A 1m 4f elongated track, there is a long, steady rise to the finish. The fences are severe. The run-in is fairly short at 190yd. The hurdles course, which is inside the chase circuit, is quite sharp. A stiff but fair test of a jumper, the course attracts a very good class of animal.

Grade: B

Success rate of all favourites: 41.6 per cent.

Best races for favourites: Handicap hurdles 41.2 per cent.

Worst races for favourites: Handicap chases 26.7 per cent.

Most significant form: (1st, 2nd, 3rd, 4th last time out) from Newcastle and Wetherby itself.

Trainer tip: At a very competitive venue, L. Lungo is high on the trainers' list with a 20 per cent win rate, but many of his winners are not easy to spot. Two lady trainers, Mrs M. Reveley and Mrs S.J. Smith, both train in the North and their winners usually have plenty of public form to recommend them. Of the southern raiders, take special note if one of N.J. Henderson's charges makes the long journey from Lambourn.

WINCANTON

Right-handed. A 1m 3f galloping track, its fences are quite testing. The run-in is 200yd long.

Grade: B

Success rate of all favourites: 36.7 per cent.

Best races for favourites: Novice chases 50 per cent.

Worst races for favourites: Handicap hurdles 26.7 per cent.

Trainer tip: P.F. Nicholls has always done exceptionally well here, which is no surprise since the Somerset venue is very much his home course. Currently his runners average just over 30 per cent wins and show a level-stakes profit in the region of about 15 points a season.

WORCESTER

Left-handed. This is a flat, galloping track of 1m 5f. The fences are moderate and the run-in is a furlong in length.

Grade: C

Success rate of all favourites: 36.8 per cent.

Best races for favourites: Novice hurdles 43.9 per cent.

Worst races for favourites: Handicap hurdles 29.5 per cent.

Most significant form: (1st, 2nd, 3rd, 4th last time out) from Worcester itself.

Trainer tip: Note the novice hurdlers of P.J. Hobbs when they go off favourite. They usually win. Handicap chasers from the same yard do very well at better prices. The Pipe/McCoy combination is best numerically and sometimes cleans up against weak opposition, while Mrs H. Dalton is a trainer in a smaller way who nevertheless has a lot of winners at this course.

Index